CLARENDON LAV

Edited by

H. L. A. HAR

CLARENDON LAW SERIES

The Concept of Law
By H. L. A. HART

An Introduction to the Law of Contract (3rd edition)
By P. S. ATIYAH

Precedent in English Law (3rd edition)
By RUPERT CROSS

Introduction to Roman Law
By BARRY NICHOLAS

Constitutional Theory
By GEOFFREY MARSHALL

Legal Reasoning and Legal Theory
By NEIL MACCORMICK

Natural Law and Natural Rights
By JOHN FINNIS

The Foundations of European Community Law
By T. C. HARTLEY

The Law of Property (2nd edition)
By F. H. LAWSON AND BERNARD RUDDEN

AN INTRODUCTION TO THE LAW OF TORTS

BY

JOHN G. FLEMING

CLARENDON PRESS · OXFORD
1985

Oxford University Press, Walton Street, Oxford OX2 6DP
Oxford New York Toronto
Delhi Bombay Calcutta Madras Karachi
Kuala Lumpur Singapore Hong Kong Tokyo
Nairobi Dar es Salaam Cape Town
Melbourne Auckland
and associated companies in
Beirut Berlin Ibadan Nicosia

Oxford is a trade mark of Oxford University Press

Published in the United States
By Oxford University Press, New York

British Library Cataloguing in Publication Data

Fleming, John G.
An introduction to the law of torts.—
2nd ed.—(Clarendon law series)
1. Torts—England
I. Title
344.2063 KD1949
ISBN 0-19-876154-6

Library of Congress Cataloging-in-Publication Data
Fleming, John G.
An introduction to the law of torts.
(Clarendon law series)
Includes index.
1. Torts—Great Britain. I. Title. II. Series.
KD1949.F57 1985 346.4203 85-14478
ISBN 0-19-876154-6 344.2063
ISBN 0-19-876155-4 (pbk.)

Typeset by Joshua Associates Limited, Oxford
Printed in Great Britain
at the University Press, Oxford
by David Stanford
Printer to the University

PREFACE

I HAVE tried to be faithful in this, as in the preceding edition, to the avowed aim of this series of addressing readers who are coming to the subject for the first time, be they students of the law or the general educated public seeking guidance on an important legal subject. In its broadest aspect, that subject concerns compensation policy for accidents, in which the law of torts plays a significant if waning role, nowadays complementary to social security, compensation systems, and private insurance.

This book seeks to look, critically, at the role tort law plays in this modern setting of welfare statism. The focus is on evolution—where we have come from, where we are now, and the outlook for the future. Two chapters in particular pursue this line of inquiry: the first ('The Task of Tort Law') introduces the reader to the big 'ideological' issue in tort law (fault or no-fault liability?) as a key to an understanding of the ensuing anatomy of Negligence and Strict Liability; the ninth chapter ('Tort or Compensation') asks the question to what extent the avowed aims of accident compensation policy are being accomplished by the law of torts under modern conditions, in comparison with its competitors—compensation systems for work injuries, for traffic accidents or, indeed, for accidents in general, as in New Zealand since 1974.

A related theme is the transformation of tort law under the spur of changing social perceptions and the institutional environment (e.g. liability insurance). The transitoriness of tort 'rules' is testimonial both to the judicial success in effecting change under the semblance of doctrinal continuity and to the highly pragmatic nature of the Common Law process. In emphasizing this element, I sought to avoid the impression of the typical legal text as a portrait frozen in time.

In sum, this book is not a potted version of available student texts; it does not cover the field in all detail, but hopes to let you see the wood for the trees. While primarily addressed to the British reader, it does draw on comparative perspectives, especially from the United States and the Commonwealth, with the aim of enriching the fare and appealing to a wider circle of readers.

Berkeley
April 1985

J.F.

CONTENTS

I

THE TASK OF TORT LAW

THE toll on life, limb, and property exacted by today's industrial operations, methods of transport, and many another activity benignly associated with the 'modern way of life' has reached proportions so staggering that the economic cost of accidents represents a constant and mounting drain on the community's human and material resources.[1] The task of the law of torts is to play an important regulatory role in the adjustment of these losses and the eventual allocation of their cost. For most of our history, it provided the sole legal mechanism for compensating the injured at somebody else's expense. But under the conditions of the modern welfare state it has come to share that role with social security and other compensation schemes, like that for victims of crime or vaccination. In England the law of torts has recently been described officially as already reduced to the rank of 'junior partner' to the social security system, and the future may well see its complete replacement by a more efficient comprehensive accident compensation plan such as has already been in place in New Zealand since 1974.[2]

1. EARLY LAW: CRIME, TORT, AND TRESPASS

At the dawn of the common law and for long thereafter, crime and tort covered much the same ground, both stemming from a common desire for vengeance and deterrence and distinguishable only by the nature of their respective sanctions. Crime was and is an offence so serious to the maintenance of public security and the interests of society as a whole that it will, at its own instance, vindicate them by prosecuting and punishing the offender. Tort liability, on the other hand,

[1] In the United Kingdom 3 million persons are injured and 21,500 killed annually in accidents. Of the total, 25 per cent occur at work, 10 per cent on the road. *Pearson Report* II, tables, 2, 3.

[2] *Infra* chap. IX.

provided a means whereby the victim could be 'bribed' into abstaining from retaliation by the prospect of being able to compel the perpetrator to render him monetary compensation for the wrong done. The dereliction against which the primitive legal process of that time, dispensed in the name of royal justice in assertion of emergent central authority, was prepared to intercede was closely identified with public disorder, threats to the King's peace. The writ of trespass as it was known issued against those charged with direct and immediate aggression to the person, chattels, or land of the plaintiff. From this fertile source sprang in time the nominate torts of assault, battery, and false imprisonment, trespass to goods, and what is still in common parlance understood by 'trespass', viz. an intrusion upon someone else's land.

The law of torts was, then, for quite a long time little more than a shadow in the wake of criminal law, concerned with the grosser delicts which almost always must have consisted in some form of *intentional* aggression rather than accidental harm. This was probably so because, in the first instance, people rarely came into close contact with each other in the absence of urban, industrial, and transport conditions which have made random collisions so familiar a feature of the latterday scene. What injury was suffered at the hands of strangers was therefore more likely than not the result of deliberation; and at an age when life was notoriously 'brutish and short' the very idea of unintentional harm seemed pardonably a little extravagant. No wonder that scant time was lost on legal discourse concerning the defendant's state of mind, its futility being underscored by the contemporary faith that even 'the devil knoweth not the mind of man'. What seemed more useful was the distinction, elusive though it may be to the modern mind, and even trifling, between immediate and direct injury on the one hand, which would alone support a writ of trespass, and harm indirectly flowing from the defendant's conduct, which seemed less reprehensible and for which redress was at first less readily forthcoming under the writ of 'case' (success depended on the circumstances of the *case*). In sum, responsibility was based on causation rather than fault, and what headway the latter notion made was in the context of the yet unambitious action on the case, especially that branch which eventually came to bloom as the action for negligence but which, until the industrial revolution, was largely confined to complaints of carelessness against persons like surgeons, apothecaries, solicitors, carriers, and innkeepers who were pursuing public callings and thus more vulnerable to legal scrutiny.

2. THE INDUSTRIAL REVOLUTION AND THE RISE OF ECONOMIC LIBERALISM

Viewed in the broad perspective of history, the law of torts entered its second stage around the turn of the nineteenth century as turnpike and burgeoning industry were vastly accelerating the pulse of human activity and confronting society with an accident problem of hitherto unprecedented dimensions. The legal response to this dramatic challenge was neither uncertain nor timid. In one respect it stimulated an expansion of legal protection, in another a contraction.

To speak of the first, the proliferation of novel and manifold perils on country roads and city streets, along railway tracks and in factories presented the courts with problems to which the antiquated and stunted doctrinal heritage proved unequal. Rather than look to Parliament which had its hands full with other social problems, the courts addressed themselves with vigour to the task of fashioning on their own an essentially new accident law. In substance it meant breaking the narrow compass within which the embryonic law of negligence had been gestating, extending it beyond the time-hallowed consensual relations of doctor and patient (and so forth) into the vast range of informal situations symbolized by collisions at intersections or level crossings, open coal-chutes in public streets, and bags of flour dropping from warehouses on passing pedestrians. It involved over the years a vast expansion of the area of legal control, a persistent probing of the frontiers of protection against accidental, i.e. unintended, harm which is even yet in progress.

Yet here was a veritable Pandora's Box which called for careful handling lest, in the familiar legal phrase destined to become the shop-soiled badge of the timorous, 'the flood-gates of litigation' would engulf us all. Let us remember that this was an epoch socially conservative and far from sentimental. Prominent among the most hazardous activities were precisely those enterprises, like mining, construction, and the railways, whose prosperity was intimately associated in the public mind with the seemingly fabulous growth of the economy and general welfare in the Victorian age. Who but one indifferent to the very success of private enterprise would not shrink from imposing upon it too heavy a burden such as would undoubtedly be involved if it were exposed to the bracing wind of an unmitigated duty of care? Since everybody participated in the benefits of the system to greater or lesser extent, was it so unfair to expect its occasional casualties to shoulder the loss themselves as their own, admittedly involuntary, contribution to the general welfare? This train of thought seemed particularly plausible in countering claims by injured workmen against their employers, and it was in no context more strikingly than this that the human sacrifice demanded for capital formation was so rigorously exacted. Thus, whatever the law's theoretical demands on management for ensuring safe working conditions, in practice they were reduced to an empty gesture by a number of defences designed to baulk recovery and so reduce the overhead cost of industrial operations. In effect it was not until the belated adoption of workmen's compensation in 1897 that a modest measure of security was first assured to the English working class as a hedge against disabling accidents 'arising in and out of the course of employment'.

But the twin defences of voluntary assumption of risk and contributory negligence, much-vaunted stimulants to the virtues of self-reliance and individualism, were by no means confined to the industrial context. In company with other ruses like the facile denial of causal relationship between negligence and harm (that came to be identified as the issue of 'remoteness of damage' or 'proximate cause'), they rendered yeoman service in generally keeping the incidence of liability in check, the more so for being manipulated with great dexterity by judges in often withholding cases from the jury and thus preventing participation in the decision-making process by the 'lay gents' who could not be consistently trusted by the professional guardians of public policy. Other notorious devices subserving the same policy of reducing industry's accident bill were the doctrine of 'privity', which (until 1932) screened negligent manufacturers from claims for injury by ultimate consumers, and the minimal responsibility laid on occupiers for the safety of persons who came on their premises.

3. NO LIABILITY WITHOUT FAULT

Intimately connected with the hedging process just described was the second notable contribution of the nineteenth century, the virtual erosion of strict liability in deference to the prevailing postulate of 'no liability without fault'. As previously mentioned, English law had in the preceding centuries displayed no marked disposition to hitch liability to any particular frame of mind by the actor who had caused the harm. Subject to the important reservation already voiced that most defendants would have intended the injury or have been guilty of socially deficient conduct such as we would today label as negligent, it could fairly be claimed that in theory liability was strict. Exculpatory pleas only grudgingly gained acceptance, so much so that until about 1400 even one who slew another in self-defence had to seek a royal pardon to escape the legal penalty for murder. Though it became increasingly more ambiguous to what extent the plea of inevitable accident would be an answer to a charge of trespass, the issue was not finally resolved until the second half of the nineteenth century, when at last official cognizance was taken of the fact that the fault requirement had almost imperceptibly come to permeate all claims for personal injury and, for that matter, property damage, so that a plaintiff was henceforth put to proof of intentional or negligent misconduct by the defendant, however he chose to frame his pleadings. With but few exceptions which could be plausibly dismissed as obstinate relics of a barbarous past, such as the curious liability for cattle trespass and dangerous animals, the triumph of fault liability was well-nigh complete and marked a singular judicial triumph in remoulding ancient precedents in the image of a radically different era.

The axiom of 'no liability without fault' was neatly attuned to the philosophy of individualism and to the economic needs of a rapidly expanding economy. To provide the most propitious conditions for private initiative, which it was fashionable to regard as the catalyst of all human progress, the legal system had to assure freedom of action for the individual by relieving him at least from all concern for the cost of inevitable accidents. Liability for faultlessly caused injuries was feared to impair progress, besides dangerously enfeebling the moral fibre of man, inasmuch as it denied him all chance to avoid liability by being careful and confronted him with the dilemma of either abandoning his project or assuming the cost of any harm that might incidentally befall. Fault alone justified the interposition of so drastic a legal sanction as the shifting of loss, because in company with the criminal law the primary function of tort recovery was seen in its admonitory or deterrent effect. An adverse judgment against the tortfeasor served at once as punishment for him and a warning for others, especially on the assumption that the award would be paid for out of the defendant's own pocket. Personal fortune was regarded as the primary source of compensation, so that the deterrent lash would be at once real and ineluctable.

This image of loss adjudication under the aegis of the law of torts was therefore critically balanced on two central assumptions, first, an identification in large measure of legal responsibility with moral blameworthiness, and secondly, the belief that compensating a plaintiff could not be accomplished without correspondingly impoverishing the defendant, since the effect of tort recovery was merely to shift the loss from one individual to another. With the passage of the present century, this view of the functioning of tort law has become gradually distorted, if not largely falsified, by better understanding the manner in which the accident cost is in fact being absorbed in society.

4. LOSS SPREADING

The decisive factor in this reorientation is the growing realization that tort law can, and often does, perform the function not merely of shifting, but also of spreading the loss; that the defendant instead of having to foot the bill single-handed is in actual fact more often than not only a conduit through which the cost is channelled so as eventually to be disseminated in small fractions among a large section of the community. This occurs whenever the defendant, by virtue of the position he occupies in the economy, is able to pass on the cost to others. A manufacturer, for example, will treat expenditures incurred in meeting injury claims by third parties, no less than those by his own work force, as part of the inescapable overhead of his operations—a cost item that will enter into the calculation of the price he will charge for each unit of his product and one that will eventually be paid by his consumers.

Further spreading of the cost may be achieved through insurance. Very large enterprises, notably governments, their subdivisions, agencies, and some public corporations, consider it economically preferable to operate as self-insurers and absorb the cost of compensation claims from current revenue or special reserve funds maintained for the purpose. Most others, however, have recourse to professional insurers who are in the business of indemnifying the insured against his legal liability to third parties. Indemnity, liability, or third-party insurance, as it is variously called, has spread tremendously since its modest beginnings in the declining years of the nineteenth century, gradually permeating the economy to the point where today it is widely looked upon as an indispensible prerequisite for doing business or for engaging even in many private activities, like driving the family car. In an increasing number of instances prudence has been backed by legislative compulsion, most notably in the case of motor vehicles, whose owners in most countries today are prohibited from driving or allowing others to drive without carrying insurance in a prescribed amount against liability for personal injury or death to third parties. Likewise in the industrial sphere insurance has long been a corollary of workers' compensation throughout the world and in some jurisdictions is mandatory also for employers with respect to any residual tort liability. Most important for the present context is the fact that insurance, besides offering a relatively inexpensive hedge against the risk in question, performs the vital social function of spreading it among those engaged in the same kind of activity and hence paying premiums against the same type of risk. This also makes it possible to distribute the accident cost of private motoring which, unlike commercial activities, presents no opportunity for 'passing the buck' to customers.

This change of emphasis from loss-shifting to the loss-spreading function of tort law is bound to modify much of the conventional thought concerning the attribution of legal responsibility. And this in at least three respects. First, it saps most of the strength from the argument, once so appealing, that the burden of an adverse judgment would have a crushing and debilitating effect on enterprise generally and the defendant's in particular. Secondly, it radically challenges the long-accredited argument that, in order to justify the trouble and expense of shifting the loss, only misconduct by a defendant manifestly deserving society's disapproval would be sufficient. For, if it be true that it is socially beneficial in itself to compensate the injured when this can be accomplished without correspondingly impoverishing another individual, we should be much readier to countenance a plaintiff's recovery that would not so much connote disapproval of the defendant, as an opportunity for financially assisting an accident victim's rehabilitation by drawing on the resources not of society as a whole but of that particular section which participated in the benefits of the risk-creating activity. Thirdly, it will increasingly divert attention from social deficiency as the paramount criterion for legal responsibility to a quest for who of the parties concerned occupies the most strategic position for distributing the compensation cost in the fairest and most efficient manner. Let me elaborate a little on each of these points.

5. ECONOMIC BURDEN OF TORT LIABILITY

The fear that tort liability would impose an undue burden has been a familiar judicial argument for exonerating defendants in the past. Examples range from early cases of manufacturers and repairers to endemic concern with liability for misrepresentations and other forms of economic loss. Today these protective shelters have all been either dismantled or substantially modified. Indeed, in a recent case the House of Lords unceremoniously denied all further audience to the 'floodgates' argument.[3]

[3] *Junior Books* v. *Veitchi Co.*, [1983] 1 A.C. 520.

Two other examples of changing perspectives on loss bearing are revealing. One is the stubborn immunity, only recently abolished,[4] by highway authorities from claims for non-repair of roads. Unlike the categorical immunity from tort liability of the Crown, which was deeply rooted in political theory ('the King can do no wrong') and survived until 1947,[5] this nefarious doctrine was from its inception bluntly ascribed to the intolerable financial burden for the ratepayer. However plausible at the beginning of the nineteenth century before the great reforms of local government, this argument lost all pretence to justification with the foundation of a modern tax structure for counties and boroughs and the increasing assumption of financial responsibility for the road network by the central government. Thereafter the public character of the defendant, far from being a reason for continued excuse, actually furnished a most cogent argument in favour of liability by reason of its peculiar ability to distribute the loss among a very broad segment of the community. If the public benefits, let it pay its own way!

A second example illustrates the paradoxical effects of liability insurance on the erstwhile immunity among spouses. The common law preclusion of actions between husband and wife was conventionally attributed, besides the metaphysically intriguing doctrine of the identity of spouses ('husband and wife are one, and the husband is *the* one'), to a fear that marital adversary litigation was calculated to disrupt the tranquillity of the home. This explanation always had a somewhat hollow ring in view of the fact that husband and wife were free to sue each other for any cause of action other than tort and some torts, like assault and battery, seemed by their very nature to belie the assumption that there was still a domestic peace to be saved. Yet the immunity survived the social and proprietary emancipation of married women only to become the most prominent casualty of the very success of liability insurance. Under ordinary circumstances, only the existence of insurance would provide a motive for spouses to sue each other, most frequently in connection with car accidents where the negligent spouse

[4] Highways (Miscellaneous Provisions) Act 1961.
[5] Crown Proceedings Act 1947.

would be compulsorily insured. The only argument against allowing such claims is the 'moral hazard' of collusion (the exact opposite of disharmony) in so far as it would not be against the driver's interests to resist an allegation of negligence. But more important, it is widely believed, is the social concern of assuring that all victims of negligent driving are compensated out of the premiums spread over the motoring public. In order to close an important loophole (passengers comprise more than a third of all casualties), the marital immunity and the related North-American guest statutes which inhibited claims by gratuitous passengers against their host have therefore been swept away.[6]

6. EROSION OF FAULT

A second consequence, more dynamic by far and endowed with vast long-range potential for changing the contours of tort law, is the weakening of those forces that once raised fault to the all-pervasive criterion of legal liability. This trend has been aided by a gradual but clearly perceptible shift in the social climate as reflected by the aspirations of the modern welfare State. Unqualified belief in the virtues of private initiative and self-reliance is yielding to ever-mounting reliance on collective action, as mid-twentieth-century man is displaying less concern for acquisition and exploitation than for the preservation of human and material resources. Security bids fair to supplant individualism as the badge of our time.

A portent of that trend is the revaluation of the deterrent value of fault liability. Indemnity insurance has inevitably drained off whatever direct admonitory effect might once have attached to an adverse judgment. Actually, far from proving a disincentive to care, as one would have been led to fear by those who once claimed that fault liability was the only effective spur to accident prevention, experience (especially in connection with workers' compensation) suggests that, on the contrary, strict liability is calculated to stimulate efforts to that end, for the simple reason that nothing short of an accident-proof operation will ensure immunity. Manufacturers whom the fault regime allows

[6] Law Reform (Husband and Wife) Act 1962.

to shelter behind the 'state of the art' defence might just feel impelled by the prospect of strict liability to invest yet more in devising new fool-proof safety procedures.

Gradual erosion of the fault element has manifested itself in two ways: first, in the proliferation of strict liability and no-fault compensation schemes; second, in diluting the fault element of negligence liability ('negligence without fault').

Strict liability

To residual pockets of strict liability which survived the triumph of the fault doctrine in the mid-nineteenth century (cattle trespass, dangerous animals, aspects of nuisance), judicial initiatives have added several important newcomers which reflect needs of our modern technological and consumer society. Anglo-American common law, starting with the decision of *Rylands* v. *Fletcher* in 1867, introduced a regime of strict liability for extra-hazardous undertakings such as the accumulation in large quantities of dangerous substances (gas, electricity, water), to which statute internationally has added nuclear installations and material. In the United States, manufacturers of defective products are now strictly liable to the ultimate consumer, as a result of a judicial reform which has inspired similar proposals in many countries, including England and the European Community. In France, the courts succeeded in distilling from an unpromising Code section a mandate for attaching strict liability to the keeper of things out of control, which was eventually extended even to drivers of motor cars.

In most other countries, however, no-fault compensation for traffic accidents has been the creature of statute; so, typically, in Germany since 1909. In the United States, about half the states have enacted so-called 'no-fault compensation', a form of first party insurance. In England, the Pearson Commission in 1978 recommended that traffic victims become entitled to the same preferential social security benefits as workers injured on the job, financed by a levy on petrol.

Negligence without fault

Beyond these open encroachments of strict or no-fault liability upon the broad canvas of negligence law, more discreet changes in the same direction have occurred behind the screen of doctrinal continuity by deploying its pliable conceptualistic apparatus (such as reasonableness, foreseeability, risk) to the service of a changing social policy. This process toward what has been aptly described as 'negligence without fault[7] has advanced on two fronts, the courtroom and the insurance adjuster's office.

Most influential has been the role of the jury. For it can hardly escape the most unperceptive observer that laymen called at random to the task of decision-making are inclined to be more receptive to the compassionate appeal of the victim's plight than to any, conceivably competing, long-range considerations of social policy that might weigh more heavily with a professional judge. This slant is especially pronounced in cases with a known or suspected background of insurance, i.e. again in the statistically most significant areas of industrial and traffic accidents, where the employer or driver is known to be a defendant in only a nominal sense and the real party in interest is credited with infinite resources—a true impression at least in the potent sense of an ability to absorb the loss and spread it where it will hurt least. In view of this well-known attitude of juries, which it is fashionable for opponents to stigmatize as their notorious vagaries, it is not altogether surprising that some states, for example, in Australia, at the time of introducing compulsory insurance for motor vehicles, sought to protect state insurance funds against depredation by abrogating jury trial altogether for this type of litigation. In England, jury trial has been denied on high principle even for the purpose of occasionally testing the street valuation of damages in catastrophic cases like quadriplegia.[8] But in many jurisdictions of the Common law world, including Scotland and Ireland, but particularly in the United States, jury trial survives in full flower in civil as it does, of course, in criminal cases. Moreover, even if professional judges are more dispassionate and restrained by training and tradition, they are by no means wholly insensitive to the shift in social climate which demonstrably welcomes today a large measure of socialized loss-bearing.[9]

[7] A. Ehrenzweig's title of his renowned monograph (California, 1951).

[8] *Ward* v. *James*, [1966] 1 Q.B. 273 (C.A.).

[9] American courts have gone furthest along this road, openly justifying extensions of liability by pointing to available insurance. The traditional etiquette

At least equally profound in their effect on loss allocation have been modern insurance practices. To start with, the overwhelming bulk of claims against insured defendants is settled out of court. Insurance companies prefer to settle rather than litigate especially when only smaller sums are at stake. Again, so-called knock-for-knock agreements between casualty insurers ensure that damage claims, most prominently for collision damage to cars covered by 'comprehensive policies', are absorbed by the policy-holder's own insurer, regardless of whose fault caused the accident. In this manner also the technical law of negligence is in fact being superseded by a system of compensation which is no longer geared to any serious inquiry into fault. Most arresting of all, finally, are those instances of 'private legislation' where, for reasons best known to itself, the insurance industry has, by agreement with the government, preferred 'voluntarily' to renounce the benefit of certain rules of law, rather than have these rules publicly abrogated by parliamentary reform.[10] In each particular, once more, the effect is for practice to give the go-by to 'black-letter' rules of law which would have hindered the cause of effective loss distribution.

Suitable loss distributors

Third of the consequences involved in emphasizing the importance of the loss-spreading function of tort law is to focus attention on who of the parties linked with the accident occupies the most strategic position as a conduit of distribution. All the better, of course, if he also happens to be the one best able to prevent accidents and susceptible to such pressure as insurance rating can exert in order to make him fulfil that function.

Besides pertinent examples already canvassed, such as the modern manufacturer's obligation to answer for the safety of his product, probably the most telling instance of 'enterprise liability' in the common law is the vicarious liability of an employer for the torts of his servants, which is

of British judges discourages such frankness, but occasional indiscretions reveal that at least some of them (most prominently Lord Denning) share similar motivation.

[10] Most significant are the decision in *Lister* v. *Romford Ice Co.*, [1957] A.C. 555, and the deficiencies of compulsory third-party insurance which have prompted the setting up of the Motor Insurers' Bureau, (*infra* p. 169).

singularly fitted for the dual task of at once deflecting recourse from the culpable yet all too vulnerable servant and, leeching on to the 'deep pocket' of the master, exploiting the latter's superior ability for spreading the cost as a fraction of the price he charges to his customers. Besides shouldering the accident cost of injury to third parties, employers are also responsible through workers' compensation (or its modern Social Security counterparts) for job-injuries suffered by their employees regardless of managerial failings.

These developments encourage the view that in many instances responsibility for accidents is imposed on a defendant primarily because he (or, more usually, it) offers a convenient conduit for efficiently channelling the cost. This perspective is brought into even sharper focus by schemes designed to assign that function to one defendant to the exclusion of all others. For example, under modern legislation responsibility for nuclear accidents rests solely on the operator of a nuclear installation to the exclusion of carriers, suppliers of equipment, operators of conventional vessels and so forth, in order to avoid the economic waste entailed in unnecessary proliferation of insurance.[11] Similarly, there is now a trend, no longer confined to socialist countries, to make the employer's vicarious liability for injury to third parties exclusive of that of the culpable employee himself.[12] So also it has been suggested that all liability for a defective product should be channelled to the manufacturer of the completed product to the exclusion of makers of component parts.[13]

But for the sake of maintaining a balanced viewpoint it is also needful to sound a note of caution in this context against the all too facile assumption that this new perspective provides a magical blueprint for promoting plaintiffs' recovery. In the first place, there are many situations where the defendant does not meet the critical qualifications because he neither occupies a position in the economy which would permit him to pass on the loss for eventual distribution

[11] Nuclear Installations Act 1965; the Vienna Convention, 1963.

[12] *Infra* p. 164.

[13] *Goldberg* v. *Kollsman Instruments* (N.Y. 1963), 191 N.E. 2d 81 (manufacturer of aircraft, but not manufacturer of the defective altimeter, held liable for passenger's death).

nor is the risk in question so typical that indemnity insurance is well-nigh universal or at least highly prevalent. 'Public liability' policies, for example, are still comparatively rare among private home-owners as distinct from occupiers of commercial or industrial premises, so that, if the special loss-distributing capacity of the latter were to be considered worth exploiting, the relevant rule of law should be formulated or at any rate applied so as not to bear unjustly upon the former.[14] Nor for that matter is it anything but a perversion of the argument, if what were considered crucial was that a particular defendant just happened to be insured rather than that he belonged to a class of persons who typically are, since recovery would not in that event necessarily serve the function of broad and equitable loss distribution, besides having an unsettling effect on premium rating practices and injecting an undesirable element of capriciousness into the administration of the law.

Secondly, sometimes it is the plaintiff who is the better loss-distributor. Admittedly, no one would lightly advocate that a plaintiff should forfeit all claim to legal protection against one who has caused him injury merely because he could have protected himself against the risk by insurance; for it would adjudge failure to insure a more heinous dereliction than the negligence or other harm-creating conduct of the tortfeasor. This caution carries the more weight when insurance against the particular type of risk is nowhere near saturation level. Personal accident insurance against injury and death, for example, is still rather rare, and, as we shall see, the insured is actually rewarded for his providence by being allowed to recover both the insurance proceeds and any damages to which he would independently be entitled from the tortfeasor.[15] Yet there are some situations in which insurance against a specialized risk is very widely held by its potential casualties. The most prominent example, of course, is fire insurance by property owners, which offers a more economical and equitable method of absorbing fire losses than the less differentiated, and from the cost point of view less easily calculable, general public liability insurance

[14] This was actually the effect of the old common law treating social guests as *licensees*, entitled to less protection than *invitees* (business visitors).

[15] *Infra* p. 129.

(against third-party risks) currently offered to potential defendants.[16]

Indeed in many other cases of property damage also, one may suspect the 'silent persuader' in decisions favourable to defendants to be not only a lesser need for compassion than for victims of personal injury, but also a concession to the better loss-bearing, even loss-avoiding, capacity of the plaintiff. In the 'cable cases', for instance, contractors who negligently strike a power line in the roadbed have generally been excused for the economic loss sustained by adjoining businesses in the ensuing shutdown. A justifiable policy reason would be that loss of such commercial profits is better calculable and guarded against (e.g. by standby generators) and more cheaply insurable by the victims than by contractors.

7. TORT LAW AND THE WELFARE STATE

Any summation of the present role of the law of torts must necessarily be tinged with diffidence. Ours is a period of transition, of as yet uneven adjustment of legal doctrine to changing and by no means universally understood or even commonly shared goals. Yet, far and beyond all controversy, the law of torts has come to perform a not insignificant function of distributing losses in our society and has thereby assumed an active and vital role as a social regulator. This role was thrust upon it as the result of changes in the social and economic environment, especially the rise of liability insurance, which the lawyer had little, if any, opportunity to influence. Open to debate alone now is whether and to what extent it is desirable for courts and legislature to exploit its potentialities by consciously controlling its range and direction.

Yet one must also be on guard against too sanguine an estimate of the importance that tort liability now does or ever can assume as a means for distributing losses. In the first place, it cannot fairly pretend to concern itself with injuries other than those caused by one person to another; calamities

[16] The most striking example is the 'New York fire rule' which limits liability to the first house set on fire. Likewise, water companies are generally excused for not maintaining adequate pressure to save a house on fire.

due to the hand of fate or act of God must perforce be left for redress to some other mechanism, be it charity or public relief. Secondly, now that we are in any event, it would seem, irrevocably committed to the provision of a large and probably increasing measure of social welfare for the benefit of society's casualties, whatever the precise source of their misfortune, including the victims of negligence or other conduct to which the law sees fit to attach legal liability, the function reserved for tort law in the larger scheme of social security is at best to supplement and redistribute the accident cost with more discrimination.

Regarding the first, one cannot very well overlook the fact that our contemporary social order evinces a great deal of tenderness for the victims of tort by generally supporting their claim to full indemnity for their pecuniary loss as well as substantial redress for pain and suffering, in contrast to general social welfare benefits (like invalidity pensions), which are invariably restricted to scheduled amounts designed merely to meet basic needs of rehabilitation and minimal economic support during incapacity. One of the more perplexing problems arising from the coexistence of these two systems of compensation is how to justify the claim by those tortiously injured to so large and seemingly disproportionate a share of bounty. Many jurisdictions throughout the world enforced just such an adjustment by abolishing all tort recovery against an employer as the trade-off for the much lower but assured benefits of workmen's compensation; and, as already mentioned, more recently some no-fault traffic schemes followed the same pattern. The culmination of this trend is the New Zealand accident compensation act which replaces income but provides for non-pecuniary injury only in severer cases and in very limited amounts.

Tort law's second possible mission stems from its capacity for distributing the cost of accidents with greater discrimination and finesse than is either desired or possible under a general social security programme. Being essentially a form of 'enterprise' or 'sponsorship' liability, it is designed to hive off the cost among those who benefit from or participate in the risk-creating activity. The cost of traffic accidents, for example, is in this manner borne by the motoring public alone. National Insurance, on the other hand, is financed much more broadly; well-nigh by the community as a whole through contributions either as in Great Britain on a flat scale from wage-earners, employers, and the State, or as in Australia graduated according to income just like income tax. The co-existence of these two systems of compensation, so differently funded, throws up challenging questions whether, and if so, to what extent the cost of particular accidents should more properly be borne by one or the other. We will return to this theme in a later chapter which asks the question 'Tort or Compensation?'

II

NEGLIGENCE

SINCE in theory if not in practice almost all of today's human activity falls to be tested by the criteria of the law of negligence, we begin our more detailed survey of modern torts with an investigation of that pervasive principle. Until its emergence in the nineteenth century as an independent basis of liability, negligence led a somewhat ambiguous and precarious existence as a mental element in the commission of other torts like trespass or nuisance: there was then no more a tort of negligence than it was ever conceivable to have a tort of intent. The stifling thicket of the writ system's formalism discouraged fruitful speculation about theories of culpability; what tender shoots there were of such an emergent notion would have been traced by the discerning eye to the amorphous Action on the Case which demanded an obligation of care from persons professing a 'public calling' on behalf of their clients, but otherwise yielded little more than a 'bundle of frayed ends'. It remained for the nineteenth century under the stimulus of burgeoning industrial enterprise to crystallize these unpretentious particles into the potent generalization that has come to dominate modern accident law.

Two preliminary observations are here in place. First, as already intimated, negligence is a basis of liability rather than a single nominate tort. Most conventional torts are, by name or association, identified with invasion of a particular kind of interest or a specific type of misconduct like assault and battery with physical aggression and defamation with slurs on reputation. In contrast negligence encompasses all manner of harm and all sorts of injurious behaviour—diffuse strands that are tied together only by the single knot of the injurer's 'negligent' conduct.

So ambitious a generalization had to be harnessed, for not even our own generation, much less our forefathers would have been prepared to countenance without reservation so far-reaching a legal postulate as that it be incumbent in *all* circumstances to exercise prudent care to safeguard *all* one's fellow men against *any* kind of detriment. Negligence, consisting as it does of failure to guard against risks of harm to others, forcibly suggests such questions as 'What kind of risks?', 'Risks to whom?', 'Risks of what kind of harm and from what kind of conduct?' Responsive to these inquiries, certain legal devices, most prominently those of 'duty' and 'remoteness of damage', have gradually emerged to play a critical role in assisting analysis, articulating conclusions, and co-ordinating these within the theoretical structure of tortious negligence. Together with the defences, strictly so-called, of contributory negligence and voluntary assumption of risk by the plaintiff, they are instrumental in giving effect to whatever contemporary judicial policy deems necessary to mitigate the full impact of the negligence doctrine on the defendant.

But by the same token the modern demand for increasing social protectionism has been duly reflected in a steady weakening of these hedging devices, along with other strategies favourable to plaintiffs, such as the progressive raising of the requisite standard of care demanded from defendants. Much of the progressive evolution of negligence law in doctrine and its application has thus taken the form of manipulating one or the other or more of these various strings which control its desired posture at any given time and place, besides introducing a welcome element of elasticity to accommodate not only differences in judicial taste and technique, but also to aid experimentation through trial and error.

The conventional elements of the cause of action for negligence are as follows:

1. A duty, recognized by law, to conform to the requisite standard of care for the protection of the plaintiff against the kind of harm in question. This is generally identified as the 'duty issue' and pre-eminently a lever for judicial control over matters of policy.

2. Failure to attain the requisite standard of care or, briefly, breach of duty. This is the 'negligence issue', entrusted to the trier of fact.

3. Actual injury. If my negligence providentially happens

not to scathe anybody, I am entitled to acquittal from all civil liability, though not necessarily from criminal penalties, as, for example, for careless driving. By parity of reasoning no redress is afforded for mere indignity or other non-material injury; though if the same had been perpetrated by me intentionally, as in committing an assault and battery, the anti-social nature of my conduct would have supplied a sufficient reason for vindicating my victim's sense of dignity with substantial, even aggravated, damages for the affront.

4. A reasonably proximate causal link between the breach of duty and the harm. This is the problem of 'remoteness of damage' or 'proximate cause'.

5. The absence of prejudicial conduct by the plaintiff. The defendant may invoke against him either the partial defence of contributory negligence, which no longer fully defeats his claim but merely reduces his recovery, or the defence of voluntary assumption of risk, now happily almost obsolete.

The functional similarity of the first and fourth issues, and their close link with the last-mentioned defences, as devices for circumscribing the range of protection against negligent harm commends as most convenient an examination first of all of the Standard of Care or What amounts to Negligence.

III

STANDARD OF CARE

NEGLIGENCE is conduct that fails to conform to the standard required by law for safeguarding others (actionable negligence) or oneself (contributory negligence) against unreasonable risk of injury. It is crucial to apprehend at the outset that negligence is not as might have been thought a state of mind, but conduct—whether it consist in action or omission to act. The law is not concerned with matters of conscience. Just as one guilty of the most callous disregard for the safety of others need not fear, as we have already seen, to be called to account at the bar of civil justice if he luckily escapes injuring anybody, so another cannot gain excuse by pleading that he had done his personal best, if that happens to fall below the standard postulated for him as for everyone else in the community. Thus, whatever the semblance of moral connotation implicit in the word 'negligence', it is belied in actuality by the practical necessity of subordinating ethical values to the more exigent demands of public safety.

1. THE REASONABLE MAN

The genius of the common law finds perhaps no more poignant illustration than in the invention of the 'reasonable man'[1] as the model against which to test a particular defendant's conduct for conformity with what is requisite at any given time and place in order to avoid unnecessary danger. For behold! First of all, this formula makes little, if any, allowance for the 'personal equation', so critical in our assessment of the moral worth of an individual, yet of so little moment to his hapless victim. By preferring an objective standard of judging behaviour the law avoided the perplexing task of having to scrutinize each specific defendant's subjective

[1] 'Man' does not mean 'male', despite A. P. Herbert's misgivings in *Fardell* v. *Potts* (*Uncommon Law*, p. 4).

capacity; instead, it contents itself with judging merely his external manifestations of conduct by whether or not it measured up to the norm set by the reasonable man.

The second great contribution of the 'reasonable man' test was that it furnished a means for keeping the standard sufficiently flexible to be applied to the most protean fact situations and thus assuring that the negligence concept itself would, in the modern idiom, remain 'open-ended', responsive to developing and differing community ideals. If traditionally associated with that mythical 'man on the Clapham omnibus', yet full allowance is made for the fact that the bearded patriarch in the horse-drawn days of the mid-Victorian era might well have entertained a very different view of what was 'done' than his grandson making the same daily trip on top of a motorized double-decker or speeding tube, not to speak of his descendants riding the Bondi tram into Sydney or speeding bumper-to-bumper at sixty miles an hour along the Hollywood Freeway.

Third and closely related was the fact that the 'reasonable man' formula was so singularly suited for transmitting the decision on the applicable standard to the jury. In this manner community valuations could be infused into the administration of the law where they were most needed and would be most effectively applied, especially at a time when judges more obviously than today preferred to insulate themselves against the vulgarities of the market-place. Besides, it allowed rules of conduct to remain adjustable to changing social patterns, since a verdict on the question of negligence did not, like a judgment on a so-called point of law, create precedent binding for subsequent cases. In a formal sense this is of course equally true where that function is performed—as it long has been in England—by professional judges rather than lay juries. In practice, however, this change has produced a noticeable hardening of the legal arteries by providing the temptation of elevating findings of fact in an earlier case to binding propositions of law. Judges deliver reasons in justifying their conclusions, in contrast to the 'featureless generality' of the jury verdict. Especially when their judgments are reported, the profession becomes apprised not only of what decision a court has reached on a so-called question of fact, but also of why the judge reached it. Inevitably the line of demarcation between questions of fact and of law—of what has binding character and what has not—becomes blurred.

A judge expatiating, for instance, on why he found a particular motorist negligent in running into the rear of another vehicle may well have said, 'If you ride in the dark you must ride at such a pace that you can pull up within your limits of vision.' Such an observation is liable to be picked up in a later case and endowed with pervasive generality, although it might never have been intended to be of universal application nor be appropriate for that matter in all conceivable circumstances. To treat it as a peremptory proposition of law, as it was for a few years until the matter was eventually set right,[2] could hardly have occurred in the case of a jury trial—for in that event the presiding judge would have left it to the jury how to decide the issue, and whatever verdict they rendered would neither have been garnished by such an explanation nor have carried any precedential value whatever for subsequent cases.

Uniformity of decisions has of course not lacked for champions. Among them no lesser jurist than the great Justice Oliver Wendell Holmes fancied legal progress to advance in the direction of a gradual triumph of fixed and uniform standards of conduct enunciated by the courts so that people should the better know in advance how to keep within the four corners of the law. This argument, alas, carries least point in relation to the law of negligence, since failure to attain the proper standard of care is rarely due to ignorance as to what precisely is required. But however limited their potential prophylactic effect, fixed rules do have marked virtue in encouraging settlements and thus keeping litigation down—a cause highly esteemed among the values of contemporary judicial policy. In significant measure this is furthered by recourse to statutory safety regulations for fixing the appropriate standard of care to be observed, especially in the industrial field (the so-called doctrine of statutory negligence), and by zealously espousing, as English courts do, the cause of standardized damage awards.[3] Least important perhaps in this regard, because purchased at too high a price, would be to enforce a policy of uniformity

[2] *Tidy* v. *Battman*, [1934] 1 K.B. 319 (C.A.). [3] *Infra* p. 127.

in the residuary area of common law negligence, which has been so well served in the past by appeal to the more flexible standard of the reasonable man.

Attributes of the reasonable man

Since we abide, then, and must emulate the example set by that imaginary figure, it would be as well to advert briefly to the salient qualities with which the law has seen fit to endow him as representative of our contemporary community ideals. Embodying in all respects the golden mean, he might well strike the astonished observer as he did A. P. Herbert when he wrote: 'Devoid, in short, of any human weakness, with not a single saving vice, *sans* prejudice, procrastination, ill-nature, avarice, and absence of mind, as careful for his own safety as he is for that of others, this excellent but odious creature stands like a monument in our Courts of Justice, vainly appealing to his fellow-citizens to order their lives after his own example.'[4]

With respect to all but physical attributes the reasonable man makes no concession whatever to the individual shortcomings of the particular defendant. For instance, though some individuals are unduly timorous and imagine every path beset with lions while others are too unimaginative even to admit the possibility of danger, the reasonable man is free at once from over-apprehension and over-confidence. His emotional stability, like his ethical values, sets an undeviating pattern of normalcy and rectitude which allows little excuse for the very factors most responsible for accident-proneness. Even in the extreme instance of lunacy the weight of authority declines to make allowance for a defendant's inability to appreciate his duty to exercise care and to make a rational choice, as when he is held responsible for going through a red light under the insane delusion of being pursued by a mortal enemy or of the truck he is driving being under remote control from headquarters. No more tender regard for that matter is evinced in dealing with lunatics charged with *intentional* infliction of injury, who, in contrast to the famous M'Naughten Rules of the criminal law, are not permitted the excuse that, though aware of the nature of what they were doing, they did not know that it was wrong.[5]

[4] *The Uncommon Law*, p. 4.

[5] *Morriss* v. *Marsden*, [1952] 1 All E.R. 925.

Rather startling at first encounter is the degree to which, by contrast, the law is prepared to apply the subjective standard to children. To be sure, most of the cases dealing with the problem have been concerned with *contributory negligence*, when there is a general inclination to take a more indulgent view, for the good reason that strict adherence to the external standard in the case of defendants tends to promote compensation of accident victims and distribution of losses, whereas applied to plaintiffs it will thwart them. In any event, a child, whether as plaintiff or defendant, is expected to conform only to the standard befitting children of like age, intelligence, and experience, with the result for example that in practice infants under five cannot be charged with responsibility for traffic accidents. The explanation for this disparity in treatment between lunatics and infants is that we are prepared to tolerate the mistakes and failings of childhood as a condition to which every one is heir, in contrast to insanity which, besides being rare and creating administrative difficulties enough in the criminal context, is perhaps still beset with an atavistic attribution of sin from which modern man has not yet succeeded in emancipating himself. As a partial counterweight to the free pass thus given for the destructive potentialities of little children, the law at least postulates an obligation from parents and school authorities to observe reasonable care in supervising them—without, however, going to the lengths of the French law which is said to attach vicarious liability to the parents for all wrongs perpetrated by their children, just as the common law used to do in the case of wives and still does with respect to employees.[6] Moreover, an adolescent who ventures on an adult activity like driving a car or running an industrial machine must meet the standard of the reasonably prudent adult, because the licence was granted to him on the assumption that he was capable of attaining it.

The subjective standard has made most headway in relation to physical attributes, most probably because they present much less difficulty of reliable proof than intellectual

[6] The German civil code, while pretending to the overriding postulate of individual culpability under the influence of the 'will theory', also capitulated to the exigent demands of the practical policy to compensate innocent casualities by holding lunatics as well as infants to 'equitable' liability, if found capable of bearing the loss.

and temperamental deficiencies in matters of the mind. Accordingly the physically handicapped is held only to the standard of care that could be expected of a reasonably prudent person afflicted with his disability. This rule of leniency, however, is contingent on efforts on his part to compensate, so far as is possible, for his impediment. A blind man, it is felt, is entitled to some freedom of movement even at the cost of a little inconvenience to the public: he may walk the pavement and even cross the street, but must not attempt to drive. By the same token, similar allowance is due for the infirmities of the aged in our midst. Much more controversial by far, however, is the continuing disposition to excuse drivers who lose control over their cars as a result of an *unexpected* seizure or heart attack. Not only is this difficult to reconcile with the opposite conclusion in the case of a driver suddenly overtaken by an insane delusion, but, most important of all, such refinements of morality would no longer seem to have a useful part to play under our modern régime of compulsory insurance.

2. UNREASONABLE RISK

What are the factors that would influence the reasonable man in deciding whether or not to go ahead, adopt a particular precaution, or in some other manner adjust his conduct in the face of danger? Few activities are altogether devoid of risk, and not every conceivable peril would therefore justify the reasonable man to pause. In short, the risk of harm must be unreasonable before it deserves the attribute of negligence. Nor is it just a question of what dangers are 'reasonably' foreseeable, as many a glib pronouncement would have us believe, because in some situations we are quite familiar with the idea that it is permissible to take even a 'calculated' risk. In truth, far from being a simple notion, negligence is the outcome of a value-judgement which often enough is based on the most delicate balancing of competing considerations. This 'calculus of risk' may at best be reduced to the formula that we must weigh the magnitude of the risk in the light of the likelihood of an accident happening and the possible seriousness of its consequences against the difficulty, expense, or any other disadvantage of desisting from the venture or taking a particular precaution.

First in importance, and usually in the forefront of lay as well as legal thinking about negligence, is the magnitude of the risk involved. Conduct cannot be stigmatized as negligent unless there is more than a theoretical chance that it will miscarry *and* thereby subject others to harm. In sum, there must be a recognizable risk of *injury*. Thus one cannot, for instance, readily condemn the playing of cricket on a certain green merely because of the chance of an occasional 'six' coming to land upon a nearby road or front garden: there must at the very least be a substantial risk of its striking someone thereby.[7] On the other hand, it would be equally wrong to concentrate only on the likelihood of the *precise* injury that occurred, for that would tend to prejudice recovery unduly by minimizing, perhaps to vanishing point, the foreseeable chance of the relevant risk. If, for example, the question relates to the propriety of backing into a space between parked cars without first removing some fragments of glass, the proper inquiry should be directed to the likelihood of a splinter being sent flying so as to cause *some* injury to *somebody* in the vicinity rather than of its putting out (as it did) Mrs. Smith's left eye. True enough, if the injury that actually occurred was rather freakish, the defendant may yet escape responsibility on the ground that it is 'too remote', but this conclusion would not trench upon the initial determination to treat his conduct as negligent in view of its aggregate of foreseeable risk.

The quest for an inclusive verbal formula to denote the requisite degree of risk has exercised a weird fascination on the English judicial mind. Where all the speculation concerning the rival claims of magic works like 'reasonable possibility', 'real likelihood', or 'probability, not possibility', really goes astray is in assuming that, even if words were equal to the task, the issue was reducible to mathematical probability alone and involved a constant element, whereas in reality it is a variable which cannot be assessed in isolation from the other factors making up the complex calculus of risk. For instance, as the gravity of possible injury increases so the apparent likelihood of its occurrence need be correspondingly less. In no circum-

[7] *Bolton* v. *Stone*, [1951] A.C. 850.

stances need proof go to the length of establishing that *more probably than not* injury would have resulted. Comparative probability is the proper legal standard in civil litigation[8] for establishing that a certain event happened in the past, not for evaluating conduct by reference to whether it is fraught with danger in the future. No one would consider Russian roulette any the less foolhardy because the chances of fatality are only one in six. By the same token the likelihood that a paperweight idly flung out of an upstairs window will actually strike some passer-by on the head may be mathematically negligible, but is nonetheless too great to be justifiable in view of its potentially dire results and the futility of the gesture.

On the other side of the equation is the social and economic cost of abstaining from the 'chancy' conduct or adopting some precaution that would reduce the hazard. If all motor-cars travelled at three miles an hour, preceded by a man on foot waving a red flag, the traffic toll would be dramatically reduced, but so would national production. We are prepared to exempt emergency vehicles from obedience to speed limits and even traffic signals, subject admittedly to such compensating safeguards as the sounding of sirens and extra vigilance, for the sake of the exceptional urgency of their errand. No less must allowance be made, in probing the duty of parental supervision, for the socially acknowledged need to allow children legitimate scope for developing individual responsibility.[9]

Cost–Benefit Analysis

Does this formula mean, then, that there is negligence only when the cost of the accident is greater than the marginal cost of avoiding it? Something like that seemed to be implied in Judge Learned Hand's algebraic equation: if the probability of the risk be called P; the injury L; and the burden B; liability depends on whether B is less than L multiplied by P: i.e., whether $B < PL$.[10] Put into economic

[8] In contrast to criminal prosecutions, which predicate the higher standard of proof beyond all reasonable doubt.

[9] A judge's—often quite unconscious—bias is sometimes revealed in decisions exceptionally favourable to a particular activity, like playing cricket (*Bolton* v. *Stone*, [1951] A.C. 850) or breeding horses (*Fitzgerald* v. *Cooke Bourne*, [1964] 1 Q.B. 249, demanding 'a real likelihood'—not just a 'reasonable possibility of foreseeable injury').

[10] *United States* v. *Carroll Towing Co.* (2d Cir. 1947) 159 F. 2d 169, 173.

terms, this formula might suggest that the law of negligence demands only cost-justified precautions; that to demand more would encourage over-investment in safety and lead to misallocation of economic resources.[11] While such a cost-benefit analysis may well play a critical role in managerial decisions of large-scale industrial operations, its application to *legal* responsibility cannot be accepted without serious qualification. For one thing, can life and limb be brought on the same monetary denominator as the expense of safety precautions? For another, the judgment is in the final resort social, not economic—safety, not efficiency oriented.

Customary practices

Since one of the most vaunted qualities of the 'reasonable man' test, especially when applied by a jury, is that it permits the injection of a good dose of grass-root sentiment into the daily administration of the law by linking the legal standard of care to accepted community evaluations, much evidentiary weight perforce attaches to whether or not the defendant's conduct accorded with general practices for doing the particular kind of thing. Failure to conform calls for a convincing explanation and is apt to constitute the most damaging evidence. Conversely, a charge of negligence can usually be dispelled by proof that what was done or omitted was not at variance with accredited practice.

Yet even common usage or custom is not altogether above legal censure, since otherwise an entire industry would be free to set its own uncontrolled standards in defiance of its overriding obligation of reasonable care. This caution is made the more significant by modern mass-market production techniques which rely on sampling for quality control. If a sample conforms to the relevant standard and the whole batch is accepted, the risk of a particular unit being defective is in effect allocated to the consumer. Yet the standard, and therewith the level of the consumer's risk, is set by the producer himself—subject only to the discipline of market conditions *and the law.* The law would be shirking its task if it were to model its own legal standard on the economic standard of the industry, bent on maximizing profits more than on consumer satisfaction. Hence in the last resort, the

[11] Posner, *Economic Analysis of Law* (2d ed. 1977) ch. 6.

true determinant of the legal standard must be not what ordinarily is, but what ought to be, done.

Outside the industrial context conformity with accepted practice plays its most prominent role in defence against claims for medical malpractice. In a graceful gesture to a sister profession the law has been specifically sensitive to the peculiar vulnerability of doctors to the effect of an adverse verdict on their professional reputation. Conscious at once of the layman's ignorance of medical science and distrustful of jury reactions,[12] the courts have insisted on the safeguard that negligence in diagnosis and treatment cannot ordinarily be established without the aid of expert testimony and proof of nonconformity with accepted medical practice. This requirement bears with singular severity on claimants, however meritorious, by reason of the well-known disinclination of physicians to testify against each other. Equally (over)-protective of the physician is the English preference for subsuming his duty to inform the patient of collateral risks and alternative procedures to the same 'professional competence' standard rather than to a patient's 'right of choice' or 'informed consent', as American and Canadian courts do.[13]

Insistence on expert testimony in these as in other actions involving technical matters goes some way towards mitigating the dilemma posed with increasing frequency on the modern scene of either confiding the decisions of experts to the review of amateurs (whether judge or jury) in the context of a damage action in tort or of renouncing all scrutiny on account of the evident inequality in technical expertise.

[12] This has prompted some jurisdictions in Canada to ban jury trials altogether from this type of litigation.

[13] *Sidaway* v. *Bethlem Royal Hospital* [1985] A.C. –.

IV

DUTY OF CARE

1. INTRODUCTION

NEGLIGENCE does not in all circumstances entail liability for ensuing harm. In some situations the law is prepared to condone even carelessness for reasons considered more important than safety. Justification for so radical a position must, of course, be sought in supervening considerations of judicial policy which, there is reason to apprehend, might not be adequately credited in the balancing process of determining whether the particular risk was unreasonable or not. Admittedly, as we have just seen, much besides mere prevision of harm goes into the latter decision, the most weighty countervailing factor being the inhibiting effect or burden on human enterprise—in other words, precisely the kind of consideration that would also be critical in the formulation of a categorical judicial policy against allowing redress for risk-creating conduct of that kind. The explanation for this apparent pleonasm is simply this: that, much as nature is proverbially bountiful, so the common law in its formative period, when jury trial still held sway, drifted into the position of investing the professional judge with more than one handle for safeguarding vital community policies from being sold short by juries prone to be swayed by sentimentality for the particular victim. Accordingly, supplementary to his power of ruling that, in view of the competing policies involved, the conduct could not be stigmatized as negligent because the risk it entailed was not unreasonable in contemplation of law, he might anticipate the same result by pronouncing right at the outset that, in any event, the circumstances did not call for a duty to be careful.

Though by no means highly systematized, prevailing practice tends to subsume to the duty issue judicial policies that are at once peremptory and expressed in fairly clear-cut categories, easily identifiable and relatively free of variables which would demand nice adjustments to the particular facts of each case.[1] Whether, for instance, police could be liable at all for acts committed in the bona fide execution of their duties would be a 'duty' (or 'immunity') question; whereas in what circumstances, if ever, police are justified in resorting to firearms in pursuit of a bank robber at the risk of hitting passers-by would ordinarily fall for debate in terms of what reasonable care demanded in the interest of public safety in the particular situation. The concept of 'duty', as thus used in its technical or conventional sense, is therefore by no means identical with the more comprehensive meaning which the term carries in ordinary parlance as when we say, for example, that a driver is 'duty-bound' to slow down when passing a school or is under no 'duty' to give a hand signal in addition to operating his blink lights. When used in the latter sense 'duty' encompasses not only the question whether the situation called for the exercise of reasonable care, but also what was required precisely to satisfy the requisite standard.

A duty of care is an incident to the relation between two individuals, specifically that between the injurer and his victim. Whether it is postulated by law—or, rather, denied (its absence being the abnormal condition)—may depend on any one of many factors which are, however, broadly reducible to three basic kinds. The first relates to what might be called the personal status of either party or some peculiar facet of their mutual relation as individuals. As already mentioned, the defendant may have been exercising governmental powers, or the plaintiff may have been a trespasser on the defendant's land and as such not entitled to the exercise of any care or, like an 'automobile guest' in some American jurisdictions, to protection only against wilful or reckless injury. By the same token a highway authority was not until a recent legislative amendment in England under any 'duty' to maintain roads in proper repair, even if aware of the existence of an unreasonable risk of injury to motorists or, for that matter, to pedestrians.

[1] In other words, issues singularly suitable for disposal by 'demurrer' or its modern English successor, a 'preliminary point of law' (under R.S.C. Ord. 25)—a procedure that obviates going to the expense of proving the facts (alleged in the plaintiff's statement of claim) in case it turns out that they would not in any event constitute a cause of action entitling the plaintiff to recover.

The second denominator has reference to the nature of the conduct that caused the harm. There is a world of difference, for example, between being responsible for a person's death by drowning as a result of negligently shoving him off a bridge and merely neglecting to come to the aid of an exhausted swimmer. The defendant's default in the first case consists in actively creating a risk, in the second merely in failing to extricate the victim from a danger not of the defendant's making. The one is a case of commission, the second of omission—even if both share the common element that the deceased would still be alive but for the defendant's failure to exercise care. Another distinction to which much weight has conventionally been attached is that between negligence in act and in word, between what a man does and what he says; the inclination for long being to deny any duty of care to speak circumspectly, even if the listener might justifiably rely on the communication and foreseeably incur detriment as a result.

The third major distinction on which a duty of care might hinge concerns the kind of injury for which redress is claimed. Although we are now broadly committed to legal protection against almost all forms of physical injury, whether to the person or tangible property, be it chattels or land, more sophisticated interests of personality have made slower or no headway at all in their quest for legal protection, at any rate against negligent as distinct from intentional interference. Being merely frightened or put in apprehension of imminent physical danger may qualify for civil sanctions against the deliberate aggressor, as it does within the compass of actions for assault and intentional infliction of mental disturbance, but not in case of mere inadvertence—for fear of imposing a quite disproportionate burden on legitimate as distinct from plainly antisocial activity. Even claims for severe emotional shock have had rough sledding. Most controverted of all is the question whether the law of negligence allows recovery for purely economic losses, like the wages lost by employees of a damaged factory or loss of profits of a business closed by a power blackout.

In this third category where redress is denied or restricted because of the nature of the injuries sustained, the law is in effect withholding its protective mantle from corresponding human interests, like the interest in emotional or financial security. Instead of talking about the defendant's 'duty', it would be more natural to talk in these instances about the plaintiff's 'rights'. The Germanic legal systems, for example, place their emphasis on what 'rights' are legally protected against negligence; we, however, more for accidental than *a priori* reasons,[2] came to address these same questions in terms of 'duty', even when the focus is not on what is expected from defendants but against what kind of injury the plaintiff is entitled to protection. Whatever the preference, it is only of terminological interest. Thus even in our system of law, it used to be fashionable to express the duty issue by saying that damage such as emotional shock was 'too remote' or, what amounts to the same thing, that the defendant's negligence was not its 'proximate cause'.[3] But partly because we got bored with the equivocations and idiosyncrasies of 'remoteness' (of which more later on), it became more attractive and modern to talk about 'duty'.

Foreseeability

Ever since the duty concept became accredited in the last quarter of the nineteenth century as a theoretical constituent of tortious negligence, efforts have been on foot to reduce to an inclusive and systematic formula the seemingly unorganized mass of precedents which, by a largely haphazard and certainly empirical process, had emerged as an expression of the accumulated wisdom of our community concerning the circumstances when one was expected to subordinate one's own conduct to concern for safeguarding others from unreasonable risk. Most influential by far, because of the great prestige of its author and its propitious timing, was Lord Atkin's famous generalization in *Donoghue* v. *Stevenson*, which has become a sacrosanct preamble to all disquisitions into the existence of 'duty' in English law:

> There must be, and is, some general conception of relations giving rise to a duty of care, of which the particular cases found in the books are but instances. . . . The rule that you are to love your neighbour becomes in law you must not injure your neighbour; and the lawyer's

[2] See Winfield, 'Duty in Tortious Negligence', 34 *Col. L. Rev.* 41 (1934).

[3] French law, with a Gallic taste for simplicity, subsumes all these problems to its inquiry into *faute*.

question, Who is my neighbour? receives a restricted reply. You must take reasonable care to avoid acts or omissions which you can reasonably foresee would be likely to injure your neighbour. Who, then, in law, is my neighbour? The answer seems to be—persons who are so closely and directly affected by my act that I ought reasonably to have them in contemplation as being so affected when I am directing my mind to the acts or omissions which are called in question.[4]

The importance of this pronouncement lay however less in its protestation of secular[5] virtue or its emphasis on foreseeability, than in its message that the time had come to replace the growing catalogue of specific duties by a wider generalization. In the intervening years it has inspired successive decisions dismantling important 'no duty' hold-outs (negligent words, economic loss) to the point where we now think of a unified principle of liability for negligence. In novel situations a two-tiered approach is now recommended: to ask first, if the relation between the parties is of sufficient proximity that, in the reasonable contemplation of the defendant, carelessness on his part is likely to cause damage to the plaintiff; and secondly, whether there are any considerations which ought to negative, or to reduce or limit, the scope of the duty.[6] The first question is said to state the 'principle', the second to make allowance for possible contrary 'policy'.[7]

This formula, enunciated in a case which became a new landmark for expanded responsibility has been understood as a mandate for allowing exceptions to the 'principle' only on the most compelling grounds.[8] To scholars, it is also significant for converging with the Civilian tradition of 'culpa' liability as a unified concept.[9]

Duty to this plaintiff

Nowhere is the common law's individualistic bias more clearly revealed than in the axiom that the plaintiff must

[4] [1932] A.C. 562, at p. 580. For its bearing on products liability, see *infra* p. 81.

[5] Cf. Luke, 10.29 *et seq.*

[6] *Anns* v. *Merton Borough Council*, [1978] A.C. 728, 751-2 (Lord Wilberforce); *Dorset Yacht Club* v. *Home Office*, [1970] A.C. 1004, 1027 (Lord Reid).

[7] The reference to 'proximity' is either a mere token of recognition to Lord Atkins's test in *Donoghue* v. *Stevenson* or is so open-ended as to duplicate the second 'tier'.

[8] Most notably in *Junior Books* v. *Veitchi Co.*, [1983] 1 A.C. 520.

[9] Compare Lawson & Markesinis, *Tortious Liability for Unintentional Harm in the Common Law and the Civil Law* (1982).

bottom his claim to redress on breach of a personal duty to himself as a particular individual. As a matter of policy it will not allow him to claim as the vicarious beneficiary of a duty owed to others: the defendant might have been only too remiss in his conduct, but this will avail the plaintiff naught if for some reason his personal credentials do not qualify him as one who can complain.

In the *Palsgraf* case,[10] immemorially linked with this cardinal proposition, a porter forcefully pushed a passenger into a departing train, thereby dislodging a parcel which unexpectedly contained fireworks. The resulting explosion caused a pair of heavy scales, a good way along the platform, to topple upon Helen Palsgraf. Yet Helen failed to recover: for though the porter might have been negligent in that he could have foreseen damage to the parcel, he had no reason to suspect its unusual contents and its unexpectedly far-reaching hazard potential. The plaintiff, being outside the radius of foreseeable danger, was not therefore a person to whom the defendant 'owed a duty'; perhaps a better way of putting it would have been to say that the defendant was not negligent towards her because she was not a foreseeable victim. Negligence imports a relation between conduct and its consequences; one can be negligent only with respect to foreseeable consequences of one's action; and to hold the actor liable for a non-negligent (because unforeseeable) consequence to an 'unforeseeable plaintiff' is therefore incompatible with the rationale of negligence.

This approach is singularly tender to the interest of defendants, tolerant of windfalls if, through some random chance, the hapless victim of wrongful conduct fails in his personal qualifications for redress. It would, for instance, exonerate a motorist who negligently failed to slow down when passing an infant school but instead of running into a heedless toddler happened to knock down a cyclist who suddenly darted into his path. Should we take the cavalier view that against the latter risk the defendant need not have guarded and thus was not negligent towards the cyclist, notwith-

[10] *Palsgraf* v. *Long Island R.R.* (1928), 248 N.Y. 339, 162 N.E. 99. The House of Lords decision endorsing the same principle was *Bourhill* v. *Young*, [1943] A.C. 92 (plaintiff failed to recover for nervous shock sustained from hearing the crash of a collision from a position of safety).

standing the fact that he was wrong in not slowing down and that, had he done so, he would have been able to miss him?

But although this principle usually militates against the plaintiff, it may occasionally work in his favour. For if he happens to be more vulnerable to injury than the ordinary person, he is apparently entitled to insist that reasonable care may require special precautions for his sake which would not otherwise be necessary. A detergent or cosmetic product, for example, requires a warning notice on the label no less because only a small number of potential users would be allergic to it. True, the extra burden or cost to the manufacturer is entitled to consideration, but only as one factor to be weighed against the chance and gravity of the injury. Thus reasonable care may demand a temporary suspension of road building operations from a contractor warned by an adjacent breeder of mink that his animals are especially susceptible to fright from noise during the whelping season and might devour their young. In such a case it may be one thing to call a halt for a day or two, but quite another to enjoin the use of modern road-building equipment all the year round.

In a similar manner special precautions may be proper to safeguard blind people against certain conditions that are hazardous to them but not to others endowed with sight. On the one hand, the blind must be expected to compensate for their handicap to the best of their ability, and cannot expect padded lamp posts; but on the other, they are entitled to reasonable mobility without necessarily having a constant attendant. Thus it is not too much to ask from a repair gang that they should place a low barrier around a trench in the pavement instead of a mere sloping hammer which the blind plaintiff missed with his stick and thus came to fall. Quite obviously, a normal sighted individual would not have succeeded, because the precautions actually taken were perfectly adequate for the likes of him; nor would it have helped him to argue that additional precautions, which in the event would have saved him from injury, were required for the sake of the blind. The short answer, again, is that he must build on a wrong done to himself, not on a wrong done to somebody else—especially when the latter remains purely hypothetical.

With this said we may now take a closer look at certain illustrations of the degree to which foreseeability has sometimes been subordinated to other competing policies in formulating legal duty relations.

2. OMISSIONS

Negligence is commonly defined to include both acts and omissions fraught with unreasonable risk of injury, and for most purposes such generalizations provide an adequate working rule. Yet the distinction, deeply rooted in the common law, between misfeasance and nonfeasance, if more muted than of old, is still sufficiently vital to command our attention.

The early common law was too preoccupied with suppressing flagrant violations of the peace to worry about complaints that harm had ensued from what someone had failed to do rather than what he had actually done. The trespass wrongs were, therefore, uniformly linked to affirmative misconduct. Liability for failing to act entered the law much later in the context of charges that the defendant had gone back on a promise to render a performance, for which legal sanctions came to be contingent upon proof that the promisee had furnished some consideration. In other words, an obligation to do something for someone else had to be purchased for a price; and to this day contract has remained, if no longer the sole, still the most prominent source of affirmative duties.

The aversion to any more far-reaching commitment finds support in that strain of individualism in our culture which is content to condone the indifference of the Priest and Levite and dismiss the Samaritan as setting a standard for private choice but not public compulsion. The force of organized society which we call law is fully employed by restraining men from committing affirmative acts of harm and shrinks from converting courts into an agency for forcing men to help each other. When Lord Atkin enunciated the modern credo that 'the rule that you are to love your neighbour becomes in law that you must not injure your neighbour', he noticeably refrained from demanding that you must also assist him in escaping injury. Critical to any assessment of legal responsibility is still the fact that, in the case of commission, the defendant is charged with having worsened the plaintiff's position, with having *created* the risk; whereas in the case of omission the worst that can be said of him is that he failed to confer a benefit on the plaintiff by saving him from a detriment. Though collectivist tendencies in our midst have somewhat blunted the edge of this conviction, the change has translated itself more into an expectation of public assistance than of private initiative.

The line of demarcation between active misconduct and passive inaction is, however, far from precise. Everyone agrees that an omission in the course of active conduct is treated like active negligence. Failure to brake, give a hand signal, or keep a lookout are not instances of supine inaction; they are merely incidents of negligent driving—surely an active enterprise which demands from the driver that he both *do and omit to do* all that is needed to prevent it from becoming an active instrument of harm to others.[11] From this it is not a far step to insist that anyone who has created a situation of peril, however blamelessly, falls under a consequential duty to prevent it from culminating in injury and, most probably, even to render aid to anyone actually injured. Thus if a car breaks down just beneath the crest of a hill, without any blame at all attaching to the driver, he must exert himself to warn approaching traffic. Although he did not *tortiously* create the hazard, he did create it; and it rightly falls upon him to take affirmative steps to eliminate it, unlike some passing motorist who may with impunity decline a call for help, disdaining to be his brother's keeper.

Yet it would serve clarity at least to face the problem; the failure in some recent cases to do so may well have contributed to an unprecedented expansion of liability. Home purchasers, complaining of slipping foundations, sued not only the responsible builder but also the local

[11] This clearly is what Lord Atkin had in mind when he admonished 'to take reasonable care to avoid acts or *omissions* which you can reasonably foresee would be likely to *injure* your neighbour'. Pure omissions might fail to protect but do not injure.

authority for certifying the foundations as complying with local bye-laws. Was the inspector's failure to check an omission or was it converted into a commission by the act of certification? Clearly, the builder, not the inspector, caused the inadequate foundations; the only charge that could be levied against the inspector was that he failed to protect the plaintiff against injury by the builder. By holding him liable the courts, perhaps unwittingly, expanded the 'neighbour principle' to include a duty not only to injure but also to help your neighbour.[12]

It is, however, presumably still true that if one is in no way involved in another's plight, one may with impunity refrain from tendering a helping hand even when to do so would avert the peril with little effort. The law, as we shall see, will strain to support altruistic action, but is not yet prepared to compel it. A doctor may evidently flout his Hippocratic oath[13] and even refuse first-aid to a stranger, just as a good swimmer on the beach is free to ignore the shout for help from someone in danger of drowning.

Even if he starts upon a Samaritan mission, it is by no means clear that he may not break off before completing it in defiance of the dictates of reasonable care. Once out in the water he may find much in the law that would allow him to change his mind with impunity, perhaps upon espying that it is a hated rival of his in difficulty; though if he carries on, he must betake himself to exercise reasonable care in the way he handles him going back ashore. The critical question is whether he overstepped the line into misfeasance by making the other's condition worse than it was before he interfered or merely withheld from him some attention that would have made it better. Thus by depriving him of the benefit of help by others he would have 'advanced to such a point as to have launched a force or instrument of harm', beyond 'where inaction was at most a refusal to become an instrument

[12] In *Anns* v. *Merton B.C.*, [1978] A.C. 728, their Lordships seem to have lost sight of this problem, and of the injury being economic, in their pre-occupation with the administrative law aspect of the case (*infra*, p. 68).

[13] I.e. so far as the law of torts is concerned. He may of course be amenable to professional discipline.

for good'.[14] This may occur not only when he actually removes a casualty from a public place to where his plight would be hidden from the gaze of those who might otherwise have helped him, but no less when—like the swimmer—he gets out into the surf and thereby dissuades others from coming to the rescue.

Beyond this there is a mounting tendency, hitherto expressed mainly in North American decisions but one which English courts would most probably follow, to insist on a duty of care to render aid as between parties who stand to each other in a special relationship like that of employer and employee, carrier and passenger, or occupier and lawful visitor. In the tragic *Ogopogo* case it was applied to the captain-owner of a cabin cruiser and a passenger who fell overboard.[15] In these situations there already subsists a duty of affirmative care which obliges the one to safeguard the other against unreasonably dangerous conditions whatever their origin, and it would be no more than conformable to the spirit of that conventional doctrine to demand also that it include an obligation to rescue and render aid regardless of whether or not he bears any responsibility whatever for the other's predicament. Nor would it be a great deal more radical to impose such a duty also on anyone who happened to be in control of the instrumentality that caused, however innocently, the plaintiff's injury, since that is really no more than a corollary of the duty to take corrective action *before* the risk materializes which, we have already seen, devolves on anyone who has become instrumental in creating a situation of danger. Surely it is not asking too much of a motorist to stop and render aid to a pedestrian with whom he has collided even if he was in no way to blame for the accident. Criminal legislation against hit-and-run drivers should, in this instance, be properly reinforced by making the violator liable for

[14] *Moch Co.* v. *Rensselaer Water Co.*, (N.Y. 1928) 159 N.E. 896, 898 (Cardozo C. J.).

[15] *Horsley* v. *McLaren*, [1972] S.C.R. 441. The captain responded but failed to rescue in time. Another passenger died in attempting to rescue his friend. In the end, claims against the captain failed because he was found not negligent, but various views were expressed on whether the defendant's negligence, if any, was causal; whether his attempt at rescue in any event placed him under duty; whether the defendant could be held liable although he did not cause the original accident and whether one rescuer could become liable to another. See Alexander, 22 *U.Tor.L.J.* 98 (1972).

any injury that his callousness may entail. It will be noticed also that none of the above-mentioned instances raise the difficulty why one particular individual rather than another should be singled out for carrying the burden of assistance, for in all of them the conditions raising the duty point their finger at the defendant alone.

Gratuitous undertakings

Another classical illustration of the nonfeasance rule is the conventional refusal to attach liability for foreseeable loss resulting from failure to perform a gratuitous promise. To do otherwise, it is thought, would give the go-by to the cardinal rule of contract law that gratuitous promises are unenforceable for lack of consideration. Is there any room here for a tort remedy?

The characteristic function of the law of contract is to permit recovery for loss of the anticipated benefits of a bargain; in other words, to protect the promisee's expectation interest by indemnifying him for prospective advantages lost.[16] In contrast the law of torts concerns itself solely with reparation of injuries suffered. Accordingly it has long been recognized that to permit a claim for damage done incidental to a gratuitous relationship in no way trenches upon the contractual requirement of consideration. If I agree to help out a friend by storing his car for a time, I am free to change my mind because the promise was gratuitous and therefore beyond the pale of contractual sanction. But I am under no lesser obligation for all that to handle the car with care while it is in my charge. If any damage results either from the way I treat it or just from exposing it to risk of injury by others, I cannot take refuge behind the absence of consideration, for the good and sufficient reason that I am being sued for the damage I have done, not for the promise I did not keep.

A closer question arises when the gist of complaint is that the defendant's promise lulled the plaintiff into reliance so that he desisted from taking steps himself to procure alternative means of performance. Easiest perhaps to construe as 'sounding in tort' are claims for personal injury to person or

[16] This is not to say that in some situations damages may not be claimed and assessed on the basis of damage suffered, e.g. in personal injury claims for breach of warranty, or where the plaintiff is unable to prove lost profits.

tangible property resulting from injurious reliance, as when some apparently reliable person fails to call a doctor as promised and the victim dies for want of prompt medical attention, or, as in the quaint case from Louisiana,[17] the owner of a cat which had bitten the plaintiff undertook to keep it under observation for rabies but allowed it to escape so that the plaintiff had unnecessarily, as it turned out, to take the precaution of undergoing the harrowing Pasteur treatment. More frequent, however, are claims for purely pecuniary loss, as in the old case where Deas promised Thorne that he would procure insurance on Thorne's brig, but failed to carry out his undertaking, and the vessel perished before Thorne had become aware that his reliance was misplaced.[18] Although economic loss is usually associated with breach of contract, second thoughts would suggest that the instant claim was really founded not so much on the defendant's failure to honour his undertaking as on the detriment inflicted by his leaving the plaintiff lulled in a false sense of reliance that he had himself engendered.

Even so, however, it is still true (as we shall presently see at greater length) that the common law has been significantly more reserved about allowing damages for negligently inflicted economic loss than for physical injury. Yet British courts have for almost two hundred years displayed remarkable zeal for fastening upon some elements of 'misfeasance' in support of such claims against would-be insurers, (for instance, on the irrelevant fact that the latter took some active steps towards his assignment) or for alternatively torturing the relation into the semblance of contract.[19] The hope is perhaps not entirely ill-founded that this auspicious catena of decisions might eventually come to be reinterpreted as the nucleus of a more promising principle of injurious reliance, confident enough to dispense with the crutches of fiction yet conformable with long-accredited notions concerning the respective spheres of contract and tort.[20]

[17] *Marsalis* v. *La Salle* (1957), 94 So. 2d 120.

[18] *Thorne* v. *Deas* (1809), 4 Johns. 84 (N.Y.).

[19] *Wilkinson* v. *Coverdale* (1793), 1 Esp. 75.

[20] This is not to dispute that reliance also plays an important role in why the law enforces promises and in 'reliance damages'.

Controlling others

Duties to exercise care in controlling third persons are yet another well-established category of obligations of affirmative action. Understandably our law has been chary in demanding that one interfere in somebody else's conduct in order to prevent him from causing harm, but certain relations call for special assurances of safety in accordance with prevailing expectations in the community. The defendant may be involved in such a critical relation either because the plaintiff is entitled to rely on him for protection or because the third party is subject to his control.

A prominent instance of the first kind is the familiar relation between an occupier of premises and his visitors. For example, patrons of a pub or place of entertainment are entitled to the benefit of reasonable care from the management against danger from the way other guests or intruders conduct themselves. No less is a parent or teacher under a duty to his charges to protect them from molestation and other risks of injury whatever their source. Must a bank therefore hand over money to a robber rather than endanger customers in case of a shoot-out?

Even if an occupier owes such a duty to his visitors, apparently he does not to his neighbours. In one recent case, burglars entered the defendant's basement and hence broke into the plaintiff's storeroom. Complaints had been made repeatedly by the defendant's tenants about undesirables on the premises, but he was held to have no responsibility to people next door.[21] It would of course have made a difference if he had *tolerated* the condition, like the occupier who allowed football to be played next to a major road or campers to foul neighbouring property.[22]

Occasionally a duty to control another person arises on account of some special relation with him rather than with the person injured. This will be rare, as it trenches most sensitively on our general commitment to the philosophy of individualism.

Of all such instances where one person is held answerable for the injury done by another the most drastic is that of

[21] *Perl* v. *Camden L.B.C.*, [1984] Q.B. 342 (C.A.).

[22] *Hilder* v. *Associated Cement Manufacturers*, [1961] 1 W.L.R. 1434; *A.-G.* v. *Stone* (1895) 12 T.L.R. 76 (nuisance).

vicarious liability, like a master's for the torts of his servants committed in the course of employment. But that is a case of strict liability, altogether independent of any fault on the part of the master in selecting and supervising the servant. In contrast, here we are concerned with instances where the law does not attach liability automatically to one person for the torts of another, but only on proof that he failed to exercise reasonable care in controlling him such as would have spared the plaintiff from injury. The father as head of the family, for example, is no longer responsible as such for the actions of other members of his household, not even his unemancipated minor children. But the power to control children, combined with the demonstrable social necessity for keeping them under discipline, is exploited by the common law in demanding from those having them in their charge, principally parents and teachers, that they exercise reasonable care, commensurate with their opportunity and ability for doing so, to control the children for the sake of public safety. Most often the parent is charged with negligence in conniving at the child's possession of such latter-day toys as guns and other instruments of destruction and torture, or in failing to divert him from some other form of mischief. But the principle has also been invoked in less sensational situations, as when an infant of four celebrated his teacher's momentary inattention by escaping from the nursery through an unlocked door into the street, causing a lorry-driver to swerve violently into a tree in order to avoid the boy. By analogy, a duty to control may also be fastened on someone who voluntarily takes charge of an individual known to harbour dangerous propensities, as when a mental hospital was held liable for allowing a lunatic with a history of sexual crime to escape and commit an indecent assault on the claimant. Some American courts have not even shrunk from imposing a duty on psychiatrists to warn someone threatened by an outpatient during therapy, despite the notorious difficulties of predicting dangerousness and the conflicting obligation of confidentiality. A defaulting therapist was accordingly held liable for the victim's death.[23]

Least clear are the outlines of responsibility for entrusting

[23] *Tarasoff* v. *University of California* (1976), 551 P. 2d 334.

an instrument to someone who subsequently wields it to the plaintiff's injury. For instance, we tend to assume that it is none of a car dealer's business to inquire into the driving competence of adult purchasers,[24] though in contrast it is no longer questioned that one must observe reasonable care not to *lend* one's car to a person known to be an alcoholic or otherwise prone to dangerous driving. Again, for long courts opposed claims based on negligently selling liquor to drivers, even when known to be intoxicated; arguing that the proximate cause of any subsequent accident is not the selling of the liquor, but the drinking of it. The spuriousness of this explanation is shown up by the fact that it has not precluded claims for negligently entrusting a car to an intoxicated driver, for in both cases alike the defendant's 'entrusting' increases the foreseeable risk of an accident due to the driver's reduced ability to control the vehicle. In this instance, some courts have now reversed their position.[25]

3. NERVOUS SHOCK

Today there remain few reservations to the general postulate that one must so conduct oneself as not to expose anyone within the foreseeable range of one's activities to an unreasonable risk of physical injury. Administrative considerations, however, have loomed large in the past, and are still far from spent, in opposition to claims for nervous shock or mental disturbance.

These are based in large measure on prevalent fears that alleged injury to the nervous system is more easily simulated than external wounds inflicted by actual impact, and that judges, let alone juries, are ill equipped to pass upon vexing questions of causal relation between the defendant's negligence and the alleged psychosomatic trauma of the plaintiff, especially in face of conflicting medical evidence and such endemic distrust of psychiatry as has survived from the days when these problems were first encountered in legal practice. These apprehensions are thrown into relief all the more by contrast with the readiness with which damages have been

[24] But responsibility for subsequent accidents clearly devolves on retailers who sell guns to little children.

[25] E.g. *Jordan House* v. *Menow*, [1974] S.C.R. 239.

consistently allowed for mental suffering in the wake of physical injury caused by actual impact, not to speak of cases where some mental reaction like fright is merely a link between the defendant's negligence and eventual external injury, as when a mother, fearing for her children, suffered a black-out at the sight of an open lift-shaft and in consequence fell into it herself. In these situations the very existence of some external injury seems to carry sufficient conviction as to the genuineness of the particular claim.

This may be conveniently contrasted with the adamant refusal on the other side to lend any countenance whatever to claims for fright, anguish, and similarly offensive sensations, unless they actually result in 'physical injury'—which seems to mean in this connection that the mental suffering must at least be evidenced by objective and substantially harmful physical or psychopathological symptoms such as a period of hospitalization for nervous breakdown, prolonged suffering from cramps or migraine, or a miscarriage. Only in the case of assault, in the technical sense of being intentionally subjected to apprehension of imminent physical aggression, has legal protection against emotional disturbance been ready to disclaim this minimum safeguard against fabricated or trivial claims.

The problem is aggravated by the widely varying threshold of individual tolerance to psychic impact. Should a loud and unexpected traffic noise, perhaps from a nearby collision, become actionable at the suit of someone especially excitable?[26] True, the defendant's conduct must have been negligent in the first instance, but is it not arguably foreseeable that such a person might be among the crowd? As already noted, one's conduct may have to be geared to its foreseeable effect even on abnormal individuals, although balanced against the burden of taking safeguards. In sum, to consign claims for mental disturbance to the elusive standard of foreseeability without additional controls seemed irresponsible.

That severe mental distress could qualify as physical injury was first recognized in an action for *intentional* infliction, when a practical joker told a wife the pernicious lie that

[26] Cf. *Bourhill* v. *Young*, [1943] A.C. 92.

her husband had been badly hurt in a street accident.[27] This case, incidentally, gave opportunity for the first enunciation of the general principle that if a person wilfully does an act 'calculated' to cause harm to another and thereby infringe his legal right to personal safety, a cause of action arises in the absence of lawful justification for the act. But for mere negligence, in contrast to outrageous and plainly antisocial conduct, the courts at first encounter in the late nineteenth century refused to allow any claim at all for mental distress, unless the injury was at least the result of an actual impact. Otherwise the damage was categorically dismissed as 'unforeseeable' and hence 'too remote'.

This impact rule long dominated the American scene but was successfully challenged in England as early as 1901 by a pregnant woman whose fright at being confronted inside her husband's pub by a horse-drawn van caused her two months later to give premature birth to an idiot.[28] Much more stubborn proved the judicial reluctance to allow claims for mental distress sustained otherwise than from fear for one's own safety. Typical are those by a mother who witnesses an accident to her child from an upstairs window. Loyal to the *Palsgraf* approach, it was not enough that the defendant had been negligent to the child: the mother had to establish her independent credentials as a 'foreseeable plaintiff'. This she long continued to find difficult as courts persisted in holding that a person outside the zone of physical danger could not foreseeably suffer injury from shock.[29] Could there be any doubt that foreseeability was being manipulated to justify a foregone conclusion?

At long last, however, these equivocations lost their appeal. American courts still favour categorical restrictions: even if no longer insisting on the plaintiff being in the zone of danger, they usually demand that she be at least an eyewitness to the accident and a close relative to the person immediately imperilled. The latest English decision seems to be even more forgiving, allowing the claim of a wife and mother who rushed to the hospital

[27] *Wilkinson* v. *Downton*, [1897] 2 Q.B. 57.
[28] *Dulieu* v. *White*, [1901] 2 K.B. 669 (Div. Ct.).
[29] *King* v. *Phillips*, [1953] 1 Q.B. 429 (C.A.).

to see her injured family two hours after the accident.[30] Some of their Lordships seemed disposed to regard foreseeability as the sole test, but others still acknowledged a role for 'policy' without however agreeing as to any precise limits. Would this new permissiveness extend to claimants who merely read or heard of a calamity or who suffered distress over an accident to a stranger, perhaps even to a pet dog?

4. PRE-NATAL INJURY

A closely allied syndrome has also retarded recognition of the claim for injuries suffered before birth. Above all else this situation was beset by the woeful ignorance concerning the nexus between trauma to a mother during pregnancy and a later premature birth, miscarriage, or congenital defect in the infant like cerebral palsy, clubfeet, or mongolism. Rather than countenance uncertain and often bitterly contested medical disquisition over the details of each particular case, the virtually unanimous response of the courts until quite recently was to turn their back on all of them without distinction. Better to disappoint the occasional meritorious claimant than to open the door to a flood of spurious litigation and 'enter a field that has no sensible or just stopping-point'.

The favoured judicial technique employed to this end was to seek refuge in the denial of any duty due to the *nasciturus*. Invoking the now familiar *Palsgraf* rationale, it could be argued that, though the defendant might have been negligent to the mother, this could not avail the foetus in her womb, of whose existence he knew nothing and whom he could therefore make bold to disown as a 'neighbour'. This argument, however, was by no means impregnable, because it failed to account for the curiously unexplained assumption that in this situation the duty of care did not as ordinarily extend to all of whose presence within the danger zone the actor was or *should have been* aware.

American courts were the first to raise the barrier, but experimented with two limitations: first, that the foetus had been born alive; and second, that it had been viable at the time of the accident. The first, eventually adopted also

[30] *McLaughlin* v. *O'Brian*, [1983] 1 A.C. 410.

by the only appellate Commonwealth decision[31] and by subsequent English legislation,[32] has two attractions. It bypasses the question whether a foetus is a legally protected *persona* at the time of the injury by taking the position that its complaint is of having been *born* handicapped. From a more practical point of view, the need for compensation is real in order to take care of future medical and maintenance expenses, but these do not arise in the case of still-birth. Any recovery would therefore only have enriched the parents who can claim in their own right for the cost and disappointment of the frustrated pregnancy.

The restriction of claims to injury of a viable foetus, however, is less defensible. It stems doctrinally from the simplistic notion that the foetus attains independent existence only at this stage rather than from conception or perhaps quickening.[33] It is also objectionable for its tendency to foreclose recovery for injury at the earliest stage of embryonic development when the foetus is most vulnerable, for example to German measles or dangerous drugs like thalidomide. Indeed, there is no reason, pragmatic or doctrinal, why the defendant's culpable conduct might not have preceded even the infant's conception, as when the mother was exposed to radiation or a wrong blood transfusion years before.[34]

The English Act which adopted the first but not the second of the above-mentioned restrictions, also addressed the question of claims by the infant against its parents. It differentiated between motoring accidents and other causes. The former involve compulsory insurance where the cost will not be borne by the culpable parent but spread among all motorists as a matter of transcendent social policy; other situations, however, are apt to raise invidious reproaches of parental conduct, like excessive smoking, drinking or taking drugs during pregnancy or infection with venereal disease.[35]

[31] *Watt* v. *Rama*, [1972] V.R. 353 (Victoria).

[32] Congenital Disabilities (Civil Liability) Act 1976.

[33] But the sanctity of life of a viable foetus is the special concern of the Infant Life (Preservation) Act 1929.

[34] The English Act imposes the condition that the parents did not know of the risk.

[35] The Pearson Commission recommended extending the mother's immunity under the Act also to the father.

Wrongful Life

In the preceding cases, the infant would have been born healthy but for the defendant's negligence; in others, the infant's tragic fate is that its only alternative to being born deformed is not being born at all. In that event, can the infant complain that the defendant should have prevented its birth? Can it raise a claim for 'wrongful life' against a doctor who negligently failed to diagnose the mother's German measles or some hereditary disease; perhaps even raise a claim against its mother for deciding against an abortion despite her knowledge of the risk to her child?

Objection to such claims is twofold: perhaps paramount is that the complaint against being born at all runs counter to our concept of the sanctity of human life;[36] even less controversial is the difficulty of computing the damages which would call for a comparison between the value of an impaired life and non-life. How can we 'determine that the child has lost anything without the means of knowing what, if anything, it has gained?'[37] We have experience in comparing life in an impaired and healthy condition, but that cannot be the test here: for, making the negligent doctor pay for the injuries would be to treat him as if he had caused them. The American pattern of rejecting 'wrongful life' claims on these grounds has been followed in England[38] and other countries.

But though no duty is owed to the child, might not one be owed to the mother to afford her an opportunity of choosing abortion?[39] The prevailing American disposition is to allow her damages for the cost of the unwanted pregnancy, perhaps even for the cost of taking care of the child's disability, but not for raising the child as such. The benefits of love and companionship balance any countervailing distress—both non-pecuniary values—as well as the economic cost of future care.

[36] At most, life may be so dreadful as to justify the termination of life-preserving procedures. Cf. *Re B (a minor)*, [1981] 1 W.L.R. 1421 (mongol).

[37] *McKay* v. *Essex Area Health Authority*, [1982] Q.B. 1166, 1181 (C.A.).

[38] Ibid.; Congenital Disabilities (Civil Liability) Act 1976 s.3(2)(b).

[39] The English Abortion Act 1967 permits abortion when 'there is a substantial risk that if the child were born it would suffer from such physical or mental abnormalities as to be severely handicapped.' This statute confers a *right* on the mother but does not impose a *duty* either on her or anyone else.

5. RESCUE

A suggestive contrast is raised by the rescue cases where foreseeability is nowadays wont to be stretched as far again beyond the norm as it falls short of it in the contexts just discussed of nervous shock and pre-natal injuries. This more than any other example reinforces the cautionary note sounded earlier that there is in truth much besides foreseeability to influence the formulation of a judgment whether a duty of care is appropriate to any given situation.

Actually the claim to redress by one injured in an attempt to rescue somebody negligently imperilled by the defendant has not always received a peculiarly sympathetic response. Far from it; legal doctrine reflected perhaps overlong the values of a rugged individualism that, if not actually deprecating anyone's aspiration to be his brother's keeper, thought it at least extravagant of him to expect someone else to pay the bill if his indulgence in Samaritan virtue went awry. So long as it stood in the shadow of this uncharitable philosophy, the law strained to discourage such pretensions by disqualifying the rescuer on the ground that he voluntarily assumed the risk or that his intervention, prompted by conscious volition, 'severed the chain of causation'—in other words, that the defendant's responsibility did not extend beyond injury to his immediate victim. But following the lead of the great Justice Cardozo, long the unrivalled oracle of tort jurisprudence on both sides of the Atlantic, English courts suddenly faltered, and veered off on precisely the opposite tack.

Sustaining recovery for the first time in the singularly propitious case of a policeman who had suffered injury in an attempt to halt a team of runaway horses from stampeding into a group of little children, later pronouncements have declined to limit it narrowly to rescuers who were under a legal duty or acted in virtually instinctive response to a crisis. Courage deserves no lesser reward when danger is deliberately faced. If humanitarianism gets the better in the event even of the instinct of self-preservation, it ill befits the law to ascribe to it that voluntariness without which a confrontation of danger cannot qualify for the defence of assumption of risk (*volenti non fit injuria*). By the same token nothing short of sheer foolhardiness could be condemned as contributory negligence. Nor does it seem to matter very much that the object of the rescue was to save property rather than human life; though one would think that, in considering whether the plaintiff acted reasonably, the relation between the value of the object rescued and the risk to be encountered cannot be wholly dismissed as irrelevant.

The problem of 'duty' has attracted but scant attention in the English cases, being submerged by preoccupation with the voluntary nature of the plaintiff's choice in its bearing upon the issue of 'legal cause' and the twin defences just discussed. Nonetheless, the tone was set early by Cardozo, J.'s classical pronouncement:

> Danger invites rescue. The cry of distress is the summons to relief. The law does not ignore these reactions of the mind in tracing conduct to its consequences. . . . The wrongdoer may not have foreseen the coming of a deliverer. He is accountable *as if* he had.[40]

Subsequent decisions by British and Commonwealth courts displayed the same capacity for vividly imagining a rescuer's likely arrival. This indulgent attitude is neatly illustrated in a judgment[41] which in the same breath declined to accept the presence of a toddler on the railway line at a small station as reasonably foreseeable, but had no similar reservation at all concerning the stationmaster's leap from the platform in a fatal attempt to save his son from a negligently approaching trolley. Even if allowance be made for a contraction of the range of imputed foresight with respect to the child, who had no business being there and hence bore the stigma of a technical trespasser, it is surely equally remarkable how readily the focus expanded at the sight of a rescuer—by squarely demanding that the defendant ought reasonably to have foreseen that 'if he did not observe care, *some emergency or other* might arise, and that *someone or other* might be impelled to expose himself to danger in order to effect a rescue'.

The same decision incidentally also demonstrates that the duty to the rescuer is not derivative, contingent on breach

[40] *Wagner* v. *International R.R.* (1921), 232 N.Y. 176, 180. (Italics added.) Cardozo was a great craftsman who chose his words with care.

[41] *Videan* v. *British Transport Commission*, [1963] 2 Q.B. 650 (C.A.).

of a primary duty owed to the person imperilled, but rather an independent obligation of care to avoid creating a situation that would prompt a rescue. This formulation neatly avoids the snares that would otherwise prejudice recovery in case the person to be rescued had himself no claim against the defendant on the ground, for example, that he was himself guilty of contributory negligence (so long at any rate as that constituted a complete bar), or that the defendant had brought the danger not on a third person, but on himself (one cannot owe a duty to oneself).

Thus it came to pass that, whereas little more than a generation ago rescuers might not unfairly have deplored their fate as Cinderellas of the law of torts, many a claimant today seems bent on qualifying as a rescuer in order to gain the fancied advantages of that status. What is the reason for this new-found benevolence?

The least the law can do, even if unwilling (as we have seen) to *compel* one citizen to help another, is to encourage him to do so. An important contribution towards that end is to assure him of compensation for any injury he may sustain in the venture. Tort law can help in this regard by offering redress against anyone who negligently created a rescue situation. Compensation schemes for victims of crimes of violence, including persons who valiantly come to the aid of others, offer another solution.[42] Finally, the law must seek to remove, or at least mitigate, any such deterrent for the rescuer as the spectre of his becoming liable himself. For example, he is entitled to demand, when coming to somebody's defence, that he may use such force to ward off the attack as he could have done to protect himself. It would also seem better policy in encouraging good citizenship to give the rescuer the benefit of any honest mistake he might make as to whether the occasion necessitates his using force, in the same way as we do for anyone acting in self-defence, rather than merely placing him in the same shoes as the person he purports to protect. Again, so far as emergency medical aid is concerned, we tend to make sympathetic allowance for the occasion, and do not put too fine a point

[42] The English scheme, set up without legislation since August 1964, is outlined in a White Paper ('Compensation for Victims of Crimes of Violence', Cmnd. 2323).

on whether he came up to the standard of professional competence. Some American legislatures, indeed, have yielded to the plea of flatly exonerating good Samaritans from all liability for negligence in order to encourage doctors to render first aid without fear of being held to ransom by the occasional ingrate.

6. WORDS

Verbal injury has been treated much more gingerly by the law than physical damage. For one thing, people tend to take less trouble over what they say than what they do; for another, communication is so essential and constant in social intercourse, whether on private or business occasions, that wider tolerance is necessary in the interests of freedom of speech. This explains much of the traditional caution manifested by the law towards all forms of verbal injury. The impediments placed on actionable defamation reflect the countervailing concern of a free society in the free flow of information and criticism particularly on matters of public interest. Injurious falsehood, like deprecating the quality of a competitor's merchandise, must make allowance for the pursuit of competitive advantage in the market place and is therefore actionable only on proof of malice. Even verbal threats remained outside the purview of 'assault' and eventually called for a new rule of liability for intentional infliction of mental disturbance, covering outrageous acts as well as words.

Not surprisingly, liability for negligence in word has made only slow progress, long retarded by its fateful link with the action for deceit.

Fraud

The action for deceit has had a long and troubled history. Long confined to special relations, like those between contracting parties, it was not until 1789 that in *Pasley* v. *Freeman*[43] English law recognized a *general* obligation of honesty in word and conduct, against a defendant who had deliberately lied to the plaintiff in answering an inquiry concerning a third party's credit-worthiness. This propitious headstart, however, was never fully matched by later development.

[43] 3 T.R. 51.

Caution, to the verge of timidity, prevailed. Courts of equity, it is true, never shared these scruples and granted their own remedies for misrepresentation, whether deliberate or innocent. Always concerned with 'good conscience', the Chancellor felt that specific performance of a conveyance or contract ought to be denied to petitioners whose 'hands were not clean' because they had misled the other party, and that even rescission, at least of an executory bargain and in grave cases even of a completed transaction, ought to be decreed on that ground. But damages were not in the equitable armoury, and when the day of testing arrived in the great case of *Derry* v. *Peek*,[44] the House of Lords insisted that there could be no damages for fraud unless the defendant was guilty of deceit—having either told a deliberate lie or, what amounts to the same thing, lacked belief in the truth of what he said. Negligence in the sense of speaking honestly but without reasonable grounds was not sufficient, unlike actual recklessness—an attitude of conscious indifference to the truth, not caring one way or the other.

That proof of such a guilty state of mind presents a formidable problem in practice weighed heavily with those who criticized the decision for undermining commercial morality or at least hampering the law in its potential for raising it. In order to propriate this rubuke, it was, however, conceded that total absence of reasonable grounds—if not fraud *per se*—might, all the same, support an inference that, despite his protestations, the defendant knowingly lied; yet there remains a clear distinction between saying that he *must* have known and that he *should* have known. The first means that he really did know despite his protestations to the contrary, the latter that he did not but would have done had he only taken more trouble.

Derry v. *Peek* was commonly interpreted as not only settling the limits of the action for deceit, but as proscribing all damages at common law for non-fraudulent misrepresentation. Even in bargaining contexts, the law remained unsympathetic to the representee. Negligent pre-contractual representations were not actionable in contract any more than in tort, unless they were promissory and meant to become terms of the resulting contract (in which event

[44] (1889), 14 App. Cas. 337.

they could found an action for breach of contract).[45] Thus a buyer would have been foolish to place reliance on assurances given by the seller in the course of dickering—*caveat emptor.* The most he could hope for was to cancel ('to rescind') the bargain if still in time, i.e. before he had accepted the goods, with perhaps a few days of grace thereafter. In practical effect, this meant—not at all, as he was unlikely to become aware of the truth until it was too late: in other words, his right of redress was stillborn.

This conclusion evinced not only insouciance over prevailing ethics of bargaining and the law's capacity for improving them, but also a perplexing lack of orientation when one considers on the other side the law's anxious concern with protecting buyers through 'implied' warranties. It meant that less reliance could be placed on what a seller said than on what the law would hold him to have assured 'impliedly' (i.e. tacitly) concerning the quality of the goods. This tragic aberration has now been corrected in England by a statute which confers a right to damages on a person induced to enter an agreement by misrepresentation of the other party, as much when that misrepresentation was negligent as when it was fraudulent.[46] As we shall see in a moment, this reform anticipated the eventual judicial extension of tort liability to negligent pre-contractual representations. In the United States, the law had long been more protective of buyers because 'any promise or representation of fact which has the natural tendency to induce the buyer to purchase the goods'[47] qualifies as an express warranty for breach of which he may recover damages.

Physical injury

Against physical injury a duty of care has long been recognized for word no less than deed. Indeed it usually passes without much notice that the defendant's negligence consisted in a misrepresentation rather than in something he 'did'

[45] In more recent years, however, under Lord Denning's unremitting prodding, judges became readier to help buyers by 'inferring' such a mutual intent.

[46] Misrepresentation Act 1967 which requires the defendant to prove that 'he had reasonable grounds to believe and did believe . . . that the facts represented were true'.

[47] Uniform Sales Act, §12; Uniform Commercial Code §2-313 (1) (*a*) ('becomes part of the basis of the bargain').

or failed to 'do'. For example, the responsibility of an occupier for injury sustained by a visitor is usually footed, not on his having hurt him while doing something like swinging a coal shovel, or even having sometime in the past 'created' the danger as by insecurely fixing a curtain rail, but simply on his having failed to warn him of a trap whatever its origin. In short, his failure in that respect is reprehensible because his premises are not as safe as they *appeared* to be. That this is the crux of responsibility, viz. his implied misrepresentation of safety, is thrown into focus by the fact that rarely, if ever, has an injured visitor a cause for complaint once he has been warned or otherwise become apprised of the peril.

As the last example illustrates, the line between doing and representing, between gesture and speech, is at once too fine and irrelevant for purposes of accident law. Nor should it matter that misrepresentation rarely causes injury without somebody's intervening action in reliance on it, instead of inflicting injury 'directly'. As we shall see in more detail when discussing 'remoteness of damage', it has long ceased to be an excuse that a dangerous condition created by one person's negligence was actually set off by another; especially when (as in the present context) it was intended or at least calculated to prompt or induce the action in reliance. The only relevance attributable to this factor is its bearing on whether such reliance was foreseeable and the resulting injury therefore a consequence within the risk for which the defendant must bear responsibility. This, however, is a question of fact, and no justification for any categorical generalization.

Not only may it be actionable therefore to label kerosene 'water', but even to label water 'kerosene'. This was tragically borne out when a science teacher, using a sample kit of petroleum products, poured the contents of a flask thus wrongly labelled over metallic sodium, which has a high degree of oxidization and is therefore stored in oil, and set off an explosion. Care in labelling was all the more imperative as the suppliers knew full well that the exhibit would be used in the school laboratory and taken for what it purported to be.[48] More difficult was the problem presented in a Canadian

[48] *Pease* v. *Sinclair Refining Co.* (2 Cir. 1939), 104 F. 2d 183.

case[49] where a newspaper carelessly printed a false report of a man's death which caused his wife a severe shock. Although this was actually one of the rare instances of a misrepresentation 'directly' causing physical injury, an important countervailing factor which, in the event, tilted the balance against recovery was the burden that any duty of care in checking incoming information would impose on a newspaper. This obviously furnishes a more convincing, if debatable, explanation for the decision than any pretence that the injury was unforeseeable or that reliance was unjustifiable. It also helps to explain the opposite conclusion reached in what at first blush looks like a very similar case, where officials of a lunatic asylum falsely informed a wife, under a mistake of identity, that her husband had just been certified.[50]

Liability for physical injury may ensue no less when the misrepresentation caused a third person, rather than the plaintiff himself, to act on it to his detriment. Thus, if someone were to shout 'Fire' into a crowded audience, causing a stampede, he would be responsible to any victim (or his dependants), whether he had done it deliberately as a practical joke or carelessly without due consideration for the risks entailed.

Economic loss

The core of resistance to the idea of a general duty of care in words had always related to claims for purely economic loss. What haunted the courts for so long was the spectre of liability unlimited in amount, in time, and in the number of potential claimants.[51] Information is apt to get around far and fast, may influence the judgment of numerous people in untold transactions, and, if inaccurate or false, entail incalculable losses. Thus, whereas negligent *action* is ordinarily spent in one blow, even if we grant that once in a long while its destructive range may be devastating as in aircraft disasters, negligent information relevant to business dealings typically has a greater potential for widespread loss, both in the

[49] *Guay* v. *Sun Publishing Co.*, [1953] 2 S.C.R. 216.

[50] *Barnes* v. *The Commonwealth* (1937), 37 S.R. (N.S.W.) 511.

[51] These triple indeterminates stem from Cardozo J.'s judgment in *Ultramares Corp.* v. *Touche* (N.Y. 1931) 174 N.E. 441, 444.

number of people affected and in the amounts involved. Bearing in mind, finally, that for precisely these reasons the law has been generally hesitant in protecting economic interests against any form of negligence, even negligent acts, its reluctance until quite recently in lending any countenance at all to negligent verbal injury in this area will hardly appear surprising.

Plainly enough, however, there is a middle ground between the extremes of denying recovery in all circumstances and opening it up without qualification to the general formula of 'reasonable foresight'. Allowance is made, as a matter of general understanding in social intercourse, for the fact that a good deal of what people say must be discounted either because they are speaking on a matter in which their duty and interest palpably conflict or because the occasion is one in which they do not expect for some other reason to be taken at their word. Hence, no duty of care is warranted unless the speaker can fairly be taken to have assumed responsibility for his advice, opinion, or information. It is one thing for a tax consultant to venture some legal advice to a casual acquaintance on the golf course, but quite another to a client in his office. It is doubtful whether investment hints offered in the column of a newspaper are meant to do more than stimulate reader-interest, or even whether text-books or encyclopaedias on technical subjects purport to assume responsibility for the accuracy, if indeed so much as care in accuracy, concerning the information they contain.

If the key, then, is the assumption of responsibility by the representor, the duty of care will fall primarily on persons whose profession it is to render appraisals, give opinions, or issue certificates, such as accountants, valuers, bankers, safety inspectors, and so forth. Thus in the English landmark case of *Hedley Byrne* v. *Heller*[52] which finally admitted liability for negligent statements causing pecuniary loss outside the traditional area of contractual or fiduciary relations, a bank had carelessly given an inaccurate credit report on one of its clients at the request of another bank acting on behalf of an advertising agency about to extend substantial credit to him. As it was, the defendants successfully took shelter behind the express assurance which had accompanied the inquiry that it

[52] [1964] A.C. 465.

was wanted 'in confidence and without responsibility'. Thus the House of Lords, while going out of the way in making their important affirmation of liability for negligent verbal injury, did not find it necessary to commit themselves on whether a bank reference would have involved an implicit assumption of responsibility in the absence of such a disclaimer. Unquestionably a bank owes a duty of care in giving information or advice to its own customers, including prospective customers, but the conflict of interest involved in furnishing a credit reference concerning one of its own clients to an outsider, as well as the burden that would be involved in checking, furnish impressive arguments against such liability.

How cautious, perhaps over-cautious, courts have remained was illustrated by a Privy Counsel appeal from Australia which insisted that the 'special duty' of care was demanded only from persons whose business or profession it is to provide information or advice of a kind calling for special skill and competence, or who at least give the recipient to understand that they claim to possess these qualities. It did not apply, therefore, to financial information given to an insurance policy holder on the affairs of a fellow-subsidiary finance company.[53] This decision has been widely deplored and indeed disregarded. The Court of Appeal has refused to accept it as a statement of English law and imposed liability, for instance, for negligent pre-contractual statements by sellers and other non-professionals;[54] nor has the Australian High Court been deflected from holding public bodies accountable for supplying relevant information, such as answering zoning inquiries.[55]

Another important limitation concerns the size of the protected class. Fear of extravagant liability is most easily assuaged when the statement is communicated to a specific person or persons for a known, or at least foreseeable, purpose. Such was the case of the public weigher who issued a false weight receipt to a buyer of beans, in consequence of which he overpaid;[56] and the warehouseman who furnished false information concerning the location of goods to their

[53] *M.L.C.* v. *Evatt*, [1971] A.C. 793.
[54] *Esso Petroleum* v. *Mardon*, [1976] Q.B. 801.
[55] *Shaddock* v. *Parramatta C.C.* (1981), 55 A.L.J.R. 713.
[56] *Glanzer* v. *Shephard* (N.Y. 1922), 135 N.E. 275.

owner who needed it for insurance purposes, with result that they were not covered against fire.[57]

On the other hand, less progress has been made with extending liability to members of an indeterminate class, such as potential investors relying on a misleading company audit. It was in just such a case, *Ultramares Corp.* v. *Touche*,[58] where thirty copies of an audit had been requested from the accountants, that Cardozo J. dismissed the claim of one investor with his celebrated dictum against liability 'indeterminate in amount, time and class'. The more recent trend, however, both in America and the Commonwealth has relaxed this opposition at least in cases where it was foreseeable that some one, perhaps even more than one, member of a 'limited class' might reasonably rely on the audit for the purpose of making an investment or take-over.[59]

What perhaps remains puzzling is the evidently greater solicitude for accountants compared with manufacturers and other enterprises. Deterrence is not served by excusing auditors, seeing that their paymasters would usually be the last to complain about too favourable a picture of their financial affairs. Are we less concerned because the loss is merely pecuniary rather than physical injury? Perhaps the strongest defence is that auditors, unlike manufacturers, are unable to distribute the cost among a sufficiently large number of clients or indeed among most of those who use their work product.[60] The effect of imposing unrestricted liability might be either to drive accountants out of business or compel them to resort to extensive disclaimers. Neither consequence would help the public.

7. ECONOMIC LOSS

The intriguing question left in the wake of the House of Lords decision in *Hedley Byrne* was whether it represented

[57] *International Products* v. *Erie R. Co.* (N.Y. 1927), 115 N.E. 662.

[58] (N.Y. 1931) 174 N.E. 441. But Parliament has long since conferred a right to damages on investors against company directors for false information in prospectuses: Companies Act 1948 s. 43.

[59] *JEB Fasteners* v. *Marks, Bloom & Co.*, [1981] 3 All E.R. 289; *Scott* v. *McFarlane*, [1978] 1 N.Z.L.R. 553 (C.A.); *Haigh* v. *Bamford*, [1977] 1 S.C.R. 466.

[60] See Bishop, 'Negligent Misrepresentation through Economists' Eyes', 96 *L.Q.R.* 360 (1980).

a new departure not only for negligent misrepresentation but also for negligent economic loss. That past opposition to liability for negligent misrepresentation was linked more to concern over the plaintiff's loss than the defendant's conduct was evident from the greater readiness to support claims for physical injury, already noted. While it has since become clear that there is no longer a categorical bar against damages for purely economic loss, the continuing process of reorientation has not yet produced any confident guidance, let alone a comprehensive principle.

Some distinctions, however, are appropriate. Not in question, for example, is the long-established practice of allowing damages for economic loss *consequential* on personal injury or damage to tangible property, like medical expenses, loss of earnings and even lost profits resulting from damage to business machinery. At issue is only 'purely pecuniary loss' standing alone.

One prominent example concerns *secondary* losses, i.e. those suffered by persons other than the direct victim because of their relationship or dependence on him, like family members of a person injured or killed. The common law was in general opposed to such claims, apprehensive of the burden, in view of the frequency with which injury to one person has economic repercussions on others with whom he maintained family or business relations. Thus it required a statute, Lord Campbell's Act (1846), to permit recovery for dependant next-of-kin of a person killed, but this has no parallel for non-fatal accidents.[61]

Whether there remains a categorical bar to all other secondary economic losses is still an open question. In one case a cattle auctioneer sued unsuccessfully for loss of business as a result of an outbreak of foot and mouth disease caused by the negligent escape of virus from a laboratory.[62] Likewise in the 'cable cases' a contractor who fractured an underground power line in the course of road construction was excused for the financial loss of nearby businesses caused by the interruption of electricity supply.[63] He would be

[61] The husband's archaic action for loss of *consortium* was abolished in England in 1982. Some other jurisdictions eliminated the sex discrimination by extending the action to wives.

[62] *Weller* v. *Foot and Mouth Disease Research Institute*, [1966] 1 Q.B. 569.

[63] *Spartan Steel* v. *Martin*, [1973] Q.B. 27 (C.A.).

responsible to the owner of the cable, but not to the businesses which depended on the integrity of the cable. The latter could recover for physical damage, for example for spoiled perishables or damaged machinery, provided it was foreseeable, but not for purely economic loss such as the profits they would have made during the shutdown. Such losses, while foreseeable in incident, are hardly foreseeable in extent, and in any event better calculable by the affected business than by the contractor. Businesses can make advance arrangements against such contingencies, for example by acquiring standby generators or by calculating them into their cost structure, as they must do for power blackouts from excessive user demand or strikes.

On this reasoning, it should make no difference that the defendant knew of the plaintiff as a specific person who would suffer foreseeable loss. Suppose as a result of negligent navigation a ship disabled a buoy for unloading tankers. Would it be defensible to distinguish between the claims for extra costs incurred by a tanker which was at the time anchored there and another which arrived the day after?[64]

In cases of *direct* injury plaintiffs have fared better. Thus negligent solicitors have been held liable to disappointed legatees whose legacy failed because the will was not properly attested.[65] Here there is no problem of multiple claimants and, in the absence of a tort claim by the legatee, there would be no effective sanction against the negligent lawyer. But should not liability be confined, as in cases of negligent misrepresentation, to defendants who undertake to perform a business or service, a principal object of which is to protect the plaintiff's economic interests? This test would have been satisfied by the frustrated legatee but less certainly in the following case.

In *Junior Books* v. *Veitchi Co.*,[66] a building owner successfully claimed from a subcontractor the cost of replacing defective floor tiles and loss of business profits during the

[64] *Caltex Oil (Australia)* v. *The Dredge Willemstad* (1976), 136 C.L.R. 529 might suggest recovery for the first, but *Osborne Panama SA* v. *Shell & BP*, 1982(3) S.A. 890 denied it for the second.

[65] *Ross* v. *Caunters*, [1980] Ch. 297; contra; *Seale* v. *Perry*, [1982] V.R. 193, (based on lack of reliance and absence of a vested interest).

[66] [1983] 1 A.C. 520.

repairs, on the ground that the relation between them fell 'only just short of a contractual relationship' and that the loss was sufficiently foreseeable and proximate to withstand any justifiable fear that it would open the 'floodgates' of liability. But this decision by the House of Lords is not free from criticism. It used to be assumed that tort liability for a defective product was confined to damage it might do to *other* property and that complaints about its own condition fell to the province of contract alone. Tort deals with accidents and safety, contract with bad bargains. Moreover, what justification is there for this new tort 'assault on the citadel of privity'? It might well demand from the subcontractor a standard of performance substantially higher than that contracted for by him with the head contractor; also the contractual structuring of the complex relationship between the three parties might have been due to a deliberate choice that the owner should only look to the head contractor for adequate performance and make complaints only within the stipulated period of one year which had long elapsed. At least the Court disclaimed any intention of extending its ruling to consumers of defective products in general on the, unconvincing, ground that they, unlike the building owner, constituted a class of unforeseeable plaintiffs.

8. PUBLIC POWERS: PRIVATE DUTIES

The twentieth century has been marked by a progressive increase in governmental functions and responsibilities, as one characteristic of the welfare state. As public bodies are being entrusted with powers to perform tasks that had hitherto gone unheeded, the question has increasingly come to the fore whether such powers entail a corresponding duty of care to exercise them so as to save private individuals from injury.

The initial response was to invoke the familiar distinction, already noted, between misfeasance and nonfeasance, thereby confining liability to action that made the plaintiff's condition worse as distinct from mere failure to make it better. Thus when a farmer's land was flooded by a bursting river and the catchment board undertook to repair the dyke but did it incompetently so that it took unnecessarily long, the board was excused because, not being under a legal *duty* to assist, it had merely failed to benefit the farmer rather than make his condition worse, as by additional flooding.[67]

This approach was criticized as over-protective of public administration and insufficiently responsive to the public's expectation of benefits to which they feel entitled as taxpayers. The result was a new start which took its inspiration from American law. The Federal Tort Claims Act, unlike corresponding British and Commonwealth legislation abolishing state immunity,[68] retained immunity from tort liability for the 'exercise or performance or the failure to exercise or perform a discretionary function or duty'. Eventually, this came to be interpreted as calling for a distinction between 'planning' and 'operational' levels of government. Thus in the 'flood case' previously mentioned, a distinction would have been justified between, on the one hand, a decision by the catchment board that its resources did not permit more help than was given and, on the other, incompetence by its staff in carrying out their tasks. The reason for judicial unwillingness to review the first decision is that it is constitutionally entrusted to the board subject to political or administrative but not judicial sanctions. In short, it would violate the separation of powers. Such 'policy' decisions typically call for a balance between efficiency and thrift, for the allocation of scarce resources, or a cost–benefit analysis of 'polycentric' dimensions. Judicial adjudication is bounded by the requirement that proofs and arguments be based on rules sufficiently specific to permit rational argument about their application by an impartial tribunal.[69] This requirement cannot be met when challenging the merits of complex administrative decisions presenting a seamless web of interrelated issues.

In two important decisions by the House of Lords this fundamental idea was imported into a new definition of

[67] *East Suffolk Catchment Board* v. *Kent*, [1941] A.C. 74.

[68] The U.S. Act was enacted in 1946, the British Crown Proceedings Act in 1947. Public authorities did not enjoy immunity as such, apart from highway authorities for non-repair of highways, abolished by the Highways (Miscellaneous Provisions) Act 1961.

[69] The concept of polycentricity stems from Polanyi's *Logic of Liberty* (1951), developed by L. Fuller, 'Forms and Limits of Adjudication', 92 *Harv. L. Rev.* 353 (1978).

'duty' in the exercise of administrative powers. In *Dorset Yacht Co.* v. *Home Office*[70] Borstal boys on a working party under minimum security arrangements escaped at night when their officers were in bed, and vandalized a nearby yacht harbour. If the negligence charged against the Home Office challenged the social wisdom of the Borstal system itself, it had to fail because the system was based on a policy decision of balancing public safety against the public interest in rehabilitation of youthful offenders, which should not be reviewable in tort litigation. On the other hand, whether the officers on the spot had adopted adequate safeguards against escape raised a question of 'operational' negligence which did not overtax the capabilities of judicial review.

Anns v. *Merton London B.C.*[71] concerned a building which had subsided due to inadequate foundations for which the current owner charged, among others, the local authority with either careless inspection or failure to inspect. Lord Wilberforce disclaimed any disposition to review the 'discretion' entrusted to a public authority as distinct from the practical execution of its programmes. Thus unreviewable would be its decision on what resources to invest in safety inspections, unlike a particular inspector's decision to accept the builder's word that the by-laws had been complied with. The line of demarcation may not always be as clear, and some of Lord Wilberforce's own examples could be misinterpreted to give too wide a scope to 'discretion'. But at this early stage of reorientation, only the general profile is as yet visible, not all its detailed features.

9. OCCUPIERS

The law relating to responsibility for accidents on dangerous premises long resisted the pervasive trend of measuring the existence and scope of duties of care by the broad standards of foreseeability of harm and reasonable conduct. Until well into the middle of the nineteenth century the prominence and social prestige attached to landholding defied all serious challenge to the claim by occupiers to be left free in the enjoyment and exploitation of their demesne without subordination to the interests of the general public.

[70] [1970] A.C. 1004. [71] [1978] A.C. 728.

Such limited concern for others as the law felt constrained to exact was merely that, for the sake of 'live and let live', they refrain from subjecting their neighbours to unreasonable interference with the enjoyment of *their* land. Apart from this commitment to desist from creating nuisances[72]—not exactly a hostage to sentimental humanitarianism, but simply a token of long-term self-interest—the landowner was virtually excused from giving so much as a thought to the safety of people who came upon his land, except that he was not to injure them wilfully or—and this was conceded only after protracted judicial tussle after the dark days of Peterloo—to go to the length of setting man-traps likely to cause death or grievous bodily harm in defence against trespassers. With respect to the condition of the premises, even a lawful visitor entered for all practical purposes at his own risk.

This singular tenderness for a sectional interest began to yield only rather less than a hundred years ago. But the adjustment engineered by that great architect of the mid-Victorian common law, Willes J. of the Common Pleas, which was to last for well-nigh a century in England and seems destined for an even longer career elsewhere, still fell remarkably short of unreservedly exposing occupiers to the full rigour of the developing negligence doctrine. Seemingly apprehensive of the manner in which juries, who could not so confidently be expected to share the same social biases, might exploit the wide latitude with which they were invested in ordinary negligence litigation, the eventual solution was found in retaining a much larger measure of judicial control by the unique stratagem of dividing visitors into a number of categories, each entitled from the occupier to a different and specifically defined measure of care.

The most favoured group, called *invitees*, were thus entitled to demand from the occupier that he warn them of unusual dangers of which he knew or ought to have known. Noticeably he was not called upon to undertake any structural changes, but merely to warn; and according to one view, to which the House of Lords in the waning days of the doctrine lent their authority much to professional consternation, an invitee who had become aware of the hazard forfeited his right to redress even if there was no practical way open

[72] *Infra* chap. X.

for him to avoid it. In contrast, a *licensor's* duty did not encompass the making of inspections, being no more than to warn of traps actually known to him. Finally, the *trespasser* was treated virtually as an outcast who could complain only of 'wilful or reckless' misconduct against him.

This approach with its pronounced emphasis on categories and labels, brought with it a high degree of formalism which experience proved to be a fertile source alike of unrealistic distinctions and capricious results. The judicial record over the years, especially in England, not infrequently lent credence to the view that the courts seemed bent on demonstrating the absurdity of their own creation rather than on mitigating its undesirable features and keeping it abreast of changing social ideas. Most questionable in particular was the manner of classifying individuals. It is true that the category of invitees was always conceived as open only to visitors from whose presence the occupier derived some 'material advantage', in contrast to licensees who came entirely for purposes of their own or, like social guests, were considered homologous to other members of the occupier's family. But an altogether too narrow view came to prevail as to the qualifications demanded from an invitee, by excluding, for example, members of the public in libraries, parks, and playgrounds maintained specifically for their use by local authorities, even a tenant's family, visitors, and customers on stairs, lifts, and other conveniences retained under the landlord's control.

In some measure this disastrous trend was being compensated for, especially in later years, by a perceptible raising of the relevant standard of care. This was most noticeable in relation to injuries sustained on public premises by claimants who, being there as of right, should—on second thoughts—have deserved a higher ranking than that of ordinary (or 'bare') licensees. Originally licensees were treated with scarcely higher regard than trespassers, being able to demand only that their host would not 'lead them into a trap'. Later this came to be interpreted as requiring that he warn of any insidious hazard actually known to him, and eventually the critical requirement of knowledge was further diluted when it was held sufficient that he had a sensory perception of facts which would have led a reasonable person to make inquiries. In short, by a process of gradual osmosis, 'know' had come to include 'has reason to know', which in practice is often indistinguishable from 'should know'. Admittedly the last alone implies a duty to inspect even in the absence of indicia that there may be something amiss, but the former would not excuse an unreasonable inability to appreciate the hazards inherent in physical facts actually known—in other words, when a reasonable person should have known better.

Another catalytic factor in hastening the transition towards full negligence liability was a new emphasis given to the old distinction between misfeasance and nonfeasance. In most cases involving the responsibility of an occupier the gist of complaint is not that he engaged in some dangerous activity, but that he failed to take positive steps to guard his visitors against structural defects. In short the question is whether he must repond to a duty of affirmative action—to warn or make safe. This aspect of the matter supplies some explanation for the historical reluctance to expose occupiers to a burdensome régime based on the broad standard of reasonable care and arguably ahead of general doctrine relating to liability for nonfeasance; it also accounts for the esoteric classification of visitors by reference to what advantage their presence would confer on the occupier, inasmuch as the law is accustomed to smile more benignly upon one who has paid a price for the benefit of a duty of affirmative action. Yet with the passage of time this argument became overshadowed by regard for the fact that the occupier is in a peculiarly strategic position to prevent accidents by reason of his exclusive control of the premises and that others depend on his efforts for their effective protection.

Full effect, however, could not be given to this change of viewpoint without the aid of Parliament. In the meantime at least it stimulated a resuscitation of that pregnant distinction between misfeasance and nonfeasance which, found in some of the early occupier cases, had almost vanished into the limbo of forgotten things. Henceforth the courts were insisting that the esoteric régime of 'occupiers' liability' be limited strictly to accidents for which no responsibility could be pinned on the defendant except possibly by reason of his being an occupier. The distinction thus drawn between so-called 'occupancy' and 'activity' duties ordinarily corresponds with injury due to the dangerous condition of premises on the one hand and hazardous operations on the other. The former category is of course very wide and applies no less to dynamic than to static conditions, such, for example, as moving belts and machinery, provided the injury was not caused by its sudden starting up. On the other hand, if the plaintiff is struck by a tree being felled rather than a tree falling, or is hit by an open compartment door of a moving train rather than slips on an icy platform, or is thrown into a ditch by a passing car rather than stumbles into it in the dark, his right to recovery did not depend on any inquiry into his precise status as an entrant or on the application of any standard other than the overriding obligation to exercise reasonable care not to injure anyone within the foreseeable range of one's activities.

Common duty of care

Mounting irritation with the exceeding complexity, fragmentation, and even occasional capriciousness of the common law, combined with a lessening sense of the need to protect occupiers against the exactions of the general negligence standard (especially now that the civil jury had disappeared from the scene), eventually prompted the passage in 1957 of the Occupiers' Liability Act. Its principal object was to introduce a 'common duty of care' in respect of dangers due to the state of the premises[73] in favour of all visitors using them for the purpose for which they are invited or permitted to be there. This eliminated at one bold stroke the previous arid learning concerning licensees and invitees, conferring instead on all who enter with the occupier's leave or the law's authority (like a policeman in pursuit of a felon) the benefit of a duty incumbent on the occupier to 'take such care as in all the circumstances is reasonable to see that the visitor will be reasonably safe'. Without detailing as a matter of law the relevance of *particular* circumstances and fearful of letting in by the side-door the defunct heritage of the old particularized standards, the legislation contents itself merely with a specific injunction against perpetuating such earlier blunders as treating a warning without more as a sufficient discharge of the occupier's duty, and conversely with an approval of the previous policy that an occupier

[73] This probably includes 'activity' as well as 'occupancy' duties.

may expect a person like a window cleaner in the exercise of his calling to appreciate and guard against any special risks ordinarily incident to it, so far as the occupier leaves him free to do so.

The greatest opportunity offered by this new start is to shift the weight of emphasis from the plaintiff's position to the defendant's as the more relevant factor in fixing the measure of his responsibility. The viewpoint of the old law was quite distorted in displaying more concern with considerations of individual morality (what had the plaintiff done to *deserve*?) than with the practical question of what precautions would be appropriate, having regard to the nature of the premises in question and the expectations of safety by their typical users. After all, if it is a shop that is involved, reason and law alike demanded and still do that the occupier maintain a reasonable system of inspection in order to secure his customers against, not only dangers of which he knows, but also those that he ought to know. Clearly it would not be adding to his burden if a safeguard which is the due of ordinary shoppers were also demanded on behalf of the odd individual who happened to enter for some other reason, such as using a public phone box or toilet. And if he failed to take that precaution and 'chanced it', the law would in effect be handing him a windfall—as it used to do—by allowing him to take advantage of the fact that the person who happened to come to harm turned out to belong to the underprivileged group. Although an argument can be made for discriminating against trespassers, it makes no sense at all to distinguish in a case like the preceding between different categories of lawful entrants.

Along the same lines, quite a different situation presents itself when the plaintiff meets with an accident on a part of the premises which visitors would not ordinarily enter at all, like a policeman entering an attic in chasing a burglar. To demand a system of continuing inspection for latent dangers in such an area might be altogether disproportionate in cost to the added safety. No doubt it was for this reason rather than any other that policemen were classified as licensees rather than invitees under the old law, since they might gain entry at unusual times and in unusual places which it would be too onerous to keep constantly safety-proof.

Likewise the important distinction between business premises and private houses can now be more frankly taken into account. In some measure the classification of commercial customers as invitees and social guests as licensees was perhaps responsive to the same idea, but it can now be tackled in a more forthright manner. A modern decision[74] excusing a home-owner for an unskilful job of fixing a door handle is a pointer in the same direction, postulating as it does one standard for the expert (and, one might add, commercial premises) and another for the millions of small home-owners who undertake such minor repairs themselves and could not afford to call in a skilled contractor.

Trespassers

Excluded from the purview of this legislation are most prominently visitors without any right to enter. These the common law treated uncharitably alike as 'trespassers', whether they were burglars staggering away with their loot, picnickers in a country field, a stockbroker taking a shortcut to the station, or a toddler straying into a dump. Far from a duty of care being owed to them, their only entitlement in token of civilized behaviour was that, otherwise than for the purpose of ejecting them, the occupier abstain from acts committed with deliberate intent to hurt or 'with reckless disregard' of their presence.

Stringent as this ideology was even in its original rural setting, when a poacher could still more or less foretell what might be coming to him, it degenerated into an excuse for outright callousness with the advent of industrialization and its attendant proliferation of insidious dangers, its power transmission lines, machinery, chemicals, and explosives. Moreoever, even if one preferred to be hardhearted enough to withhold one's sympathy from an adult intruder, considerations of humanity urged a fairer deal for little children prone to disregard boundaries and indulge their curiosity in the face of hazards which, through lack of understanding and experience, they are unable to recognize. To shift the blame entirely to parents for failing to keep their offspring out of mischief became the more pharisaical as industrialization immeasurably increased the incidence of danger in the very

[74] *Wells* v. *Cooper*, [1958] 2 Q.B. 265 (C.A.).

lower-class areas in which parental control was least likely to be encountered.

In the course of time, a few modifications to this basic rule were grudgingly admitted. Perhaps the most favoured, if fickle, device was to upgrade the victim to the status of licensee by imputing to the occupier a consent to his entry from acquiescence in the intrusion. A special version of this technique, employed for the undoubtedly admirable purpose of aiding little children, was to infer an 'implied' license from so-called allurements, building on the analogy of an old case where a landowner was held responsible for luring his neighbour's hounds to destruction with bait of stinking flesh. In the words of the great Justice Holmes 'while it is very plain that temptation is not invitation, it may be held that knowingly to establish and expose unfenced to children of an age when they follow a bait as mechanically as a fish, something that is certain to attract them, has the legal effect of an invitation to them although not to an adult'.[75] Especially when children are lawfully on premises and tempted to meddle with an allurement thereon—some object combining the properties of temptation and retribution, at once fascinating and fatal—the occupier may not excuse his failure to render it innocuous by pleading that the victim had no business to tamper with it, by e.g. trying out berries from a poisonous belladonna shrub in a botanical garden or climbing a horse-drawn van left unattended in the street.

Other stratagems that have especially in more recent years been put to the service of aiding recovery are to deny the benefit of the immunity to anyone other than the occupier himself, so that the latter's licensees must observe reasonable care not to create dangerous conditions to people likely to find themselves in the area, including even intruders. Their trespass vis-à-vis the occupier is no longer a disqualification as such, and has a bearing only on whether their presence should have been anticipated. This humanitarian intrusion of the negligence doctrine makes a good deal of sense when applied against persons maintaining a dangerous situation for purposes of their own, such as the electricity company which had strung high-tension wires across farming country. At one point they passed through the dense foliage of an oak tree,

[75] *United Zinc & Chemical Co.* v. *Britt* (1921), 258 U.S. 268, 275.

invisible to a girl of thirteen who, coming across from a school camp in a neighbouring field, climbed it and was decapitated when accidentally touching the wires. If applied also against contractors who were on the land for the occupier's purposes, as has been done in some cases, this exception emerges as yet another transparent ploy for side-stepping the discredited charter of immunity.

Another exception drew on the distinction between misfeasance and nonfeasance by requiring the occupier to abstain from positive acts (like felling a tree or shooting) which would foreseeably imperil even an intruder who is known, or very probably so, to be within the danger zone. Whether this be explained on the ground that it is 'wanton' to persist in active operations likely to endanger a known trespasser who is powerless to avert the accident or that there is simply a duty of responsible care in such a situation mattered rather little in the result.

Dissatisfaction with this state of the law became increasingly insistent. Its puritanical philosophy was no longer compatible with the more compassionate and humanitarian temper of our own time, and the exceptions engrafted on it made it at once more arbitrary and emphasized the need for a more principled reform.

Occupiers might be legitimately concerned with the fact that, unlike permissive visitors in the stock situations, trespassers are apt to get into trouble in unlikely places at unlikely times, that injury to them is therefore in a sense often unforeseeable, and that it would be altogether too burdensome to maintain all parts of the premises around the clock in a condition fit and safe for their contingent arrival. Yet making full allowance for this is not incompatible with requiring a residuary duty to take reasonable care for trespassers, since all the above-mentioned considerations and the fact that an intruder could not fairly demand more than a peremptory warning, would be given their due weight in deciding what due care demanded in the circumstances.

Too many of the decisions upholding the immunity evoked a feeling of outrage precisely because the accident could have been prevented with the slightest effort or because it was wholly fortuitous that the person who came to harm turned out not to belong to the expected class of legitimate visitors —in other words, where his being a trespasser was converted into an undeserved windfall for an unmeritorious occupier. If a dangerous firecracker explodes among a circus audience, is it not repugnant to our sense of justice that all might recover except little Johnny who squeezed in without paying admission, or that all casualties in a train collision could complain of the driver running through a red signal except a passenger without a ticket?

After years of vacillation, the House of Lords finally relented.[76] But precluded by the deliberate exclusion of trespassers from the 1957 Act, the Court lighted on a compromise formula, demanding only a 'duty of common humanity' rather than of reasonable care. While the precise nature of this modified duty remained undefined, it was elucidated by helping the plaintiff in the case to recover. He was a child who made his way from a playground through a dilapidated fence on to an electric railway line where he was severely injured. Common humanity, it was held, demanded that the fence be repaired after reports had reached the authority that children had been seen on the line. The same conclusion has since been reached where the removal of an electric powerline which had come to within five feet of an embankment was delayed over a fateful weekend,[77] even where workmen had simply failed to keep a proper lookout against children coming near a bonfire.[78] In the result, the duty to trespassers does not seem to demand much less than the exercise of reasonable care, especially for the sake of little children.

This development was essentially confirmed by the Occupiers' Liability Act 1984. Rather than follow the example of the Scottish legislation and of judicial reform in many American states which abolished all special rules for trespassers, it recognized a duty of care in favour of persons other than 'visitors', cautiously conditioned however on the occupier being aware of the danger or having reasonable grounds to believe that it exists and that the intruder is or may be in its vicinity. Moreover, the risk (of personal injury) must be 'one against which, in all the circumstances of the case, he may reasonably be expected to offer the other *some* protection.'

[76] *Herrington* v. *British Railways Board*, [1972] A.C. 877.
[77] *Southern Portland Cement Co.* v. *Cooper*, [1974] A.C. 623.
[78] *Harris* v. *Birkenhead Corp.*, [1976] 1 W.L.R. 279 (C.A.).

10. VENDORS AND LESSORS

Until quite recently the law declined to recognize any obligation on the part of one who had sold or leased his premises regarding their safe condition, once he parted with possession. The special duties previously discussed were cast on occupiers by virtue of their control, but once this ceased they were quit of all further responsibility even for dangers existing at the time of the sale or lease, let alone any arising thereafter. As Erle C. J. once pithily put it, 'fraud apart, there is no law against letting a tumble-down house'.

Progress in this area has been slow. A landlord may, of course, enter into a covenant to keep the premises in repair and, once apprised of the need for action, must do so with proper dispatch. Otherwise he runs the risk of being held liable to his tenant not only for any resulting pecuniary loss, but also for personal injuries and property damage that the tenant might suffer in his own person or that of his wife and children. Modern housing legislation, through the technique of *implying* repairing obligations for an increasingly wide range of tenancies, has vastly increased tenant protection in this respect.[80] Statutory reform has, moreover, made the benefit of such express and implied covenants available to all lawful visitors, not only to the tenant himself as at common law.[81]

Further, the courts have on their own initiative relented to the point of imposing on the landlord an obligation of care for any condition on the premises which he has himself created. Here he is responsible not as landlord but like any independent contractor or builder. This obligation was first attached to repairs during the tenancy but eventually extended also to conditions existing at the commencement of the lease which the landlord designed or constructed. Indeed the tenant is apparently not even debarred by having later become aware and protested the danger because, it has been said, he is not truly free to act on such knowledge.[82]

Still recalcitrant, however, is the remaining immunity of 'bare' landlords for conditions which they had no hand in

[80] Housing Act 1957, s. 6; Housing Act 1961, s. 32.
[81] Occupiers' Liability Act 1957, s. 4.
[82] *Rimmer* v. *Liverpool C.C.*, [1984] 2 W.L.R. 426 (C.A.).

creating, for example such as arise simply from wear and tear. All that has ever been advocated is that he give warning to the in-coming tenant of hidden dangers actually known to him. This would impose but a trivial burden, yet go far towards accident prevention by acquainting the tenant with what remedial measures and repairs to take himself. The present position leaves an undesirable vacuum of responsibility, because it denies in effect all means of redress, alike to the tenant himself, his family and visitors, who could not even look to their host unless and until he, in the exercise of common care, ought to have discovered the peril by independent effort. Better-reasoned American decisions, therefore, cast a duty on the lessor to warn the incoming tenant of concealed dangerous conditions known to him, as well as the more demanding requirement to exercise reasonable care to inspect and repair premises let for a purpose involving public admission like shops or places of entertainment in recognition of the special need to ensure public safety.

The position of vendors is much the same. Merely as sellers, they have no responsibility, apart from any special covenant, for the condition of the premises after parting with the title and possession. A duty does arise however if they built the structure or had it built by an independent contractor. Indeed such liability covers even damage to the defective structure itself, like subsidence due to inadequate foundations.[83] Rather than deal with such damage on the footing that it was 'purely economic loss', it was described as 'damage to property' (although clearly it was not damage to *other* property) and thus sidestepped the still unresolved general issue of liability for negligent economic loss. Admittedly, in these cases the structure was not only defective, it was unsafe. Still, the line between contract and tort was becoming blurred. It seemed to disappear entirely from view when in *Junior Books*, a decision already encountered,[84] the House of Lords extended this line of cases to one where the defect did not threaten safety at all. The complaint was therefore that the defendant had installed a bad, not a dangerous, product. In the past, such a complaint sounded in contract alone and therefore required 'privity'. Would this

[83] *Anns* v. *Merton London B.C.*, [1978] A.C. 728.
[84] *Junior Books* v. *Veitchi Co.*, 1 [1983] A.C. 520, *supra* p. 65.

new tort liability on the part of builders in the future benefit not only the original owner but also subsequent purchasers, as it already does where the structure is dangerous?

In recent years builders of *dwellings* have assumed additional responsibilities in response to mounting complaints about jerry-building. By statute[85] and the 'voluntary' NHBC scheme[86] they guarantee in effect to the purchaser and his successors that the dwelling 'has been or will be built in an effective and workmanlike manner and of proper materials and so as to be fit for habitation'. Thus, even if a purchaser's protection against his seller remains slim, that against his builder or developer is now much improved.

11. DEFECTIVE PRODUCTS

Until within living memory the law was prey to the incubus that, if A was obligated by *contract* to B to render a certain performance like keeping a vehicle in repair, he could be under no *tort* duty to anybody else injured by his failure to do so. This *non sequitur* furnished the doctrinal basis for excusing all suppliers of chattels from liability, even for negligence, to any person other than those with whom they were in privity of contract. With increasing specialization in the marketing of goods, manufacturers of defective products were therefore rarely amenable for their negligence to those most calculated to suffer injury, viz. the ultimate consumer, who, if *he* had purchased the goods at all, would have done so from a retailer.

This piteous condition of consumer protection was later mitigated by allowing a purchaser to recover from his own seller (the retailer) for any personal injuries he suffered on the ground that the latter was in breach of his implied warranty to deliver goods of merchantable quality. Indeed, the gap in tort protection was thus in a sense *over*corrected, because the basis of this warranty liability was strict—it was a guarantee against defects—with the resulting paradox that, while the manufacturer was not directly answerable to the ultimate consumer even for negligence, the innocent

[85] Defective Premises Act 1972.

[86] National House-Building Council, operating since the mid-60s and now covering over 20,000 builders.

retailer—a mere link in the chain of distribution—was liable without proof of fault, though he might eventually pass on this liability to the responsible manufacturer through the conduit of contractual indemnities.

This disguised pattern of strict products liability under the beneficent screen of 'contract' law, which emerged almost surreptitiously at the turn of the twentieth century, still dominates this whole area of accident law. It was, however, marred by two major *lacunae*. First, sellers could exclude warranties by suitable disclaimers which typically accompanied consumer contracts, often hidden in dense print. British, unlike American, courts never carried their hostility against unfair 'adhesion' contracts to the point of developing a theory of unconscionability on the German model. Eventually, however, the English Unfair Contract Terms Act 1977 voided all exclusions of implied warranties in consumer sales and related transactions.

The second limitation, however, survived: recourse to 'warranty' is available only to the buyer, and thus excludes from the purview of protection all other victims of defective goods, such as his friends, members of his family, employees, or strangers. Thus if a car with dangerously defective steering suddenly got out of control, the buyer might have redress for his personal injuries and for damage to the car itself, but any of his passengers, pedestrians, or other road users injured in the accident are relegated to some other theory of liability, if any.

In 1932 the landmark case of *Donoghue* v. *Stevenson*[87] eventually opened for them the door to pursue the manufacturer directly if they could mount a case against him for negligence. The plaintiff allegedly suffered injury as the result of consuming the contents of a bottle of ginger ale bought for her by a friend in which were found the decomposed remains of a snail. Overruling the defendant's objection that this disclosed no cause of action for want of any contract between the parties, the House of Lords at last endorsed the principle that a negligent manufacturer was responsible in tort for injury suffered by the ultimate consumer from the foreseeable use of the product. Cautiously at first, but with progressive momentum, this decision has in the intervening

[87] [1932] A.C. 562.

years been interpreted as a broad mandate for a general duty of care on the part of all suppliers of chattels to everyone exposed to danger within the foreseeable vicinity of their use. Although traditionally most solicitous about the safety of food and drink, the law did not hesitate to extend this duty to other substances, indeed all substances fraught with foreseeable peril from negligent defects—ranging from dermatitis-genic underpants to dangerously stacked piles of gunny-sacks in a warehouse. As much as to articles fraught only with risk of personal injury, like ingestibles or articles of intimate personal use, it applies equally to substances which could cause damage only to property, like poisoned cattle food or 2-4D carelessly mixed into a pesticide for spraying broad-leafed crops. For some time there appeared to be some irrational reluctance to extend it to realty fixtures, but these misgivings were at last also allayed. A contractor, for example, can no more escape responsibility for negligent installation of cupboards in a kitchen or repair work on the roof of a house than could the negligent manufacturer of a motor-car or of a toxic detergent, and the only stubborn exception appears to be the remaining immunity of vendors and landlords concerning the condition of premises sold or let.

Whether it would also cover damage to the defective article itself remains controversial. If a car with defective steering is damaged in a resulting accident, or if in order to avoid an accident expense is incurred in necessary repairs, the modern view would be sympathetic. But it is unlikely that this favour would be extended to claims for repairing a defective product that did not threaten safety, like a carpet that will not lie flat. Such claims must still be bottomed on contract, requiring privity, because the complaint is only that the product is of poor quality, not that it is dangerous.[88]

Manufacturers and retailers

Upon whom does the duty devolve? Without doubt on all who in the process of design, manufacture, and distribution

[88] *Junior Books* v. *Veitchi Co.*, [1983] 1 A.C. 520 (*supra* p. 65), although allowing recovery for such a loss by a building owner against a sub-contractor, disclaimed any pretence of extending it to the relation between manufacturer of products and ultimate consumers (on the unconvincing ground that they were unforeseeable plaintiffs).

make the product a source of foreseeable peril to others. This too, however, must not be understood in any narrow sense, since care may well require a duty to check for defects as well as a duty not actively to create them. Thus, the manufacturer of a product may not blindly rely on the maker of a component part for its safety, but ought himself to subject it to some tests, even if these need not perhaps be as thorough as his supplier's. Hence, if a bottle of carbonated drink explodes in the hands of a consumer and this is traced to a flaw in the glass, liability may well be brought home to the manufacturer of the drink as much as of the bottle, neither being able to shelter behind the other.

Much less in the way of safeguards is of course expected from retailers than manufacturers. Leaving aside negligence on their part in actively creating a danger, as by unsafe storage of perishables, their relatively lesser know-how and equipment, as well as the extra cost involved, justify only superficial safety checks being demanded from them in the exercise of due care. Motor-car dealers, for example, can be expected to check the steering and brakes, but not to open up the top of the engine block or gearbox.

In the early days it was fashionable to consider that responsibility ceased as soon as either the ultimate user or some intermediary like a retailer had an opportunity of examining the article for defects. So arbitrary a limitation, however, did not long survive, and it is now accepted that nothing less than justifiable reliance on somebody else's inspection prior to use sufficient to detect any defect would insulate a defendant from responsibility. Thus, by suitable warning notice, the manufacturer of a hair-dye might shift the onus of testing it for toxicity to a hairdresser before applying it to the scalp of a customer.

Incidentally, the last-mentioned case also suggests that, provided suitable precautions are taken, there is nothing reprehensible even about releasing into the stream of commerce goods that are known to be defective. There is a market for 'seconds' as well as for 'firsts', and the law would be encouraging waste if it categorically condemned any distribution of defective goods as negligent *per se.* Rather, the law's sanction is conditional upon due observance of all reasonable precautions to ensure that those who take them over are fully conversant with the risks and evidently competent to deal with them. Indeed, the problem is closely akin to that posed by inherently dangerous products, like dynamite, poison, and toxic chemicals. Both call for care in regard to the process of distribution rather than production—for precautions to acquaint the unsuspecting and ignorant of their lurking hazards so that their undoubted economic usefulness is not vitiated by their menace to public safety.

Ordinarily, of course, responsibility will not extend beyond the intended or contemplated use of the article in question. If danger develops because it is part of an unforeseeable and abnormal use, no blame can fairly attach to the supplier, and if anything goes wrong, it must be laid at the door of the user. In one such case,[89] scaffolding was erected by a specialist firm for the purpose of enabling repair work to be done on the outside of a high building, with platforms four-planks wide. Inexplicably, however, the repair contractor placed only two planks on a particular platform, which left a dangerous gap between the guard rails with the result that one of their workmen fell to his death. The erector was excused because he had no more reason to anticipate that the platform would be used in such an unorthodox and perilous manner than the manufacturer of a knife would expect it to be used as a toothpick.

On the other hand, the familiar stress on the 'intended use' should not be taken in any literal or arbitrary manner. If, for instance, the environment in which the product will probably be used poses a substantial risk of misuse, as, for example, of infants tampering with poisonous furniture polish if left in their reach, reasonable care may well call for a warning label that would put mothers on their guard. It is obviously a matter of degree whether in any given case the use to which the article was put is so foreign to its normal purpose as to fall entirely outside the supplier's range of responsibility, or whether it should merely be ascribed to the user's contributory negligence, such as would at most reduce instead of entirely defeat his claim to damages.

Proof

In no other context has the tendency towards relaxed standards of proof taken such dramatic strides. For barely

[89] *Poole* v. *Crittal Metal Windows*, [1964] N.Z.L.R. 522 (C.A.).

had the principle of liability for negligence been established than it came to be allowed that, in some cases, such negligence might be inferred without specific proof from the mere fact that the accident had occurred. If it could be traced to a defect in the article which most probably existed at the time it passed out of the defendant's hands, the suggestion was open either that the process of production was at fault or that someone had slipped in carrying it out. Even an attempt by him to prove that his was a fool-proof system was doomed to futility, for the very happening of the accident was evidence to the contrary. Indeed, in these days of quality control through random sampling, a defective item in the production line is usually nothing more nor less than the calculated risk assumed as a matter of pure economics in minimizing production costs. Not only is it statistically expected, but it is the corollary of a managerial decision that the risk of substandard items below a certain incidence was worth taking. Is it not only fair then that such a unilateral decision in the interest of cutting costs should at least carry a commitment to compensate the hapless casualty?

The effect of all this has been to straddle in large measure the gap from negligence to strict liability. It is the modern law's response in part to the inequality in access to relevant evidence which puts the injured consumer at a serious disadvantage concerning inside information of how the failure occurred or might have occurred; in part to the law's ability thereby to exert the maximum pressure for the observance of safety procedures in order to reduce the accident toll; and lastly to the well-recognized ability of the manufacturer or other supplier to absorb the cost of the accident bill by incorporating it into the price of his goods. Indeed, if the cost is inordinately great because of a high accident toll and this is likely seriously to prejudice his competitive position, it becomes a useful mechanism for driving an inefficient and socially undesirable enterprise out of the market (thereby engaging accident compensation in the efficient allocation of economic resources).

Such a short cut to proof is of course not available in all accidents caused by defective products, but only in those which can fairly be said not to occur ordinarily in the absence of negligence by someone in the defendant's position. Often enough more than one hypothesis is open to account for a particular accident, in which case it behoves the claimant to eliminate or at least to weaken all those implicating some other possible cause. To give but one example: the explosion of a bottle of carbonated drink may be due either to a flaw in the glass or to excessive pressure. The first might have occurred no less owing to improper handling by the plaintiff himself or intermediate carriers of the consignment than to fault on part of the maker of the bottle or of the drink manufacturer in failing to check it for flaws. Hence, before it is possible to assert that the accident bespeaks the latter's negligence, it is at least necessary to dispel the first three competing explanations as likely causes of the mishap. Only if the explosion can be traced to excessive pressure would it unequivocally point an accusing finger at the latter alone.

Strict Liability

The momentum of development towards strict liability for defective products, from sales warranties through the quasi-negligence of *res ipsa loquitur*, reached its climax in the renowned American innovation of 'strict products liability', accomplished in the euphoria of the judicial activism of the 1960s.[90] In its eventual effects, more than in its original conception, this breakthrough was destined to radically shift the centre of tort litigation in the United States. It was also to make a profound impression on law reformers in the rest of the common law world, indeed in all Western industrial countries.

Strict liability shifts attention from the manufacturer's conduct to the objective condition of the product. Only *defective* products incur liability. Thus the important question becomes 'What is defective?'. The most obvious type of defect is a construction defect, like a loose wheel on a new car, a mouse in the Coca Cola bottle or a mislabelled drug. Its characteristic is a random failure to conform to the manufacturer's own specifications—a flaw that just should not happen, a kind of 'negligence per se'. Since *res ipsa loquitur* was already available in most of these cases, in effect 'presuming' negligence,[91] strict liability could be viewed as

[90] Encouraged by *Restatement of Torts, Second*, § 402A.
[91] *Infra* p. 151.

just another negligence-shortcut. Greater advantages from the consumer point of view were that strict liability could now be invoked by the ultimate buyer despite an exemption clause in his sales contract with the retailer dealer and that victims outside the chain of distribution ('innocent bystanders') were eventually also admitted to the same benefits.

Far more profound in its effects was the extension of strict liability to design defects. Here the problem is by what standard to determine whether the manufacturer's own design furnished adequate safety. This poses the greatest challenge where the particular feature was the result of a *conscious* design choice, such as the position of the petrol tank or engine in the rear of a car (thus making it more vulnerable to rear or front collisions); as distinct from self-defeating features of a product, usually the unintended consequence of a design choice, like a car hoist which collapses or a carburettor that sticks. In the absence of available or controlling governmental safety standards, it is up to the judge and jury to second-guess the manufacturer's own design.

While American courts have reached no unanimity on the precise formula for this task, most resort to a version of the cost–benefit analysis, viz. a balancing of the risk of the product against its functional and cost benefits compared with alternative designs. While this test might not look so different at first sight from that of negligence, the focus of strict liability on the product's objective condition rather than on the manufacturer's design process may suggest that it be tested by hindsight rather than foresight. Thus, according to one prominent formula, the question is whether a reasonable manufacturer, with the knowledge he now has of the product's risk, would still have marketed it. This might lead to liability in two types of cases, those where the risk itself was unknowable at the time of marketing (e.g. side effects from drugs despite rigorous testing) and those where no technology then (or now?) existed to eliminate the risk, e.g. serum hepatitis in blood plasma. This would convert tort liability into an accident compensation system without the financial planning that went into the drug compensation plans of Germany and Sweden, following the thalidomide catastrophe.[92]

[92] See 'Drug Injury Compensation Plans', 30 *Am. J. Comp. L.* 297 (1982).

In any event, the cost-benefit test for design defects poses in many cases 'polycentric' problems which overtax the judicial process.[93] Just as pitting courts against administrators over policy decisions,[94] so here in pitting courts against design engineers may exceed the legitimate province of the judicial function.

In the United States, concern over the extravagant cost to industry of the tendency by the most 'liberal' courts to convert this form of tort liability into a no-fault system has prompted legislative efforts to return to more manageable bounds.[95] In the same spirit, the EEC Draft Directive, otherwise modelled on the Strasbourg Convention, contains an upper limit on the producer's total liability. The English reform proposals,[96] however, spurn monetary limits and possible exclusion for drugs and human blood, besides countenancing hindsight and recommending a definition of 'defect' (consumer expectation) which American experience has shown to be illusory.

12. DUTY IN CONTRACT OR TORT?

In many situations, as we have seen, the plaintiff's injury is linked to breach of a contractual obligation that the defendant owed either to the plaintiff himself or to a third party. These situations where tort and contract touch—'contorts'[97]—have proved troublesome.

Between Contract Parties

Negligent injury is a frequent result of careless or incompetent performance of a service undertaken by the defendant for the benefit of the plaintiff; whether it be professional, as by a doctor or lawyer, or by a tradesman such as a plumber who forgets to block an open-ended pipe or a cleaner who ruins the wedding dress. Whether the plaintiff can, or must, sue in contract or tort may well affect his claim because of

[93] See Henderson, 'Judicial Review of Manufacturers' Design Choices: The Limits of Adjudication', 73 *Col. L. Rev.* 1531 (1973).

[94] *Supra* p. 66.

[95] E.g. the model Uniform Products Liability Act, sponsored by the U.S. Dep. of Commerce (1979).

[96] *Pearson Report* I, ch. 22.

[97] Gilmore, *The Death of Contract*, 90.

many differences in the rules between them. For example, the statute of limitations operates differently: in contract, the period begins to run from breach (e.g. when defective goods are delivered), in tort when damage occurs (i.e. from the accident, maybe many years later). Again, contributory negligence affects the plaintiff's recovery in tort but, most probably, not in contract;[98] contribution was permitted only among tortfeasors until a recent statutory amendment extended it to parties liable in tort or contract.[99]

There are three possible ways of dealing with this problem. The first is that where the parties' relationship is governed by a contract between them, whether their obligations are defined expressly or implied by law, the plaintiff can only sue for breach of contract, not tort. This is the position of French law. An intermediate view allows plaintiffs the option of suing in tort at least in some situations. Thus American courts, looking for the 'gravamen' of the claim, regard personal injury as the badge of tort, while the English used to permit tort claims only against those pursuing 'common callings', like bailees and doctors, but not solicitors or accountants who, perhaps significantly, typically cause economic rather than physical injury. Another familiar distinction was that between misfeasance, as when the cleaner dropped the chandelier, and nonfeasance, as when the solicitor failed to prosecute a client's claim in time.

In the last few years, however, English courts have abandoned these distinctions in favour of allowing plaintiffs generally the choice of proceeding either in contract or tort, whichever suits them best.[1] Thus actions against solicitors have now been repeatedly pleaded in tort so as to gain the advantage of a later commencement of the period of limitation.[2] The breakthrough in *Hedley Byrne* which opened up the new field of tort liability for negligent pecuniary loss, will substantially increase the occasions when plaintiffs will now be able to sue in tort rather than contract.

On the other hand, whether plaintiffs can avoid reduction of their damages on account of contributory negligence by pleading their claim in contract has not yet been authoritatively

[98] *Infra* p. 134. [99] *Infra* p. 113.
[1] *Esso Petroleum* v. *Mardon*, [1976] Q.B. 801 (C.A.).
[2] E.g. *Midland Bank* v. *Hett, Stubbs & Kent*, [1979] Ch. 384.

resolved. The answer depends in part on the wording of the relevant statute which, on one view, can be construed to invoke the defence whenever the plaintiff *could* have sued in tort.[3] This should be welcomed for introducing a uniform rule regardless of the plaintiff's pleading.

Contract with Third Party

It was *Donoghue* v. *Stevenson*, of course, as already noted, which in 1932 laid to rest the century-old heresy that when *A* entered a contractual obligation to *B*, breach of it would not confer a cause of action on *C*, in tort any more than in contract. Henceforth a negligent manufacturer could be liable to tort for an injury caused by a defective product to an ultimate consumer, although he had sold not to the consumer but to an intermediary.

Does it make any difference that the defendant's negligence consists not in actively creating the risk, as by manufacturing and marketing a defective product, but in omitting to do something to save the plaintiff from injury? One of the most prominent progenitors of affirmative duties is a contractual promise. But would such a promise to *B* create a concurrent tort duty to *C* to perform that promise? Supposing *A*, a car rental agency, leased a car to *B* with an undertaking to keep it in repair during the lease—could *C*, a passenger of *B*'s, invoke that undertaking, not to compel performance but to recover for personal injury resulting from *A*'s neglect? According to the modern view, by assuming the duty to repair, *A* entered into a relationship which made him responsible for care to all those who depended on him for their safety. This would be all too obvious if he gave an actual assurance to *C* himself, but it would nowadays be considered equally sufficient that the undertaking had satisfied *B* that he could rely on him for proper maintenance and could in this manner discharge his own duty as host driver to ensure that the vehicle was as safe as reasonable care could make it. As we have already seen,[4] it is only when the defendant's fault consists in nothing more than his bare refusal to carry out his undertaking, seasonably communicated

[3] See Swanton, 'Contributory Negligence as a Defence to Breach of Contract', 55 *Austr. L. J.* 278 (1981).

[4] *Supra* p. 39.

to the hirer in time for him to make alternative arrangements, that his sole liability will be in contract, for the only complaint against him in that event is that he failed to confer a benefit, not that by failing to act he had launched an instrument of harm. If such be the case, the only sanction is an action for breach of contract, available to none but privies, i.e. those party to it.

13. EMPLOYERS

The responsibility of employers for the safety of their men has been no less vulnerable to changes of public opinion than all other facets of industrial relations. Even more perhaps than products liability, with which it shares this common bond, the law has veered in less than a century from the extreme position of economic liberalism, which offered little in the way of protection for the working man because it was feared that this would impair the free operation of the market and thereby impede progress, to a point where nowadays it is unquestioned that industry owes the highest social obligation to exert itself towards accident prevention and the care of its casualties. If enterprise liability is to have any place in our social ordering, here is its strongest claim.

Workmen's compensation and industrial injury benefits

Its first official recognition came with the introduction of workmen's compensation in 1897, more than a decade after Bismarck had ingeniously contrived it as a counter to deflect the political aspirations of the German working classes. It ensured for the victims of industrial accidents the cost of medical treatment, rehabilitation, lump sums in specified amounts for so-called 'scheduled injuries' like loss of particular limbs (comparable to tort damages for 'loss of faculty') and periodical payments for loss of earnings which in England, in case of total incapacity, eventually amounted to one-half the pre-accident wage. The employer not only had to foot the bill for the insurance, but was nominally the party responsible for meeting claims. In reality, of course, he was merely a conduit distributing the cost among that section of the consumer public who bought his goods or services.[5] The most radical

[5] As in the saying attributed to Lloyd George, 'The cost of the product should bear the blood of the working man.'

departure of all from the prevailing *status quo* was that the 'liability' to compensate claimants was independent of any fault by the employer nor defeated by any of the 'unholy trinity' of common law defences, common employment, voluntary assumption of risk, and contributory negligence. How revolutionary an innovation this appeared to some contemporary minds is clearly demonstrated by the fact that for a time in America it was even considered a violation of the constitutional guarantee of 'property rights', not to speak of its sapping the moral fibre of the working man.

Experience soon gave the lie to these dark forebodings. Neither did the cost prove crippling to the economy, nor was there any basis for believing that it lessened at all the working man's sense of urgency to take care of himself as best he could. Indeed, making all due allowance for such factors as heightened social conscience on the part of management, improved machinery, and the industrial inspectorate, there is no reason to doubt the substantial contribution which workmen's compensation made to reducing the toll of industrial accidents in the half-century of its operation.

Great Britain abandoned this system of compensation when it adopted in its stead an industrial injury scheme as part of the National Insurance plan advocated in the famed Beveridge Report of 1942.[6] The most prominent changes introduced by the new régime in 1948[7] were these three: first, dissatisfied with the legalism that had come to encrust workmen's compensation, it dissociated administration from the adversary process fostered by the (county) courts and transferred it to the administrative hierarchy of hearing officers, appeal tribunals, and the Industrial Injury Commissioner at its apex. Secondly, it replaced income-related 'compensation' with three kinds of primarily flat-rate 'benefits'[8] which are paid for in equal shares by employer *and* employee. The reason for thus breaking with the past and

[6] See especially pp. 35–48. A summary is found in D. Payne, 'Industrial Injuries', 10 *Cur. Leg. Prob.* 85–103 (1957).

[7] National Insurance (Industrial Injuries) Act 1946, which came into force in 1948.

[8] 'Industrial injury benefit' is available for the first 6 months; succeeded by 'disablement benefit', somewhat like damages for 'loss of faculty' but fixed on a scale according to the degree of disablement, irrespective of earning loss, though there are now two income-related supplements (for unemployability and special hardship). The third is 'death benefit'.

with the general practice in the rest of the world was the then-accepted dogma that social insurance should be based on need, linked to family responsibilities, rather than earnings. This view has lost its support in the meantime on both sides of industry, with the result that we will probably see an accelerated trend towards earnings relation, both of benefits and contributions.[9]

The third innovation of the industrial-injuries scheme is its abandonment of the idea that rate calculation should play a part, if only a modest part, in accident prevention. Actually, a rate differential serves at least two important purposes: in so far as it is based on previous accident experience of the particular enterprise, it may be wielded in quite discriminating fashion with an eye to improving its safety record. Not that too much should be expected in this regard, as clearly other more important means are at hand for policing safety standards. More significant from an economic point of view is that a flat contribution tends to subsidize dangerous industries, like mining and heavy engineering, at the cost of those less hazardous. This was done deliberately, in the teeth of a special recommendation in the Beveridge Report,[10] in order to accomplish a complete pooling of risks as in other branches of social insurance. One may well take exception to this decision for so interfering with sound resource allocation in the absence of any studied documentation that a particular industry thereby advantaged deserves a subvention on grounds of supervening national interest. Closely linked with this feature was that henceforth the employee himself had to make a modest weekly contribution to the scheme, in derogation of the generally accepted view that it was industry's sole responsibility to foot the bill and allocate it, like other overheads, to the production cost, which would eventually be reflected in the price of the product.

The basic structure and operation of the industrial benefit scheme appears nonetheless to have earned a remarkable measure of support and has been compared favourably with most other countries in the benefits offered.[11] Each year

[9] *Pearson Report* I, para. 800.

[10] The recommendation was twofold: to impose a special levy on hazardous industries and institute a merit rating (paras. 86–9).

[11] *Pearson Report* I, paras. 283, 792.

in the United Kingdom 720,000 persons are injured at work and 1,300 killed. This amounts to about twice as many injuries at work as on the road, although less than one-fifth as many deaths. Compensation is paid through the scheme each year in over 600,000 new cases of injury or disease at an annual cost of £250 million.[12]

Tort Liability

In comparison, the share of the tort system is rather modest, its payout each year being only £70 million to some 90,000 claimants. Most countries, following the German pattern, abolished the employer's tort liability right from the start as the 'trade-off' for workmen's compensation. But trade union opposition in Britain ensured its survival even into the National Insurance era because of the enduring attractions of lump sum awards and damages for pain and suffering. The Pearson Commission in 1978 adhered to this position on the ground, among others, that abolition of tort actions would discriminate against victims of work injuries, and made light of the argument that the adversary nature of tort litigation hindered corrective safety measures and rehabilitation.[13]

Indeed, tort liability has progressively assumed greater importance than ever before as the result of modern support given to it alike from Parliament and the courts. From the former, in consequence of the legislative abrogation of the defence of common employment and the introduction of apportionment of loss in lieu of the complete bar for contributory negligence; from the latter, in consequence of the virtual attrition of the third defence of voluntary assumption of risk and the undeviating support for causes of action based on violation of industrial safety statutes and regulations. Finally, legal aid, introduced in 1949, has contributed a far from negligible share in escalating the volume of common law claims for industrial injuries, which now vie with running-down actions as the principal class of all litigation.

There are two quite distinct sources of potential liability for an employer: the one for breach of the overriding duty of care imposed upon him, by virtue of his managerial position

[12] Ibid., pp. 169–70. By 1980 the cost had reached £300 million.
[13] Ibid., pp. 193–4.

and responsibility, to ensure safe conditions of employment for his men; the other for vicarious liability in regard to injuries caused by one employee to another. A defence against the latter head of liability was for a long time provided by the so-called doctrine of common employment, which exempted a master from vicarious liability for the torts inflicted by one of his servants in the course of employment upon a fellow servant as distinct from a stranger. Originally contrived in the first half of the nineteenth century as a deliberate device for reducing the burden of an employer's accident bill—behind the transparent fiction that an employee impliedly assumed the risk of carelessness and incompetence of fellow workers—the defence became primarily responsible for the eventual introduction of workmen's compensation.[14] It survived, however, until 1948. Its abolition added a new and substantial source of liability to employers.

Managerial duties

The other head of tort liability stems from the employer's obligation to furnish reasonably safe conditions of work for his men. Unlike his vicarious liability it is based on a personal duty—'personal' in the sense that responsibility for its being performed cannot be shifted to somebody else. True enough, the National Coal Board itself or any of its members would be quite unable to ensure that ceilings in mine-shafts are properly shored up or to prescribe any of the myriad safety devices that reasonable care demands in its innumerable establishments around the country—indeed, they would almost certainly be remiss in so much as attempting to undertake a task calling for expertise which as individuals they do not command. Clearly, its performance not only may, but (as a general rule) *must*, be delegated to managers, foremen, and the like. What is meant, therefore, by saying that such duties are non-delegable is not that their performance, but only the responsibility for their performance, cannot be delegated.

Lately it has become fashionable to divide the employer's managerial responsibility into the four component duties of providing competent staff, safe working conditions, safe

[14] See Friedman & Ladinsky, 'Social Change and the Law of Industrial Accidents , 67 *Columbia L. Rev.* 50 (1967).

tools and equipment, and a safe method of work.[15] To illustrate: responsibility for an injury caused by horseplay on the working site may as well, and perhaps more easily, be pinned on management for failing to discipline the culprit after the first such incident became known rather than on the basis of vicarious liability which would precariously hinge on whether such a misdeed actually fell within the course of employment. Or, in the case of an airline pilot's sudden collapse at the controls, the only source of liability may well be his employer's failure to enforce periodical medical examinations, since no blame at all might attach to the pilot, himself unaware of his latent cardiac disease. The airline's duty in this instance would of course be owed as much to the other members of the crew as to the passengers—though to the first it would be in its capacity as employer, to the second in its capacity as carrier. The House of Lords declined to extend the employer's non-delegable duties beyond procurement to the actual manufacture of tools and thereby to impute the manufacturer's negligence to the employer.[16] Imposing liability would not have struck a worthwhile blow for the cause of accident prevention, because all conceivable pressure short of strict liability is already upon the employer to do all he can within *his* control to make sure that the tools are safe for the intended purpose. Moreover, since what is mooted is liability for *negligently* manufactured tools, is not the liability of the manufacturer for *his* negligence sufficient? All the same, Parliament had the last word[17] and, by reversing the decision, pushed the employer's liability one notch further away from conventional notions of fault.

The standard of care has tended to increasing stringency, although—at least in theory—the law does not insist that the system of work be actually accident-proof. What is required is safeguard against 'unnecessary risks', having regard alike to the likelihood of danger, the gravity of injury and the means of avoiding it. In particular, employers cannot shift to employees all responsibility for minimizing accidents. Accident prevention is at least as much the responsibility

[15] *Wilsons & Clyde Coal Company* v. *English*, [1938] A.C. 57.
[16] *Davie* v. *New Merton Board Mills*, [1959] A.C. 604.
[17] Employers' Liability (Defective Equipment) Act 1969.

of management as of the individual worker. Where a practice of ignoring an obvious danger has grown up, it is not reasonable to expect the worker to take the initiative in devising precautions, as used to be thought. It is the duty of the employer to devise a suitable system, warn him of unexpected risks, and instruct him how best to secure himself against injury. Nor does he fully acquit himself unless, in the provision of safeguards, he allows for the fact that inadvertence and inattention are common features of everyday work.

Contributory Negligence

Concurrent with the rising standard of care demanded from employers has been a trend to take a more forgiving view of the mistakes of employees. A worker is today entitled to assume that his employer's system of work will provide reasonable protection, and he is not required to stop his work and imagine possible risks unless they become obvious to him. Here too, the conditions of industrial employment must be given due weight in drawing the line where 'mere thoughtlessness or inadvertence or forgetfulness ceases and where negligence begins'. Although the sanction for contributory negligence is now much less punitive since it leads only to reduction, not a complete denial of recovery, employees are still *largely* excused for inattention to personal safety when absorbed in work or taking a risk in the interest of the employer or taking it for granted that dangers have been eliminated by those charged with that responsibility.

Statutory Violation

An important auxiliary source of tort liability to injured employees is the violation of statutory duties. Health and safety legislation places on employers a code of stringent requirements, ranging from the siting of fire exits in factories to the width of planks for work at certain heights. The Health and Safety at Work Act 1974 has expressly reinforced the common law doctrine, to be noted presently,[18] of conferring a right to damages on employees injured as the result of non-compliance. This dispenses with the inquiry what reasonable care would otherwise have been required in the circumstances.

[18] *Infra* p. 99.

To the extent that the regulation in question is peremptory, requiring abject compliance without regard to whether it was reasonably practicable to comply, this theory of recovery injects a goodly measure of strict liability. This is particularly pertinent to the duty to 'fence securely' dangerous machinery, but some other regulations specifically allow the defence that 'it was impracticable to avoid or prevent the contravention' for instance for the purpose of testing the machine. Some years ago the Monckton Committee recommended that *all* statutory duties be thus qualified for the purpose of civil liability, on the view that compensation under National Insurance did not justify any co-existent tort liability by the employer based on anything less than his culpable negligence.[19] This recommendation was not, however, pursued, and it remains as true now as it was then that (save for express statutory language) the duty to conform with a statutory mandate is an absolute duty to secure the prescribed result, not merely a duty to exercise reasonable care to secure it (nor, for that matter, a duty to secure that result unless it is not reasonably practical to do so).

14. STATUTORY DUTIES

Although most duties of care are of judicial origin, some have a statutory source. For example, the Misrepresentation Act 1967 specifically makes a person liable in damages for loss caused by inducing another to enter into a contract by negligent misrepresentation. Again, an Australian statute extended liability for mental shock to parents or spouses of a person negligently imperilled (whether or not within sight or hearing), long before the common law caught up with that position, if indeed it has yet.[20]

More often duties imposed by statute do not address themselves to the question of compensating losses caused by their violation. From duties imposed on public authorities courts have become particularly wary to extrapolate a liability to the private citizen, for fear of adding an excessive financial burden to the proliferating public services of modern

[19] Final Report of the Departmental Committee on Alternative Remedies, paras. 78–83 (1946).

[20] *Supra* p. 49.

government.[21] Although less well justified, this cautiousness has also left its mark on the judicial handling of safety statutes which commonly specify only a penal sanction, typically a fine, against infractions.

Such statutes were appearing in increasing volume from the mid-nineteenth century onward, prescribing safety procedures especially for the sake of reducing the staggering toll of work accidents. At the outset, these statutory duties were sympathetically construed to confer a right to damages on injured workmen, probably not uninfluenced by a judicial desire to compensate for the difficulties of workers successfully suing their employers for common law negligence. This enthusiasm however soon waned, with the result that English courts have rarely entertained claims for breach of statutory duty in other contexts.

This retreat was orchestrated by insisting that a right to damages had to be traced to a legislative intent. Since the statute, *ex hypothesi*, only provided a criminal penalty, it was difficult realistically to *infer* such an intent for a complementary remedy that, moreover, might well inflict a financial cost out of all proportion to the prescribed fine. The pursuit of such an elusive legislative intent has been—perceptively—likened to a 'game of chance'.[22] In practice, it has furnished a screen for throttling the potential of 'statutory negligence' in all but the area of industrial accidents.

This unimaginative approach has not been followed in all other common law countries. The prevailing American theory, for example, disclaims any pretence that such an action would be based on the statute. Rather, when a statute prescribes a particular safety precaution, for example to drive within a posted speed limit, to provide handrails on stairs or guards on circular saws, the court may find it appropriate to adopt such a statutory standard in lieu of the 'reasonable

[21] Pre-nineteenth century precedents from an age of legislative lethargy display less concern. From that period stems the rule that liability for public nuisance is actionable at the suit of private claimants who suffer 'special damage' (*infra* p. 191). Early apprehensions surfaced in the rule of *Russell* v. *Men of Devon* (1788), repealed in 1961, exempting highway authorities for non-repair of roads. For the related problem of statutory *powers* see *supra* p. 66.

[22] *Ex p. Island Records*, [1978] Ch. 122, 135 ('You might as well toss a coin for it': Lord Denning).

man' standard that would otherwise be fixed and applied at the discretion of judge and jury. Indeed it would be invidious to allow the latter to substitute their own judgment for that of the legislature on what is proper conduct in the circumstances. Accordingly, the statutory violation amounts to 'negligence *per se*'. The difference between the English and American theories is reflected by the fact that in England 'breach of statutory duty' is recognized as a separate cause of action distinct from common law negligence, whereas in America 'statutory negligence' denotes merely an alternative way of setting the standard for determining negligence.

Either approach rules out its application to statutory prescriptions which do not lay down standards of conduct, like licensing requirements. Take first the case of driving an unregistered car. To hold the driver liable for an accident merely because he violated that prohibition could not be linked to accident prevention except in the irrelevant sense that otherwise the car would not have been in traffic at all; it would merely add another sanction, not provided for by the statute, for collecting the registration fee. Now take the case of an unlicensed driver. Unquestionably the purpose of the driving licence is to ensure minimal competence for better road safety. But such a licence does not tell anyone how to drive; moreover, experience suggests that many unlicensed drivers drive carefully, just as licensed drivers often do not. Accordingly, to attach liability for any damage done while driving without a licence would be too draconic a penalty for the sake of its possibly remote contribution to road safety.

Sometimes even a violation of statutory standards should be excused. For example, brakes suddenly fail, rear lights expire during the trip or a tyre blows out, causing a car to swerve into an opposing lane. Criminal sanctions would almost certainly not be invoked in these circumstances, but can liability for breach of statutory duty be similarly mitigated? Perhaps it was this conundrum which dissuaded English courts from ever applying the doctrine to the Highway Code. American courts, more resourceful, allow exceptions as for uncontrollable occurrences and necessity, or ask: Did the defendant act as a reasonable person would have done who desired to obey the statute?

The least ambitious response is of course to treat statutory violation, where appropriate, as mere evidence of negligence rather than as negligence *per se*. In other words, the trier of fact may give it whatever weight he thinks proper in the light of all attendant circumstances. In England, this method is expressly prescribed for the Highway Code.[23] The Supreme Court of Canada has endorsed it for general application, after finding the English doctrine of 'statutory duty' spurious and unworkable.[24]

Risks covered

As a by-product of the 'implied legislative intent' theory, the important qualification was also engrafted that the benefit of the legislative standard can be invoked only by someone who belongs to the class of persons within the purview of legislative protection and who has sustained the kind of harm which it was the purpose of the statute to obviate. Factory legislation, for instance, has been credited with the sole aim of ensuring the safety of employees, not of a fireman or policeman even if they had business to be where they came to harm. That the injury must fall precisely within the contemplated hazard is illustrated by the seminal decision[25] in which the owner of sheep washed overboard in a storm vainly appealed to the shipowner's violation of a statutory requirement that animals be kept in pens. The reason given was that the object of the statute was to avoid the spread of disease, not to guard against perils of the sea. The same result ensued when, in defiance of statute, a railway company failed to fence its track and a cow perished thereon, not as the result of being run over but from eating poisonous weeds.

This manner of limiting legal protection to harm precisely within the risk contemplated by the particular rule that was violated is, as we shall see hereafter, somewhat at variance with a rather more 'liberal' attitude that has prevailed in staking out the boundaries of recovery for violation of common law negligence. In the present context, at any rate, there is evident a studied endeavour to put a damper

[23] Road Traffic Act 1972, s. 37(5).
[24] *The Queen* v. *Saskatchewan Wheat Board* (1983), 143 D.L.R. (3d) 9.
[25] *Gorris* v. *Scott* (1874), L.R. 9 Ex. 125.

on the potential range of liability by requiring that the harm for which recovery is sought must not only have been broadly *within* the foreseeable risk of the defendant's unlawful conduct, but itself the *very* risk which made it unlawful. This formula, without proscribing all leeway in the determination of what exactly was the 'contemplated hazard', has at least the merit of simplicity in postulating a precise correspondence between harm the risk of which made the defendant's conduct unlawful, and harm for which alone a victim may have recovery.

It incidentally also suggests a neat method for disposing of certain 'causal' problems that have proved singularly vexing in other contexts. Suppose, for example, that a motorist without any fault on his part runs into a train that has stopped athwart a level-crossing at night beyond the ten minutes allowed to it by statute. The violation can be instantly dismissed as irrelevant on the ground that the purpose of the rule was to reduce delay, not to prevent a collision. The same technique will readily solve the old puzzle of the driver who, after exceeding the speed limit on the first stage of his journey, gets involved in a collision or his car is struck by lightning long after having slowed down. Again, it is sufficient to discount his earlier violation with the explanation that the object of the speed rule to minimize the risk of losing control over the car, not to assure that it is at some place rather than another at any given time.

Stricter Liability

A corollary of treating statutory violations as peremptory is to infuse an element of stricter liability since it will not avail that all 'reasonable care' had been used. Most notably the duty 'to fence securely' dangerous machinery under the Factories Act is one of absolute obligation and applicable even when compliance would make the particular machine commercially impracticable or mechanically useless.[26] Occasionally courts have even invoked a statute that prescribed a result rather than a specific way of doing things, like a duty to ensure that all ladders are safely constructed and maintained.[27] Such a construction imposes outright

[26] *Supra* p. 98.
[27] *Cole* v. *Blackstone*, [1943] K.B. 615.

strict liability and can only be defended as an exceptional aid to industrial safety.

More generally there has been a justified reluctance to invoke a statute when to do so would have been to impose outright no-fault liability. In some instances, for example, the duty has been read down to require only 'to take all reasonable steps' to secure compliance or subject to the defence that 'it was impractical to avoid or prevent the contravention' as under the Mines and Quarries Act. In the same spirit, American courts allow the exceptional justifications already noted, and German law requires that the violation be intentional or negligent.[28] These devices ensure that the doctrine does not lose claim to its title of 'statutory *negligence*'.

Another factor favouring claimants is that the defence of voluntary assumption of risk (*volenti non fit injuria*)[29] was early held to be inapplicable on the ground that no one could waive a statutory protection. Although contributory negligence was eventually admitted, its effect has been largely mitigated by applying a very forgiving standard in judging whether a worker's lapse should be condemned as negligent, given the often arduous conditions of work, or at worst by making only a modest reduction from his award.

[28] BGB § 823 II. [29] *Infra* p. 138.

V

DAMAGE

NEGLIGENCE is not actionable unless it results in actual damage. Such damage may consist in personal injury, property damage, or economic loss. That the type of injury suffered may critically affect liability we have already noticed in discussing nervous shock and economic loss.[1] But if the injury qualifies for protection against negligence under these 'duty' rules, it must still pass the test whether it was 'caused' in the legal sense by the defendant's negligence, besides raising the question of how to assess compensation for it.

Because the cause of action is not complete until damage occurs, the statute of limitation (three years for personal injury, otherwise six years)[2] does not begin to run until that time. This differentiates tort from contract, for the latter cause of action arises on breach, and may therefore make it more advantageous for a plaintiff to sue for tort, as he may now do at his option in the many situations where he suffers injury from the negligent performance of an obligation undertaken by contract. Thus, if a solicitor fails to register a mortgage, loss might not result for many a year; indeed, the client may not become aware of the dereliction until time has run out against his cause of action in contract, yet he could still be in time for tort. The recent expansion of negligence liability for economic loss, already noted,[3] has considerably magnified the importance of this choice.

But even the right to sue for tort may be lost before one realizes one had it if the injury 'occurred' long before it was discovered or even discoverable. In the leading case,[4] the defendants designed a chimney in 1969 for the plaintiff's works but owing to their negligence cracks formed which were not discovered until 1977. It was held that the plaintiff's

[1] *Supra* pp. 47, 63.
[2] Limitation Act 1980.
[3] *Supra* p. 63.
[4] *Pirelli* v. *Oscar Faber*, [1983] 2 A.C.1.

action was time-barred since the damage was deemed to have occurred as early as 1970. Only in cases of personal injury has Parliament relented by enacting that time does not run until the plaintiff first had knowledge that the injury was significant and that it was attributable to the defendant's conduct.[5]

1. THE PROBLEM OF CAUSATION

One of the most important elements in the attribution of legal responsibility for negligence, as for any other tort or crime, is the causal relation between the defendant's fault and the plaintiff's injury. Unfortunately 'cause' has become a much over-worked concept, a shelter for a wide spectrum of inquiries which stand a much better chance of satisfactory solution if handled with more discrimination than is possible under the Procrustean formula of 'proximate' cause or any similar monistic doctrine. Here as elsewhere in the law one should not forget that legal techniques and doctrines are only tools, and that the only standard for judging their worth is the extent to which they help us penetrate to the essentials of an issue and reach an intelligent and articulate decision. By this test the past legal record in this area cannot even on the most charitable view be adjudged as anywhere near equal to the task, dominated as it has been for the most part by addiction to threadbare phrases and conceptualism which served to obscure rather than to illuminate.

One feature especially that has been a source of much unnecessary difficulty ought to be disposed of at the outset. It relates to the manner of formulating the question to be answered. Causal problems are of course not unique to legal inquiries; yet there is one profound difference at least between the scientist's and the lawyer's discourse about 'cause' which is calculated to spare the latter much of the former's difficulties. This difference is due to the discrete purposes of their respective inquiries, the scientist's being explanatory, the lawyer's attributive.[6] The former's concern is to isolate all antecedents of a given consequent so as to be able, for example, to reproduce an experiment. By contrast,

[5] Limitation Act 1980, ss. 11, 14.

[6] See Hart and Honoré, *Causation in the Law*, chap. 3 (1959).

the lawyer's task is much less pretentious, being focused solely on whether a particular person's negligence or culpable conduct was a responsible factor in causing the plaintiff's injury. There may well be a hundred and one causes of a certain occurrence, in the sense of all the conditions that make up a set sufficient to produce it, but for legal purposes we may well be satisfied with merely establishing that the defendant's contribution was one of these. Accordingly, the legal question properly formulated is not 'What was *the* cause?' or even 'What were the cause*s* of the injury?', but 'Was the defendant's tortious conduct a responsible cause?'

It is as well also to notice in this connection that, even confined to purely legal contexts, the focus of causal inquiry may differ vitally from one to the next. Some contexts, for instance, compel an ineluctable choice of one from amongst several alternatives as *the* cause of a particular event, as in the well-known insurance case where a ship, sailing in convoy during the Norwegian campaign in 1940, was ordered to follow a zigzag course with dimmed lights and eventually, after encountering an unexpected tide, was swept upon the rocks. The perplexing question for decision was whether the loss was covered by the insurance against marine perils or fell into the exception of 'all consequences of hostilities or warlike operations'.[7] Tort claims do not present any either/or issue like that. For, though it was once fashionable to ask whether the defendant's tort was *the* cause of the plaintiff's injury, it is now freely allowed as sufficient that it was only *a* cause and that there might well be other legally responsible causes besides—in other words, that there can be more than one tortfeasor liable for the same damage, thus dispensing with any invidious selection of one of them as the only liable defendant.

2. CAUSE-IN-FACT

The first screening of all claims is invariably addressed to whether the defendant's tortious conduct was a causal factor at all in occasioning the plaintiff's injury. The accredited test for this purpose is to ask oneself whether that injury would not have happened 'but for' such conduct. If it would

[7] *Yorkshire Dale S.S. Co.* v. *Minister of War Transport*, [1942] A.C. 691.

have happened just the same, the defendant's lapse is causally irrelevant. So, for example, failure to provide adequate lifeboats for ship's passengers would not have been a cause of their deaths, if the ship listed so heavily that no boats could have been lowered in any event. This test is foolproof save when, quite extraordinarily, there happens to be some other 'cause' present which would by itself also have been *sufficient* to produce the same loss, as when two fires merge and together destroy a house. Here the inquiry whether it would also have been destroyed but for fire A or B would elicit an affirmative reply and might thus lead to the exoneration of both. This would of course be quite absurd, at any rate if both were of culpable origin. For just as it is no excuse that one's own negligence would not have been sufficient to produce the injury without somebody else's negligence combining, no more is it an excuse that the latter would by itself have been sufficient to produce it.[8] More debatable is the case where the other sufficient cause is of innocent origin, because it is then arguable that to allow recovery would confer a windfall on the claimant.

The 'but for' test, it will be noticed, calls for an answer to a hypothetical question, an inquiry not into what did happen but into what might have happened. This injects a certain element of speculation. For who could say with assurance that, had the lifeguard been present, the toddler would have been saved from drowning; that the woman would not have developed cancer of the breast two years after being bruised in a collision, or, being pregnant when injured, that her child would not have been born deformed? But the standard of proof on this issue, as on all others in civil litigation, is not proof beyond all reasonable doubt as in the criminal courts, but only proof on a balance of probabilities. There are some cases, moreover, where even the '51 per cent rule' would be asking too much. Suppose, for example, that a seaman was last seen on board four hours before, and that the captain, in breach of a common law or statutory duty, refused to order the ship turned around. Can anyone seriously contend that the sailor's widow be asked to prove that he would *more probably than not* otherwise have been saved? Surely, despite the fact that the odds

[8] *Infra* p. 110.

here are so unpredictable and overwhelmingly against such a conclusion, allowance must be made for the fact that the defendant's negligence is itself responsible for the difficulties of proof, or, what amounts to much the same thing, that the gravamen of the charge against him is that he unreasonably deprived the deceased of *all* chance of being rescued in time.

Another difficulty that has plagued the professors more than the courts concerns the question whether the relevant causal link is with the whole of the defendant's conduct or just that segment of it which is wrongful. According to one view, espousing the latter alternative, what is called for is the setting up of a parallel case as close to the real facts as is compatible with just making the relevant conduct lawful. Thus, if a motorist exceeded the speed limit by driving at 35 instead of 30 m.p.h. and an infant darted out into his path, the proper question is thought to be whether, on a balance of probabilities, he would have avoided the child at the lesser speed. If an unlicensed driver is involved in a collision it may be pertinent to ask whether the same accident would not have occurred even if he had had a licence. Now it may well be that, thus formulated, the question could be answered affirmatively, i.e. in the defendant's favour, especially if he had once had a licence but had forgotten to renew it. Yet might it not have been just as correct to argue that, had he obeyed the law and stayed at home, this accident would not have happened? Hence, if we are disposed to let him off, it must be because of some as yet undisclosed factor.

Indeed, the sting of the 'parallel series' formula lies precisely in its tacit assumption that the law will not hold a person liable for an injury merely because, at the time, *he happened to be* engaged in some unlawful act, even if that act had the general tendency to increase substantially the risk of such an injury and the safety rule flouted had the purpose of reducing that risk. To be sure, there is ample authority that, ordinarily, it would be excessively punitive and outside the legitimate purview of civil liability to hold a person liable for all or any damage he happens unwittingly to cause while perpetrating some crime or other infraction of the law, like driving an unregistered vehicle or carrying contraband goods in the boot. But that not even this proposition goes wholly without question is shown by the conventional rule that a trespasser is strictly accountable for all damage he happens to cause *during* his intrusion.

Beyond that, however, authority is scant, except in so far as the refusal to treat want of a driving licence as even evidence of negligence may be thought a straw in the wind. True, the major reason given for this conclusion has been that even an unlicensed driver may on occasion drive with competent care, just as we know licensed drivers to be guilty of lapses once in a while. This argument assumes of course that what must be proven is nothing more nor less than that the collision was caused by the individual's incompetent driving, and that merely driving without a licence, in defiance of a rule aimed at assuring minimum competence and thus aiding safety, is not enough. Yet, with all this said, one cannot ignore the dominant fact that, driving being so easy a skill to acquire and so prevalent, we have reason to doubt whether want of a licence increases the risk of accidents sufficiently to warrant the drastic remedy of holding a violator liable for any accident even in the absence of independent proof of incompetence (like repeatedly failing the driving test). Much stronger, of course, are cases of unlicensed medical practice or driving under the influence of intoxicating liquor, because the risks involved are so great and the probabilities of incompetence so high that we may well feel justified to resolve any doubt against the culprit.

What this discussion goes to show is that the problems so far discussed are by no means capable of mechanical solution, despite the vogue to subsume them to the classification of 'cause-in-fact' as distinct from 'proximate cause', which still remains to be considered. While cause-in-fact seems to concern itself solely with a 'scientific' or 'fact' relationship between an antecedent and its consequent, it is yet far from untainted by value or normative considerations. These do, however, play a much more circumscribed and subdued role than in the congeries of problems customarily associated with the heading of 'proximate cause' or 'remoteness of damage'.

3. MULTIPLE RESPONSIBILITY

In many situations more than one person may be legally responsible for a given injury. This can come about for one of two reasons: first, if the defendants are 'joint tortfeasors' in the narrow sense that each committed the same wrong—not just the same damage. This may happen because one is vicariously answerable for the torts of the other, as in cases of master and servant or principal and agent, or because they acted in pursuit of a common design. In such an event each is liable not only for his own acts, but also for those of his accomplices.

A more frequent source of concurrent liability is a common link, not in any planned action by the defendants, but in one indivisible injury resulting to the plaintiff from quite independent conduct by two or more tortfeasors, as when two cars collide hurting a passenger. The acts in question may have 'concurred' or coalesced as in the preceding illustration. Or again, they may have been successive in time, though concurrent in their causative effect on the injury, as when a service-station attendant spills some petrol which later catches fire when a burning match is tossed on it.

In all these cases the plaintiff must of course be content with a single satisfaction of his loss, but this does not preclude his seeking a judgment against all in the first instance. Thus he may either proceed against all of them together—and this he could originally do only if they were 'joint tortfeasors' in the first-mentioned sense—or he might proceed against each one of them in turn and take advantage of the most favourable award. Such verdict-shopping, however, is now discouraged by ordinarily depriving the plaintiff of his costs in any second action and restricting him in any event to the collection of not more than the amount he was awarded in the first.[9] But a successful claimant is under no restraint as to the share he may demand from any individual tortfeasor. He may recover the total or any lesser amount of what is due to him, provided it does not in the aggregate exceed the amount of the verdict.

Much the same applies where he has recourse to settlement rather than litigation for satisfaction of his claim. If he settles with one tortfeasor, he may reserve his rights against all others, but must of course give credit to each in turn for what he has already collected, so that he does not in the aggregate receive more than one compensation for his injury.

[9] Law Reform (Married Women and Tortfeasors) Act 1935, s. 6 (1) (*b*).

To this there is an exception in the case of 'joint tortfeasors', the release of one discharging all; but it may be easily circumvented by aptly turning the settlement into a 'covenant not to sue' rather than a 'release'.

Often enough it occasions pause, if not misgivings, that a relatively minor fault should expose one defendant to liability for the total damage, while others who bore a larger share of responsibility should escape scot-free. Admittedly the measure of one's liability for a tort bears no relation whatever to one's fault but only to the fortuitous amount of any damage that happens to ensue. Even so, in cases of multiple responsibility, to throw the whole of the loss upon one of several equally responsible causes seems to offend our sense of justice, the more because means are at hand for distributing the burden more equitably. This may be done in several ways.

First to be noticed are cases where it is practically feasible to divide the total loss by attributing different injuries to separate causes. This is apportionment according to different causes, not according to degrees of responsibility or fault. It is appropriate, for example, where a person is run over in succession by two cars, the one breaking his right arm, the other his left leg. Although the former may well be liable for both injuries, for the first because he actually inflicted it and for the second because he exposed his victim to the risk of being run over again as long as he remained prostrate in the road, yet the second driver could only be held responsible for the particular injury that he himself caused, viz. the broken leg.

But what if the injuries were successive and theoretically distinct but cannot in practice be disentangled for lack of proof, as in many chain collisions on motorways? One way of dealing with that situation is to hold all negligent participants liable for the aggregate injuries unless a particular defendant can prove for which injuries he is not responsible.[10]

Successive causes pose other puzzles. In one case,[11] the plaintiff suffered severe permanent injury to his leg, reducing his earning capacity by 50 per cent, as a result of *A*'s negligent driving but had his leg amputated three years later after

[10] See *Restatement of Torts 2d* § 433B, ill. 8.

[11] *Baker* v. *Willoughby*, [1970] A.C. 467.

a hold-up by *B*. There were three possibilities: (1) to limit *A*'s liability to the period before *B*'s intervention, but this would leave the plaintiff worse off than if he had not been injured by *A* at all, since *B* would only be liable for the already depreciated value of the leg on the principle that a tortfeasor takes his victim as he finds him; (2) to impose 'joint and several' liability on both *A* and *B* for the injury after the amputation as if the injury had been caused simultaneously instead of successively; (3) to continue holding *A* liable for his share of the injury (50 per cent) after the amputation. The House of Lords preferred the last solution. However, where the second cause is 'non-actionable', *A*'s liability would cease because it would make no sense to differentiate between a case where, say, the injured leg is later lost as a result of blood poisoning unrelated to the prior accident and where the injured leg was in any event soon to be amputated because of an already developing cancer.[12] In both the latter cases, our law takes into account 'innocent' mitigating conditions so as to deny the plaintiff a windfall. Only where the second cause is 'actionable', will *A*'s liability continue, lest the victim 'fall between two tortfeasors'.

The third type of multiple causation consists of the more typical remaining cases where the defendant's tortious conduct contributed, together with other responsible causes, to an injury which is not practically susceptible to that kind of division. Often enough his share of responsibility would be no greater, perhaps much smaller, than that of other co-operating causes. If altogether trivial in causal potency, neither necessary nor sufficient to produce the injury because the other co-existing causal factors would by themselves have sufficed, it may fairly be dismissed entirely from consideration. Thus we could not bring ourselves to hold a person responsible for having thrown a log or a match into a raging forest fire that eventually destroyed the plaintiff's home, because, as Americans would say, it was not a 'substantial' enough factor. Otherwise, however, the only way to temper the wind to the shorn lamb is to permit contribution between tortfeasors.

[12] *Joblin* v. *Associated Dairies*, [1982] A.C. 794.

4. CONTRIBUTION

This solution was not open at common law on the ground that, whatever the merits of the Aristotelian theory of distributive justice, it could not be called in aid by a proven wrongdoer. There was perhaps some sense in this Puritanical attitude when dealing with such outrageous claims as that of the highway robber who prayed the court for a share of spoils from his accomplice, and was not only sent packing in contumely but hanged to boot. Yet its later application to negligent tortfeasors was not only unjustifiable in terms of the original deterrent theory, it also exposed a defendant to the unaccountable whim of the plaintiff to select whomever he fancied as the one who should foot the bill. For the plaintiff, it will be recalled, could determine not only whether to sue one or more or all of several tortfeasors, but also from whom to collect on judgments so rendered. And to clinch it all, the one thus marked out had no means for calling on any of the others to distribute the burden, nor even protection against a collusive deal between them and the plaintiff.

In actual fact, however, the system worked less unfairly or capriciously. For the plaintiff would usually go after that tortfeasor who, in his estimate, was either insured or otherwise best able to absorb the cost, and the latter's inability to shift part of it to someone who was in no comparable position to spread it was actually calculated to promote the policy of wide and painless loss distribution. It is not wholly surprising, therefore, that foremost among the advocates of contribution among tortfeasors have been insurance companies and other big enterprises, who, by compulsory joinder of smaller fry as defendants, hope to blunt the edge of jury bias against themselves.

More abstract notions of fairness, however, eventually triumphed in the passage of legislation, first enacted in England in 1935, permitting claims for contribution from 'any other person liable in respect of the same damage'. Originally the common liability had to be in tort, but since 1978 it no longer matters what 'the legal basis of [their] liability, whether tort, breach of contract, breach of trust or otherwise'.[13] In contrast to most of its American

[13] Civil Liability (Contribution) Act 1978, s. 6(1).

prototypes, contribution may be in unequal shares in accordance with the parties' respective responsibility for the damage as the Court may find 'just and reasonable'. This discretion extends even to the grant of complete indemnity in suitable cases, as when one person, himself completely innocent of blame, is held vicariously responsible for the other on the principle of *respondeat superior*.

So as not to discourage out-of-court settlements, a tortfeasor who has made an accord with the person injured may claim contribution just like one who has been sued to judgment. On the other hand, unless he obtained a release not only for himself but for all others as well, he runs the risk that he may be called upon again in case the plaintiff recovers a larger judgment against the others and these in turn claim from him contribution for his apportioned share. Under the generally prevailing American pattern this is not possible because, just as a tortfeasor who has failed to obtain a release effective against all is disqualified from claiming any contribution, so anyone who has settled 'in good faith' is thereafter immune from all claims for contribution from co-tortfeasors.[14]

An important side effect of contribution is that it has weakened the temptation to excuse some defendants altogether on the pretended ground that their wrongdoing was not the 'proximate cause' of the injury. This inclination was fairly strong so long as there was reason to fear that to hold a rather less responsible actor liable might mean that he would not be able to shift some of it at least to the more responsible culprits. Most notable instances were those where the defendant had merely created the opportunity or set the stage for somebody else's mischief, when for long it was the fashion to hold only the 'last human wrongdoer' to account. Nowadays, however, it is no longer necessary to go to such shifts in cases of grossly disparate fault, now that, instead of completely excusing the less guilty, it has become possible to apportion the damages in accordance with the defendants' respective degree of responsibility.

Precisely the same has occurred in dealing with the problem of multiple responsibility between a guilty *plaintiff* and a defendant. For, as we shall see, there also the common law

[14] Uniform Contribution Among Tortfeasors Act (1955), §§ 1 (*d*), 4 (*b*).

offered only an all-or-nothing solution: if a plaintiff was himself guilty of contributory negligence, however slight, he forfeited all claim to recovery. Greatly preponderating fault on the part of the defendant could therefore only be given weight, if at all, by hypocritically clearing the plaintiff from *all* blame. Since 1946, however, it has become possible openly to compare the parties' respective shares of responsibility for the accident and reduce the plaintiff's damages accordingly. In the upshot, therefore, the same régime now prevails in the allocation of multiple responsibility, whether between different defendants or between plaintiff and defendant.

5. REMOTENESS OF DAMAGE

It remains finally to deal with the rest of the problems around the vexing question of where to draw the outer perimeter of liability for the consequences of tortious conduct. For, culpable as the defendant may have been, we shrink from holding him responsible for all and every conceivable effect of his original wrong, since to do so could impose an altogether excessive burden on an individual for the good of a society dedicated to encouraging human enterprise and still largely inured to the idea that there are some risks and injuries which an individual must bear himself without recourse. Though the parable be true that 'but for the nail the kingdom was lost', it would surely be as extravagant in law as in morality to hold the wretch accountable for so far-reaching and 'remote' a consequence. For even if subjective blameworthiness or guilt has long since forfeited its claim to attention in this context, the common law still largely clings to the assumption that the tortfeasor would have to dip into his own pocket to satisfy an adverse judgment, and that, therefore, even if there is no exact correlation between the degree of his culpability and the measure of his liability, yet the two must not get completely out of kilter. To the extent, of course, that the defendant is in a position to pass on the cost and spread it over a wider section of the community, apprehensions about its possibly crippling effect become more muted to the point where the very fact that it can be exploited to such an end may itself offer a sufficient reason for using the defendant as a conduit for loss distribution.

Courts and writers alike have for the most part sought to impose a semblance of spurious unity by subscribing to some single verbal formula as the universal solvent for all the countless and protean fact situations that call for adjudication. Yet after long experience there is as much doubt as there ever was whether this approach is not at best a polite fiction, if not an outright obstacle to clear anlaysis and sound judgment. In truth this problem presents itself in so many facets that 'no magic words could do it justice'.

The most pretentious formulas, at either extreme of the spectrum, would hold the tortfeasor liable either for all the 'direct' or only for the 'foreseeable' consequences of his negligence.

Direct consequences

The first test has exerted the strongest appeal in relation to personal injuries, where the view has rarely been challenged that liability extends to all physiological *sequelae*, whether themselves foreseeable or not. Its most frequent illustration is embodied in the maxim that 'a tortfeasor must take his victim as he finds him', so that he becomes liable for all complications or aggravations due to a pre-existing disease or special susceptibility, however rare, like being a 'bleeder', having an egg-shell skull, or being afflicted with hysteria or some other neurosis. Beyond all else this attitude of the law is due to a recognition of the precariousness of human life, which realistically leaves little room for nice discriminations based on foreseeability of identifiable injuries. For who can ever predict precisely where the effect of a contusion or concussion will end?

More debatable by far are the credentials of the 'directness' test in other situations. Its strongest argument is that the one who 'set the whole thing in motion' has a lesser claim to sympathy than his innocent victim, and that once his conduct has been branded as negligent because fraught with unreasonable risk of *some* injury (to the plaintiff), the relevance of foreseeability has been exhausted and the extent of his liability falls to be decided on other criteria. 'Directness', though far from precise in every respect, encompasses at any rate all consequences following in uninterrupted sequence, without intervention of 'new forces', human or natural. Its prototype is the collapse of a house of cards or bowling pins, knocking each other over one by one. It also includes all aggravations, however unexpected, due to the way the scene was set when the defendant's negligence intruded. Thus, in the famous *Polemis Case*,[15] a stevedore was held liable for the total destruction of a ship by fire, although it was found unforeseeable that negligently dropping a plank into the hold would strike a spark and cause an explosion of gasoline vapour. Once found negligent because *some* damage to the ship was foreseeable, he was liable for all direct consequences however unforeseeable.

Although this is the precise analogue of the pre-existing disease applied to property damage, it does not explain some perplexing distinctions. How, for example, to justify the differentiation thus drawn between unforeseeable consequences due to pre-existing and subsequently arising conditions, between a latent blood disease from which the victim is already suffering and tetanus bacteria entering his wound afterwards? Moreover, once the law became committed to the proposition that a negligent defendant was liable only to those persons to whom he owed a duty of care by reason of their being within the foreseeable range of (some) injury,[16] was it not rather capricious to allow recovery for all direct damage to a foreseeable victim, but not for any damage to an unforeseeable victim—a distinction, in other words between unforeseeable injuries and unforeseeable casualities, between the shipowner in the preceding case who recovered and owners of the cargo in the hold who would have remained without redress?

Foreseeability

The competing 'foreseeability' formula, besides disposing of these perplexities, also pretends to superior logic on the ground that it alone is compatible with the theoretical foundations of negligence liability. For, so the contention runs, negligence (like intent) is an attitude to a consequence of a particular act or omission—we call an inattentive driver negligent because of the risk that he might *hit* a pedestrian—and, since that consequence must at least be foreseeable (as one that a reasonable person would have sought to avoid),

[15] [1921] 3 K.B. 560 (C.A.). [16] *Supra* p. 37.

it is claimed that he cannot be held liable on a footing of negligence save for foreseeable consequences.[17] The weakness of this argument is that the premise does not compel the conclusion, since the fact that the actor was negligent with respect to some foreseeably injurious consequences may well be deemed sufficient to warrant his being held to account for others as well. In short, the issue can be resolved only by appeal to policy, not logic.

A second and related claim that has been made for foreseeability, viz. that it would subsume 'remoteness' to the same test as 'negligence' or breach of duty,[18] rests on no less tenuous ground. It falsely assumes that there is nothing more to the notion of negligence than foreseeability of injury, ignoring all the other factors that we have seen to be involved in that complex calculus. None of these, however, has any claim to attention in determining whether a particular consequence is sufficiently unforeseeable to be too remote. By the same token, a particular consequence, though foreseeable, may not have been sufficient, alone, to make the defendant negligent. In truth, the elliptical use of the same term—foreseeable—in relation to the two issues tends to give them a semblance of verbal unity which does not in the least correspond to their function.

All the same, after a brief period of eclipse, the limitation of liability to foreseeable consequences once again became the accredited doctrine in British courts. In *The Wagon Mound (No. 1)*[19] a ship bunkering oil allowed some of it to spill and float across the harbour where it was set alight and burnt a dock. The ship was held not liable on the assumption, based on expert testimony, that the oil could not have been foreseen to ignite. It was not sufficient that *some* injury to the plaintiff was foreseeable; the 'particular' injury for which a claim was made had to satisfy the same test, standing on its own footing. Crucial, of course, for an assessment of this position is the manner in which the job of classification is handled. Foreseeability is a criterion with a wide margin of tolerance, largely influenced by individual experience and

[17] See Goodhart, 'Liability for the Consequences of a "Negligent Act",' *Essays in Jurisprudence and the Common Law* (1931).

[18] *The Wagon Mound (No. 1)*, [1961] A.C. 388, 423, *per* Viscount Simonds.

[19] Ibid., (P.C.).

imagination. The spectrum of probability stretches from 'remote' through 'possible', 'likely' and 'probable' to 'substantially certain'. Thus in a subsequent appeal arising out of the same fire, the Privy Council decided this time against the ship on the ground that, on somewhat different evidence, there had been 'a real risk, one which would occur to the mind of a reasonable man in the defendant's position and which he would not brush aside as far-fetched'.[20] In effect, this liberal formula did much to correct the retreat to foreseeability which seemed so incongruously restrictive at the very time that negligence liability was rapidly expanding its scope of 'duties'.

No less permissive is the concept of 'particular' damage, especially as neither its extent, nor its gravity, nor the precise manner in which it came about, need be foreseeable. What is aimed at is evidently a middle ground which the current American practice seeks to express in the formula that what must be foreseeable is harm of the 'general kind' that occurred. Inevitably the process of classification will hinge on the manner of describing the foreseeable and the actual injury for the purpose of comparing one against the other, and this in turn is influenced by extraneous, usually inarticulate, factors, among which the most prominent is what conclusion the judge wishes to reach.

To illustrate: if, in a given case, fire damage was foreseeable because of the known combustible nature of a particular substance, but the fire was actually set off as a result of its unsuspected explosive quality (and was for that reason the more catastrophic), is it not just as legitimate to classify the foreseeable injury as 'damage by fire' and the actual injury as 'damage by explosion' as it would be to describe both as 'damage by fire'? And in that event the next question is whether the distinction between 'fire' and 'explosion' is sufficiently critical to amount to a difference in 'kind', or whether the one is just a 'version' of the other. That this line of inquiry is no idle exercise in nit-picking is demonstrated by the fact that, applying the same verbal test of 'foreseeability', a distinguished American court held that the catastrophic explosion of ammonium nitrate in the famed Texas City disaster was unforeseeably different from the combustible fire hazard that the fertilizer was alone

[20] *The Wagon Mound (No. 2)*, [1967] 1 A.C. 617.

thought to present at the time,[21] while the House of Lords in a contemporaneous appeal, disagreeing with the lower courts, dispelled all apprehensions that the foreseeability test might be deployed with pro-defendant bias in any narrow fashion, by holding that a freak explosion of an overturned paraffin lamp, as distinct from the ordinary danger it presented of causing a fire by spilling, was still substantially the same type of accident, defined as damage by burns.[22] True, the injury was a good deal greater in extent than was foreseeable, and the known source of danger, the lamp, behaved in a totally unpredictable manner, but that could be dismissed as immaterial.

Ulterior harm

The resilience of the foresight test is put to additional strain in cases of 'ulterior harm'. Suppose, for example, that a traffic victim is struck a second time before being moved to a position of safety, or that a doctor busy dispensing first aid is himself hit by a later car, or that a would-be rescuer comes to harm on his mercy mission. In all these cases recovery has been allowed against the first driver, although it would be a transparent fiction to say that these were risks that figured in holding him negligent for not keeping a proper lookout or driving too fast. Standing alone, they would have been altogether too conjectural to condemn the defendant for ignoring them, but they involve not abnormal after-effects or responses to a crisis and are therefore accounted as broadly within the purview of the risk created by him.[23]

In many cases it will help to ask oneself whether the injury was of the kind which the rule violated by the tortfeasor was designed to obviate. This, it will be recalled, is the accredited test in cases of statutory violation; and although in the case of common law duties it has not been accepted as the last word, probably because it is feared to be too narrow, it offers sound guidance at least in some situations. Take, for instance, injuries brought about by a third party deliberately exploiting

[21] *Republic of France* v. *U.S.* (5 Cir. 1961), 291 F. 2d 395, [1961] 1 Ll. Rep. 504.

[22] *Hughes* v. *Lord Advocate*, [1963] A.C. 837.

[23] Besides, in what sense are they foreseeable? Not without allowing that, just as it has become proverbial that 'one thing leads to another', so an eventual consequence is much more easily foreseeable if we follow the sequence of events step by step, instead of merely looking at the first and last.

a perilous situation for the purpose of causing the injury in question. If that eventually was *a* reason, the more when it was *the* reason, why it was negligent for the defendant to have created the dangerous situation, it would be plainly absurd to excuse him on the ground that there had intervened a stranger's 'conscious act of volition' or that the defendant had not, in any proper sense of the term, 'caused' the injury as distinct from merely creating an opportunity for it. For example, in the *Dorset Yacht Club* case discussed in an earlier context,[24] the Home Office was held responsible for the vandalism perpetrated by Borstal boys after escaping from their inattentive guards.

In contrast, when the defendant was negligent on account of quite different hazards, a deliberate infliction of injury by a stranger in exploiting the opportunity offered to him by the defendant's negligence is generally outside the latter's range of responsibility. Whether foreseeable or not, it is then deemed beyond the accountable risk. Such for example was found to be the case when the plaintiff's car was vandalized during his absence in hospital after the accident.[25] That moralistic considerations play a role in these cases is no secret. One might speculate whether the outcome would have been different if the plaintiff had been robbed after being knocked down by a hit-and-run driver. In any event, the question is not who of the two culprits is more to blame, but whether the motorist should be held responsible as well as the thieves. It is difficult, however, to ignore the stark reality that the latter are usually unreachable, remaining either unidentified or having no assets. Hence the plaintiff's concern to seek out a more promising target.

Judges often find it easier in these cases to agree on the result than how to justify it. In one notable instance,[26] the plaintiff let her house during a prolonged absence in America. Contractors breached a water main which caused the house to subside and the tenant to leave. While unoccupied the house was vandalized but the contractor was not held responsible for that damage. One judge thought that the third party's acts would have had to be 'very likely', if not

[24] *Supra* p. 68.
[25] *Duce* v. *Rourke* (1951), 1 W.W.R. (N.S.) 305 (Alberta).
[26] *Lamb* v. *Camden L.B.C.*, [1981] Q.B. 625 (C.A.).

an almost inevitable consequence of the defendant's negligence; another preferred a 'robust and sensible approach' by relying on his 'judicial instinct'. Lord Denning—rightly—found the answer in 'policy': after a certain lapse of time, it became the owner's job to look after the house; besides, it was more efficient for her insurance company to absorb the loss than pass it to others like the contractor or *his* liability insurer.

Conclusion

What is suggested here is that multiple factors rather than any single formula play a role in deciding where to draw the boundary beyond which a defendant will cease to be liable for the consequences of his negligent conduct. The outcome will depend on the purpose of the rule violated, on the gravity of the defendant's conduct, on the parties' respective capacity to avoid the loss as well as their capacity to absorb the accident cost, on past experience in dealing with similar situations but also on evolving notions about loss allocation. In short, the process of decision-making calls for the same sensitivity to tort policies as in dealing with the functionally related issue of 'duty'. As one American judge on a notable occasion summed it up, 'what we do mean by the word ["remote"] is that because of convenience, of public policy, of a rough sense of justice, the law arbitrarily declines to trace a series of events beyond a certain point. That is not logic. It is practical politics.'[27]

6. ASSESSMENT OF DAMAGES

Of hardly lesser importance than the question for what injurious consequences of his tort the law will hold a defendant answerable is how it will assess what is due from him to repair such loss. Although the first inquiry is often identified with the problem of 'responsibility' and the second with 'compensation', the latter involves much more than a mere accountancy task of calculating a sum in pounds and pence. For it is contingent on what elements of damage are considered compensable—an inquiry that in many respects is

[27] *Palsgraf* v. *Long Island R.R.* (1928), 248 N.Y. 339, 162 N.E. 99, 103 (Andrews J.).

barely distinguishable in character from questions conventionally associated with 'remoteness of damage'. If both are apt to raise some serious issues of policy, the present question is if anything even more pragmatically oriented and reveals, often rather too blatantly perhaps, the essentially casuistic nature of the common law.

In contrast to some other legal systems (like the German) and our own law of alimony (and formerly workmen's compensation, now industrial injury and disablement benefits), compensation for torts is made once and for all, and in the shape of lump sums rather than periodical payments. While popular because it puts a substantial sum of money into the hands of the plaintiff for the possible purchase of a home or car that might otherwise be beyond his reach, it also has substantial drawbacks. The most serious is that in cases of continuing disability an irrevocable guess must be made as to the plaintiff's future condition. If there is a substantial chance of deterioration, or (for that matter) of improvement, the chance must be discounted, with the inevitable consequence that he will in the event be either over- or, more usually, under-compensated. This hazard explains why either party may be anxious to delay trial or settlement for as long as possible until the plaintiff's condition has become stabilized. It was with a view to this problem that the High Court was recently empowered, in actions for personal injuries in which there is a chance of serious future deterioration, to make a provisional award on the assumption that the deterioration will *not* occur, but to award further damages if it does.[28]

Damages are commonly divided into general and special, but unfortunately this distinction is not free from ambiguity. In its original sense 'general damages' were those normally associated with the injury in question, like loss of reputation in libel, or pain and suffering in personal injuries, whilst 'special' were those contingent on the particular features of a case, like losing one's job in the first or missing a lucrative engagement in the second. The point of it all is that the first 'goes without saying', while the second in fairness requires giving the defendant advance warning in one's pleading. From this developed the secondary meaning of

[28] Administration of Justice Act 1982, s. 6.

'special' as damage capable of substantially precise proof in monetary terms—a synonym, finally, for pecuniary damage like loss of earnings or medical expenses up to the time of trial, but not beyond.

Rather more important, perhaps, for present purposes is the distinction between pecuniary and non-pecuniary losses.

Pecuniary losses

In personal injury cases the principal items under the first head are medical costs and impairment of earning capacity; although now that National Health takes care of hospital and medical bills, the former is an item that has paled into insignificance—certainly as compared with America, where today's staggering cost of medical treatment is in large part accountable for the disproportionately higher verdicts, the more because an American plaintiff need not even give credit to the tortfeasor for his bill having been met from insurance or some other collateral source. It used to be thought that the test was whether medical expenses had been *incurred*, but the competing principle of need eventually prevailed by allowing a claim for the value of gratuitous nursing rendered to the plaintiff by his daughter who gave up a lucrative job to do so.[29] Although *she* would not have had a claim against the tortfeasor either for the value of her services or for giving up alternative employment (her 'opportunity cost'), this way at least the father was enabled to repay her for the kindness.

Next to be considered is loss of earnings prior to trial and loss of future earning capacity. In case of total incapacity the latter is estimated by multiplying the victim's current earnings by the period of his projected incapacity (which in case of permanent injury would be the remainder of his working life). This sum, however, must then be reduced to present value in order to allow for interest that will be earned on the capital sum when invested. In England, unlike most other common law jurisdictions, these calculations are simplified by using rough 'multipliers', instead of relying on actuarial evidence. For a long time, the courts also resisted making any allowance for creeping inflation, but under the impact of the disastrous inflation of the 70s

[29] *Donelly* v. *Joyce*, [1974] Q.B. 454 (C.A.).

it was at last acknowledged that the nominal interest earned on investments contained an inflation factor and that for purposes of 'reduction to present value' only the 'real interest' rate (i.e. the nominal rate minus the inflation factor) should be employed. For the inflation component of the nominal interest rate does not represent real income and merely compensates for the intervening loss in value of the capital. The conventional English multipliers were said to be based on a four to five per cent rate; Commonwealth courts tend more realistically to use three per cent and some American courts have gone as far as zero.

Another problem concerns the incidence of income tax. Neither in Britain nor America is an award for personal injuries as such taxable in the hands of the successful claimant. The reason for this charitable attitude is not so much that the award is viewed as compensation for loss of a capital asset, i.e. earning capacity rather than earnings, but that our moral revulsion against taxing such a receipt is reinforced by the injustice of subjecting it to our steeply graduated income tax, unmitigated by any spreading provision or some such device as the current British exemption of the first £5,000 of any compensation for loss of office. But if the Inland Revenue is thus to be denied its bite, is there any reason why this should go to benefit the tortfeasor rather than his victim? Yet in Britain since 1956 the latter can claim only the capitalized value of his net, not his gross earnings, on the ground that he would otherwise receive a windfall.[30] This solution, which is not followed in the U.S. or Canada, has been much criticized as apt to be quite prejudicial to plaintiffs, especially those in higher income brackets whose capacity for minimizing their tax burden is difficult to prognosticate.

Non-pecuniary loss

Putting a monetary value on pain and suffering may well seem an all too formidable challenge to judicial imagination, if not an altogether contemptible infusion of commercial values into the realm of private feelings and sensations. Yet damages for non-pecuniary injury are a typical feature of tort recovery in the Common law and most other Western legal systems. Of course it would be idle to pretend that

[30] *British Transport Commission* v. *Gourley*, [1956] A.C. 185.

money could ever furnish restitution for a lost arm or searing agony; all that it can hope to accomplish is to furnish some solace in accordance with contemporary notions of what is a right and proper tariff. Hence, calling upon the judge or jury to say at what price *they* would have been prepared to allow their own arm to be amputated or even to make a minute-by-minute calculation of the monetary value of pain and then multiply it by the victim's life expectancy, as has occasionally been urged on American courts, is completely to miss the point. In truth the strikingly inflated level of American awards does not so much reflect a more sophisticated or refined citizenry as the fact that something like one-third of the plaintiff's award will go towards his attorney's fee, and that recovery under the nominal title of pain and suffering is well understood to furnish him with the necessary funds for that purpose, leaving just enough to compensate for his strictly pecuniary loss. Under the British system, where the unsuccessful party must ordinarily reimburse the successful for his legal costs, including most of his solicitor's and barrister's fees, damages for pain and suffering need not be similarly earmarked and therefore can well afford to be more modest.

Non-pecuniary loss may be analytically unscrambled into several elements, although customarily only an undivided lump sum is awarded.

The item which has attracted most controversy is actual pain and suffering: past,[31] present, and future. It is to this that some Socialist countries take particular exception. Others, like Italy, confine it to victims of crime, somewhat reminiscent of punitive damages under the Common law.

To be distinguished are damages for loss of 'amenities' or 'faculty', similar to the lump sums awarded for loss of limbs, etc., under workers' compensation.[32] Here the principal purpose is to provide substitute satisfactions so that someone who has lost a leg and can no longer play football or tennis will be able to afford other forms of entertainment.

However, no consistent approach has been reached on

[31] Cf. Lord Halsbury's unworldly sentiment 'What manly mind cares about pain and suffering that is past?' *The Mediana*, [1900] A.C. 113, 117.

[32] Their National Insurance successor, disablement benefit, is in the form of a pension, though also based on a tariff.

whether the test should be a personal *sense* of loss. If the plaintiff's life expectancy has been reduced, he can recover for loss of earning capacity but not for non-pecuniary loss during his 'lost years' because, being dead, he would not experience it.[33] On the other hand, substantial compensation is nowadays awarded for loss of faculties to victims suffering a 'living death', totally unconscious of their plight.[34] Not even the fact that the victim will in all probability never herself benefit from the recovery has in this instance proved sufficiently persuasive to justify the award of only a nominal sum, as it did in the case of loss of expectation of life before that item was recently totally abolished by legislation.[35]

This conclusion is irreconcilable not only with any principle of *need*, which has received recent support in other contexts,[36] but also with the notion of satisfaction that the payment of damages might convey to the victim. Some other legal systems are more candid than ours that non-pecuniary damages serve at least an auxiliary function of giving 'moral satisfaction', more openly avowed in awards of punitive damages against heinous offenders.

Standardization

As already adumbrated, sums awarded for non-pecuniary injuries do not reflect any serious attempt either to assess the value of what has been lost or what it would require to compensate it. For it would be idle even to pretend that we could calculate the incalculable. Rather, awards are in the nature of conventional sums assessed in accordance with a scale representing prevailing community standards tempered by judicial policy. The current tariff, for example, for loss of a limb is between £50,000 and £60,000, for loss of an arm £25,000 to £30,000.

This pattern of regularity, faintly reminiscent of the fixed statutory amounts for 'scheduled injuries' under workers' compensation, is a deliberate goal of prevailing judicial policy in England. It seeks its justification principally in three considerations. First and foremost is the widespread popular

[33] *Pickett* v. *British Rail Engineering*, [1980] A.C. 136.
[34] *West* v. *Shephard*, [1964] A.C. 326 (£17,500 to 41-year-old woman).
[35] Administration of Justice Act 1982, s. 1.
[36] *Supra* p. 124.

acceptance of the axiom that justice implies equality and that, just as criminal sanctions should be administered even-handedly, so there should be uniform standards of awards for like injuries in civil litigation. Secondly, adoption of such standards is the more imperative because there are no other 'objective' guidelines for calculation, and there would otherwise be a real danger of discrepancies becoming intolerably wide, with no standard available even to prescribe outer limits of tolerance. Lastly, there is the important administrative consideration that regularity of awards encourages settlements by providing a knowable tariff which offers only a slim margin for dispute.

Acceptance of these premisses strongly militates against jury trial. Much as may be said for jury participation in passing upon the issue of liability, especially when the governing criterion is purposely designed to ensure some flexibility (as in the appeal to community standards evident in the cluster of negligence concepts like reasonableness and foreseeability), it is incapable of ensuring any substantial measure of uniformity in the assessment of damages. Operating without any continuity of personnel and deprived even, unlike judges, of the benefit of instruction as to the practice in comparable cases (apparently, although not altogether convincingly, for fear of confusion and distraction from the case in hand), jury awards can in practice only be controlled by setting them aside and ordering a new trial, limited to the assessment of damages, in the hope that the second or third jury will eventually come up with a figure more nearly in accord with the judicially accepted tariff of the moment.

Several remedies are available. The first is for appellate courts to interfere with less hesitation than in the past in upsetting jury verdicts and either ordering a fresh assessment by a judge alone or, with the consent of the parties, substituting their own figure. Better still, to deny jury trial in the first instance, as has become the consistent practice in England.[37] Unfortunately this may mean sacrificing the benefits of jury trial on the issue of substantive liability in some otherwise suitable cases for the sake of gaining the advantage of judicially assessed damage awards. Best of all,

[37] *Ward* v. *James*, [1966] 1 Q.B. 273 (C.A.).

perhaps, would be—if the premise of uniformity be granted—to adopt a bifurcated trial, just as in criminal cases, in which the issue of liability, as of guilt, is in the hands of the jury, but that of assessing damages (like sentencing) in the hands of the professional judge. This procedure has been considered especially for actions of defamation,[38] but has never been put into practice.

7. COLLATERAL BENEFITS

Nowadays, accident victims frequently become entitled to benefits from other sources than the tortfeasor. These range from social insurance (e.g., disability pensions) to voluntary retirement schemes and private insurance. What effect does the availability of one or more such benefits have on tort damages? Can the victim recover both? If not, which is primary—tort damages or the other source of compensation?

There are three possibilities: one is to permit the plaintiff to 'double recover', the second is to reduce his award, the third is to compel the tortfeasor to reimburse the other source. Although in tort litigation as a rule only the victim confronts the tortfeasor, in reality the alternative compensation source also has a stake in the ultimate allocation of the loss. The problem is therefore one of transcendent accident compensation policy.

The first solution of treating the alternative benefit as 'collateral' to tort liability, i.e., as none of the defendant's business, is the standard American solution (the so-called 'collateral source' rule) and has now also regained prominence in English law. It carries greatest persuasion in relation to benefits which are the result of the plaintiff's own thrift, like private insurance he has paid for voluntarily himself. In the case of gifts, it permits the plaintiff to repay his benefactor who could not otherwise gain repayment from the tortfeasor. Beyond that, the standard argument is that in the interest of deterrence a tortfeasor should not be relieved of his full liability, but modern realities ensure that the cost is as a rule distributed by insurance and passed on to the

[38] See Australian Commonwealth Law Reform Commission, *Unfair Publication* (1979), paras. 288–91.

consumer rather than borne by the defendant himself. Why, then, should the plaintiff get a windfall at the expense of the innocent public? If the defendant exceptionally had been guilty of gross misconduct, such as drunk driving—and were denied insurance cover—allowing the plaintiff double recovery could conceivably be justified on the same reasoning as punitive damages,[39] but the rule is not in practice so limited. In the United States, support for the collateral source rule also derives from the argument that tort damages rarely compensate the plaintiff in full, in view of the fact that, under the prevailing contingent fee arrangement, one-third or more of the award is earmarked for his attorney. Although this does not apply to the English scene, the modern trend has been to award full damages even where the collateral benefit came from a public pension or retirement scheme, on the somewhat disingenuous ground that it was not the purpose of that scheme to indemnify against that precise loss, still less to exonerate tortfeasors.[40]

The second solution of reducing the defendant's liability by the collateral benefit is nowadays applied by English courts only to disability pay or wages continued by the employer, whether voluntarily or under contract. Here the theory has prevailed that the employee has simply suffered no loss, that he has in fact continued to receive the very wages that he is now claiming from the defendant.

The third solution, to reimburse the collateral source, has perhaps the greatest appeal because it avoids the disadvantage of each of the other two: it compels the defendant to pay in full but without conferring a windfall on the plaintiff. This result can be achieved in different ways. One is by subrogation as in the case of fire or property insurance[41] whereby the insurer, having paid the insured, can assert the latter's rights against the tortfeasor by operation of law. Another method is to confer an independent right to

[39] In England punitive (or exemplary) damages were abrogated in *Rookes* v. *Barnard*, [1964] A.C. 1192, except against (1) oppressive, arbitrary and unconstitutional acts of government servants, and (2) where the defendant sought to make a profit from his tort. They survive, however, in the older Commonwealth and the United States.

[40] *Parry* v. *Cleaver*, [1970] A.C.1.

[41] In case of motor car collision damage, 'knock-for-knock' agreements between insurance companies waive this right.

reimbursement, like that of social security administrations in most European countries and workmen's compensation prior to its abolition in England in 1947. The modern British social welfare system has deliberately relinquished such claims. National Health thus subsidizes tort defendants, since the accident victim cannot make a claim himself for the free service. In effect, that cost of, say, traffic accidents is 'internalised' to the general taxpayer rather than to the pool of the motoring public. The resulting externalities are however not too serious, as the benefits of motorized transport reach into every aspect of modern social life.

A more controversial feature of modern British welfare legislation is a limited right of double recovery, inasmuch as the victim's tort damages are reduced only by one-half of his rights to industrial injury or disablement benefit, or sickness benefit, during the first five years, in token of his weekly contributions to National Insurance. This arrangement was the result of a legislative compromise under trade union pressure, but is no longer justifiable.[42]

8. FATAL ACCIDENTS

The common law took the rather cavalier view that causes of action in tort unlike contract survived the death of neither the tortfeasor nor his victim. Moreover, in cases where the injury was itself the cause of the latter's death, far from this furnishing an additional item of recovery on behalf of his estate (representing his surviving relatives and creditors), it did not even confer an independent cause of action on those of his dependants whose expectancy of support was cut short by the fatal accident. In one way or another these various positions have all been eventually modified by statute.

The first of these (non-survival) had to wait longest for reform; for although progressively claims for damage to property were permitted to survive, it was not until 1934 that this became the *general* rule, with some minor exceptions like defamation. Most important of all, even claims for personal injury were included, but the estate may recover (besides pain and suffering and medical expenses) for the deceased's loss of earnings only up to the time of his death.

[42] See the *Pearson Report* I, paras. 467–83.

Future earnings in his 'lost years' are beyond the reach of the estate, being earmarked to meet, as we shall presently see, the claims of his surviving dependants for loss of their expectancy of support. Thus reconciliation between the competing claims of the deceased's creditors and legatees on the one hand, and his dependent relatives on the other, is somewhat crudely based on heads of damage rather than the extent of their respective losses. What matters is not so much the detriment they have sustained as what notional fund they can lay their hands on.

The claim of the last-mentioned group did not receive legal recognition until the passage in 1846 of Lord Campbell's Act. This reform, stirred by the horrendous toll of the infant railways—indeed, many of its early American prototypes confined themselves solely to this type of fatal accident—conferred for the first time a cause of action in their own right on certain designated beneficiaries, the closest members of the deceased's family, provided the deceased would himself have been able to sue had he survived. The latter qualification has been construed to preclude recovery if the deceased in his life-time relinquished his own claim, as by accepting a settlement or recovering for his personal injuries in a legal action. In the result, if an accident victim once accepts compensation for his injuries (and he must make claim within three years lest it become stale), he takes the risk that, should they eventually turn out to be fatal, he has irrevocably prejudiced all recovery by his surviving family. This punitive conclusion obviously goes far beyond the well-recognized need to save the tortfeasor from having to pay twice over for the same injury.

In other respects also, the statute was construed in an extremely niggardly fashion. Thus the claims of dependants were strictly confined to pecuniary loss to the exclusion of damages for grief and loss of the emotional and other non-pecuniary benefits of the deceased's companionship and familial role as spouse, parent, or child. Only a recent amendment introduced a claim for 'bereavement' by a spouse or parent to a fixed sum of £3,500,[43] emulating the Scottish *solatium* and earlier Australian legislation. In Canada and the United States substantial awards for loss of companionship and society are now common.

[43] Administration of Justice Act 1982, s. 1A.

In a widow's claim the calculation usually starts with the deceased's rate of earnings reduced by the amount he would have spent on himself. An appropriate multiplier is then chosen, having regard to the probable duration of the deceased's earning period, the joint life expectancy of the deceased and the claimant, and such contingencies of life as ill health and accident that might have reduced the deceased's earnings, although no longer the widow's chances of re-marriage because of the invidiousness of such speculation.[44] The death of a younger child rarely supported any claim by his parents so long as courts continued to subscribe to the 'child-labour' standard and addressed themselves solely to the question of what financial benefit might eventually have accrued to them from his wages, until the recent, just mentioned, introduction of a claim for 'bereavement'.

Another respect in which more compassionate legislation has overcome the penurious judicial record of the past is in respect of collateral benefits. Exemptions for insurance monies, pensions, and certain other benefits were gradually introduced until eventually all benefits accruing to a beneficiary from the deceased's 'estate or otherwise as a result of his death' became exempt.[45] This will include even damages for the deceased's pain and suffering inherited as part of the estate.

The class of protected individuals, defined by the statute, has also gradually expanded so as to include besides wife or husband and children other remoter relatives, including illegitimate, adopted, and half-blood. Even an unmarried person who has lived with the deceased as husband or wife for a period of at least two years now qualifies. The claims of all dependants must be consolidated, ordinarily in the hands of the executor or administrator, although the latter acts in this instance not in his capacity of representing the estate, but as fiduciary for the surviving dependants, and his recovery is therefore subject neither to the deceased's debts nor to death duty.

[44] Sect. 3(3). [45] Sect. 4.

VI

DEFENCES

1. CONTRIBUTORY NEGLIGENCE

IN a system of liability based on individual fault, like the common law of negligence, fault on the part of the plaintiff would seem to have at least some claim to relevance, if not as great a claim as fault on the part of the defendant. Multiple responsibility is a frequent feature of the commonest accidents: sometimes, as we have already seen, involving an innocent plaintiff and more than one defendant; even more often a negligent plaintiff and defendant, as in most collisions between two vehicles. To what extent, then, should his contributory negligence be counted against the claimant? The law might either halve his damages, as the maritime law was wont to do, or reduce them to greater or lesser extent in accordance with his share of responsibility, as is the practice of the modern civil law, or resort to the drastic common law method of denying him all recovery whatever.

No satisfactory reason has ever been proffered for the last solution, save that it seemed natural to a frame of mind addicted to a theory of moral absolutes, unsympathetic to burdening juries with so perplexing a task as to compare the negligence of two or more persons; and, above all else, because it tended to reduce the burden on enterprise and activity by letting the loss lie where it fell. It used to be fashionable to seek an explanation in spurious theories of causation, saying that the plaintiff's failure to watch out—occurring usually later in time—'superseded' the defendant's earlier negligence and thus became the sole responsible cause of the accident. Sometimes, of course, the plaintiff is truly the sole author of his own harm, as when he acts so unpredictably that the defendant need not as a reasonably prudent person have taken precautions against so unlikely an eventuality. Again, the defendant's negligence may not, in the event, have been causally relevant, as when he failed to give a signal to a plaintiff whose attention was carelessly diverted in some other direction. Usually, however, the defendant's negligence is as much a cause of the accident as the plaintiff's in the sense that, but for it, the injury would not have happened, nor so trivial that it can for all practical purposes be ignored.

In theory, then, the common law lent no countenance to comparing faults, no more when the plaintiff was only slightly negligent in comparison with the defendant than when the position was reversed. In practice, however, this harsh régime often imposed too great a stress even on hard-headed judges, let alone more sympathetic juries, with the result that a qualification came to be engrafted whenever the defendant had the 'last opportunity' or 'last clear chance' to avoid the accident—in other words, where not the plaintiff's but the defendant's negligence was clearly the later. But again the transcendent logic of the all-or-nothing theorem compelled that, in such an event, the plaintiff recover full damages without any prejudice whatever for having carelessly placed himself to start with in a position of peril. Thus, in however crude a fashion, comparison of fault became respectable but could not be officially reflected in apportioned damages. Apportionment did play a covert role in many a jury verdict (pruning a plaintiff's verdict to barest pecuniary loss) as also in negotiated settlements. Indeed, it was the disappearance of juries that ultimately compelled legislative reform.

After first, in 1911, permitting unequal division in maritime collisions in place of the established moiety rule, pursuant to the Brussels Convention of 1910, and following some twenty years' experience in Canada with a system of apportionment of general application (for land as well as sea), it was at last enacted in England[1] that:

> [w]here any person suffers damage as the result partly of his own fault and partly of the fault of any other person or persons, a claim in respect of that damage shall not be defeated by reason of the fault of the person suffering the damage, but the damages recoverable in respect thereof shall be reduced to such extent as the court thinks just and equitable having regard to the claimant's share in the responsibility for the damage.

Thus it became permissible to administer a deterrent lash to a plaintiff commensurate to his own shortcoming

[1] Law Reform (Contributory Negligence) Act 1945.

instead of being faced with the distorting dilemma of either subjecting him to the disproportionate penalty of barring him altogether or closing an eye to his failing.

Apportionment may be in unequal shares, and is not (as under one American model) precluded by the fact that the plaintiff's fault was greater than the defendant's. It is usually expressed first in terms of an arithmetical fraction, like 25 per cent and 75 per cent or ¼ and ¾, and then applied as a divisor of the respective losses. Accordingly, if in a collision the damage to A's car was £100 and to B's £300, and their responsibility is apportioned in the aforementioned ratio, and they will be awarded £75 each. To set these off one against the other, so that neither party recovers anything, would appear sensible enough at first blush, but on reflection turns out to be only a sinister device for enabling the insurance companies of both parties to escape their just obligations. It would mean that, instead of A recovering £75 from B's insurer (against third-party risks) and B £75 from A's, both insurance companies would go scot-free and, instead of A bearing only £25 of his own loss and B £225, A would actually bear £100 and B £300: thus, instead of £150 being met by insurance, the total loss of £400 would be defrayed from private resources. So harsh and—from the point of view of overall loss distribution—unsound a solution has accordingly encountered little favour.

Basis of apportionment

The controlling criterion for apportionment, as in the related context of contribution among tortfeasors, is the plaintiff's share of 'responsibility' for the accident. This is not identical with 'fault'—a term that could have been employed, as it was for instance in Eire, but was deliberately rejected in the English legislation. The subtle alchemy of 'responsibility' is composed of many elements. Foremost of course is that of fault, having regard alike to the plaintiff's degree of deviation from the norm—ranging from slight inadvertence to wanton recklessness—and to the gravity of the risk created by him. This danger factor accounts primarily for the more lenient view persistently taken of inattentiveness by pedestrians and cyclists in comparison with motorists.

In theory, the standard of the 'reasonable man' applies

to plaintiffs and defendants alike, except that what is relevant here is the precautions he would have taken for his *own* protection rather than that of *others*. This may in practice be a far from negligible difference, because the tendency of a particular course of conduct to imperil oneself alone, and no one else, tends to evoke much less censure, and also accounts for the difference in judging pedestrians and motorists. Another difference is that a plaintiff's negligence need only have contributed to his injuries, not to the accident. Thus it may have consisted merely in remaining as a passenger in a car after becoming aware of the driver's intoxication. Even failing to use a seat belt or harness is now held to be sufficient, provided of course that in the event its use would have prevented or mitigated the injuries. A flat reduction of 15 to 25 per cent for such preventable injury has become routine in England, once the initial hesitation was overcome of treating the omission as unreasonable.[2] Finally, it must also be remembered that the effect of attributing responsibility is very different on a plaintiff compared to a defendant. The defendant is typically able to pass on his share to insurance, while the plaintiff must bear his reduction alone. Consequently, contributory negligence still operates harshly on victims, although no longer as punitively as before apportionment.

Imputed negligence

At one time when the law was more sympathetic to appeals for limiting liability as a kind of protective tariff for enterprise, it was prepared to exploit the defence of contributory negligence even to the point of 'imputing' it, as an incident of certain relations, to someone who was not guilty of it in fact. In its hey-day a parent's negligence was thus imputed to his child, a bailee's to his bailor, a driver's to his passenger, and even a wife's to her husband, so as to debar the latter in each instance from suing a negligent third party who had caused him injury in combination with the former. But decreasing enthusiasm for the whole doctrine of contributory negligence led to the eventual disavowal of the 'imputed' variety, except when one person's tort is imputed to another also as defendant.

[2] *Froom* v. *Butcher*, [1976] Q.B. 286 (C.A.).

Accordingly the incidence of fictional identification is now limited to principal and agent. If, for example, a collision occurs between two vehicles owing to the combined negligence of both drivers, one being a servant in the course of employment, the latter's master would not only be responsible for any injury to an innocent bystander (vicarious liability), but would also be prejudiced in any claim against the other driver for damage to his own car (imputed negligence)—for, though he might have recourse against his own servant for that damage no less than for an indemnity of the amount he had to pay to the bystander, his recovery against the other driver would be reduced proportionately to the share of responsibility for the accident attributable to the servant. Not that imputed contributory negligence logically follows from vicarious liability, except for minds seduced by the allurement of symmetry; some Canadian and an increasing number of American courts at all events have shrunk from invoking it against car owners (who under widely prevalent legislation are made responsible for anyone driving the car with their consent), for the sensible enough reason that the underlying policy of furnishing financially responsible defendants has no relevance whatever to claims by, as distinct from claims against, an owner.

2. VOLUNTARY ASSUMPTION OF RISK

A second defence which once enjoyed great vogue is a plaintiff's voluntary assumption of risk or, as it is still commonly called by English lawyers with traditional fondness for classicisms *volenti non fit injuria*—no injury is done to one who consents. But sound as this description is of the defence of consent to *wilful* conduct that would otherwise be assault and battery, such as the bodily contact in the familiar instances of submitting to dental treatment or of a girl permitting herself to be fondled, it would rarely if ever be applicable literally to situations of negligent injury. For, far from consenting to *negligent injury*, whoever would so much as agree, if he had any free choice in the matter, even to run the *risk* of it?

In some situations, it must be admitted, the law roundly imputes an acceptance of typical risks incident to certain relations. Spectators at sporting events cannot complain of injury due to the normal hazards of the game, like an ice-hockey puck hit into the crowd, provided at any rate that all customary safety precautions, like a screen behind goal, were installed by the organizers. American courts have taken the same views with regard to the peculiar occupational hazards of firemen. Thus, unlike ordinary people who suffer injury while coming to the rescue of persons or property imperilled, firemen cannot base a claim to compensation merely on a defendant's negligence in *starting* the fire. For fighting fires is their job, and most probably the vast bulk of fires are attributable to carelessness. Being called out to deal with a negligently started fire is therefore as much part of their day's work as putting out a purely accidental fire, the risks involved in either being much the same—in contrast to unusual hazards created by an occupier, like a defective electric switch which fails to cut off the current.

In these, and some other situations, then, certain risks normally associated with them must be accepted without possibility of recourse. But the conventional explanation is not that the person injured fails by reason of having assumed, or consented to, the risk of injury from the defendant's negligence, but rather that the defendant's duty did not require from him care in obviating the risk in question; in short, that he had not been negligent at all. In other words, the plaintiff's defeat is bottomed, not on any individual attitude on his part manifested towards the risk in question, but on the defendant's duty being so defined as to exclude responsibility for this particular risk because it is not deemed sufficiently 'unusual' or 'unreasonable' in the circumstances. Though hardly different in purpose and effect, the dominant policy is in this instance legally formulated so as to confront the plaintiff at the threshold of his case rather than as a defence, properly so called, to be raised by the defendant in order to meet a prima facie case against him.

Yet the defence of *volenti*, strictly so-called, is also nowadays explained as a 'waiver of duty'. Unlike contributory negligence, which admits the commission of a wrong but mitigates the culprit's duty to repair it on the ground that it would be *pessimi exempli* to overlook the victim's own fault, the defence of voluntary assumption of risk means that the plaintiff agreed to absolve the defendant from the duty of care that would otherwise be his due, with the result that the latter's carelessness would not qualify as a breach of duty at all. Put in other words,[3] the defendant does not say: 'Even if I was negligent, you had agreed to take the risk of the consequence of that, and cannot recover'; but rather: 'You had agreed to absolve me from the duty of taking care for you, so that, if harm happens, I was not negligent, and you cannot recover.'

But it may well be asked when, if ever, anyone would freely consent in advance to such a reduction of the protective care due to him from another. The life-cycle of the defence, indeed, is marked by the progressive displacement of *imputed* consent by nothing short of *real* consent as the basic requirement. This is reflected in the defence's dramatic shift within less than a hundred years from a point of dominance in many fields of injury litigation, most prominently industrial accidents, to its present state of virtual atrophy. In largest measure this transformation is of course due to the lessening need for protecting industry from meeting the cost of its accidents, to a growing sense of social responsibility, especially in our concern for the working man, and to the fact that the developing techniques of negligence law nowadays offer more attractive ways of preserving anything worthwhile remaining of the core idea, as in the sibling defence of contributory negligence and the formulation of the duty of care relevant to certain special relations like the above-mentioned instance of the stadium. Finally, the fate of the defence was for all practical purposes sealed by the introduction of apportionment of loss, since it makes little sense to debar a plaintiff completely for any so-called assumption of risk (which may or may not even have been negligent), while merely reducing his recovery on account of contributory negligence.

In the upshot the defence is today moribund. It has almost completely disappeared from the field of industrial accidents as the result of stringently insisting that it has no place except in situations of complete and genuine freedom of choice, where the defendant can fairly confront the plaintiff with 'Take it or leave it'. This condition, it has at

[3] D.M.W., 1964 *Jur. Rev.*, at 167.

long last come to be acknowledged, does not exist in cases of master and servant where loss of employment is too stark an alternative to warrant the inference that a servant's continuing with his job despite awareness of its hazards (and perhaps under protest) could mean that he was prepared to absolve his master from the managerial duties of care in providing safe working conditions. Hobson's choice is not sufficient.

The only stock situation in which the defence is still occasionally encountered is that of a passenger injured by an intoxicated driver. But even there it is apt to miss the mark. Clearly it is contributory negligence for a passenger not to get off at the first opportunity after becoming aware of his driver's incompetence. Since the introduction of apportionment of loss, his recovery will in such an event no longer be totally barred, but merely reduced—a solution which is the more desirable because it administers a deterrent lash not only to the plaintiff but also to the defendant. In contrast, defeating a plaintiff entirely on the ground of voluntary assumption of risk is not only unduly severe to him, but misses the opportunity for the law to play a more effective role in accident prevention, at least by inducing the driver's insurance company to raise his premiums and thus act as a stimulant to greater care in the future. Alive to these considerations, it is hardly surprising that English courts have lent no countenance to the defence even in this context since the advent of apportionment of loss.

More dubious was a recent decision dealing with a learner-driver. Her instructor, a family friend, was injured when the young lady lost her head during the second lesson and steered into a lamp-post. One would have thought that his claim should have failed on the ground that the risk was inherent in the enterprise. Either the standard of care (or competence) that he was entitled to expect from her was not breached or he had waived his right to complain of her negligence. The Court reasoned, however, that if she had injured a pedestrian, she would have been judged by the standard of an ordinary competent driver, regardless of her learner status, and that the same 'duty' was owed by her to one and all, including her instructor. That he was allowed to recover for his injuries may not have been uninfluenced by the existence of compulsory insurance and a desire not to discourage private driving instruction.[4]

Express Disclaimers

We frequently assume the risk of somebody's negligence expressly by accepting an exemption clause on entering a contractual relationship like parking a car in a public garage, taking a voyage on a cruise ship, or consigning a cargo for transport. Such clauses are a common feature of 'adhesion contracts', by which one party in a superior bargaining position offers services to the public on unnegotiable 'take it or leave it' terms.

For a long time the courts fought an unequal battle against these clauses, with such limited weapons only as construing them strictly against the proponent and insisting that they had been brought to the plaintiff's attention.[5] Frontal attack was in England left to Parliament. The first to fall were exclusions of the statutory warranties in contracts of hire-purchase and sale of goods to consumers. Finally, the Unfair Contract Terms Act 1977 generalized this trend by nullifying all contract terms and notices which exclude or restrict liability for death or personal injury resulting from negligence, as well as such terms with respect to other loss or damage unless they satisfy the test of reasonableness. This reform at last dispensed with the need for experimenting with more devious and clumsy forms of judicial intervention.[6]

[4] *Nettleship* v. *Weston*, [1971] 2 Q.B. 691 (C.A.). '*Volenti*' was negatived because the plaintiff had specifically assured himself that there was insurance cover!

[5] Compared with the deployment of more potent weapons, such as 'unconscionability', by American and German courts.

[6] See *Photo Production* v. *Securicor Transport*, [1980] A.C. 827.

VII

PROCEDURE

1. JUDGE AND JURY

ALTHOUGH the great bulk of all tort claims is resolved by settlement, tort is still pre-eminently a litigation subject.[1] To the extent that success or defeat is determined not only by the principles of substantive law, but also by rules of evidence and procedure, which in turn are reflected in the bargaining process of settlement, it will repay us to take a brief look at those facets of adjective law which are most apt to leave their mark on the outcome of litigation.

From this point of view foremost among the procedural rules is the allocation of functions between judge and jury. In England, it is true, the civil jury has for all practical purposes disappeared from the scene.[2] Since 1933 it is available as of right only in actions for defamation, malicious prosecution, and fraud; and the judicial bias in the intervening years has progressively hardened to the point where a jury trial in accident litigation is not considered justifiable even as an occasional check against the adequacy of judicial assessments of damages. This change of procedure has had some far-reaching results. In one respect it has bridged much of the gap that used to divide the English law and the Civil law of the European continent by substituting professional judges for the lay arbitrament of the man in the street. In another it has fulfilled its intended object of assuring maximum uniformity of awards, particularly now that most verdicts are publicized in periodicals and thus become available as guidelines for the future. This in turn has encouraged settlements.

Finally, as that great American Justice, Oliver Wendell Holmes, would have had cause to applaud, the law itself has

[1] 86 per cent of claims are settled without issue of a writ and only 1 per cent reach the courts: *Pearson Report* II, 20.

[2] Whereas in 1901 60 per cent of all civil cases before Queen's Bench judges were tried with a jury, by 1973 this had fallen to less than 2.1 per cent.

become more professionalized and certain. So long as juries had their say on what reasonable prudence required in the circumstances and rendered a 'general verdict' without giving any reasons, the law could fairly claim both to be attuned to contemporary values and to remain flexible in so far as a jury verdict never created precedent. In both respects their disappearance has spelled change. Judges think aloud, registering in their judgments the thought processes which lead to their conclusion for or against the plaintiff. In one way this has made their judgments more vulnerable to being upset by an appellate court than used to be the case with jury verdicts, because it has become the practice to demand that a judge's determination of negligence must be supportable not only on the facts, but also on the steps of reasoning which he recorded in his notes or judgment. In another way it has encouraged the tendency to convert conclusions of fact (in any one case) into propositions of law (binding in others), thus making law arguably more certain but at considerable cost in flexibility, already heavily hobbled by an excessively rigid system of precedent which would be well-nigh intolerable but for the small number of decisions that find their way into the law reports.

Less serious to some observers, perhaps, is the loss entailed in the jury's function of infusing into the law a large measure of kerbstone morality—'fireside equity' as Lord Devlin once called it in a homely phrase.[3] In some measure this is offset by the general trend towards egalitarianism, from which even judges as a class have not escaped and which is illustrated by the fact that pretended judicial ignorance of the 'world outside' is no longer considered as fashionable as it once was, more to the delight of the populace than the litigant. But nothing has taken the jury's place in making obsolete law more acceptable by bending it to its own notions or plainly ignoring it. The all-or-nothing rule of contributory negligence simply had to be replaced by the modern régime of apportionment once juries were no longer available to mitigate its harshness by finding for the plaintiff in cases of great disparity of fault. Juries have less reason than judges to respect and safeguard the accredited black-letter rules of the law,

[3] Lord Devlin's Hamlyn Lectures, *Trial by Jury* (1956), furnish an excellent survey and summation of the present position in England.

and are thus much apter to keep the law abreast of changing social climate. Their reputed vagaries are less often attributable to sentimentality and irrational prejudice than to sensitivity to a growing gap between the lawyer's view of what the law is and the layman's view of what it ought to be. Finally, notwithstanding some angry judicial protestations, juries tend to be more alive, in assessing damages, to increases in the cost of living and to the higher value that one has come to attach to the amenities of life in the affluent society. This indulgence in realism is the less objectionable when defendants are insured and thus able to spread the cost.[4]

Outside England, however, many common law jurisdictions have retained jury trial in accident litigation: among them our closest neighbours, Scotland and Ireland, and in the Dominions particularly those Canadian provinces and Australian states with the largest measure of urbanization, population, and motor traffic. In the United States trial by jury is a constitutionally entrenched right.

Indeed, far from being a declining institution, the jury has assumed a progressively more prominent position as judicial control in the litigation process has relaxed. Among the factors most responsible for this shift are the many changes in substantive law which have replaced specialized rules by broad standards of foreseeability and reasonableness, ever since the dramatic breakthrough of *Donoghue* v. *Stevenson* in 1932. Accompanying this has been the pervasive trend of trial judges to give the jury a much freer rein in the determination of the critical issues of whether the defendant had been negligent or the plaintiff's injury was foreseeable and not 'too remote'. In other words, the traditional techniques of controlling a jury by means of nonsuit or directed verdict are less frequently deployed, in part because the better educated, modern jury is considered worthy of a larger share of responsibility and, perhaps most important of all, because the law has become far less apprehensive about verdicts for the plaintiff. Only where it is feared that defendants are singularly vulnerable and entitled to protection against the unsympathetic bias of juries is there any continuing disposition to keep a jealous eye on their participation in the judgment

[4] See also *supra* p. 128 for a more detailed evaluation of the jury's role in assessing damages.

process. Such is the case in actions for professional negligence against doctors whose reputation is peculiarly sensitive to adverse verdicts and for which the law makes allowance, if not by an outright prohibition of jury trial as used to be the practice in Ontario, at least by insisting on safeguards like the universal requirement of expert testimony and what in practice is a rather exacting standard of proof.

2. BURDEN OF PROOF

The burden of proof itself often plays a strategic role in the outcome of litigation, especially in jury trials. In criminal cases the requisite standard is proof beyond all reasonable doubt, but in civil cases it is sufficient to carry persuasion on a balance of probabilities. The party on whom the burden of proof rests on a particular issue must establish it as more probable than not, and if the probabilities are evenly balanced, the trier of fact must resolve the doubt against him. In such a case it may accordingly be critical to whom the burden of proof is allocated by law.

This is a question which policy, fairness, and empirical notions of probability all play a hand to resolve. The reason, for instance, why a bailee, like a warehouseman or carrier, is required to assume the burden of proving that damage or loss of the goods entrusted to him for storage or transport was *not* due to his negligence is because he has better access to information as to what might have happened, because it is much more probable that his negligence was responsible than any other cause, and, lastly, because this procedural handicap exerts additional pressure on him to take the utmost care. By contrast no single factor has been more instrumental in discouraging actions for malicious prosecution than placing the burden on the plaintiff of proving that the defendant had no reasonable and probable cause for prosecuting him, rather than calling on the latter to clear himself in a situation where he would obviously be the one to know much better what motivated him.

Ordinarily in accident litigation the plaintiff carries the burden of proving all the facts in issue, except with respect to the twin defences of contributory negligence and voluntary assumption of risk. Thus he must prove as more probable than not that the defendant failed to conform to the appropriate standard of care demanded from him like taking a particular precaution, that this caused his injury in the sense that 'but for it' the accident would not have happened, and that the injury was of a kind that was foreseeable and accordingly not too remote. On the other hand, he need not disprove his own responsibility on a balance of probabilities, for the burden on that issue is placed on the defendant because our law is on principle averse to requiring anyone to prove a negative, all the more against a defendant whose negligence caused him the injury.

That this allocation of the burden of proof is not self-evident is demonstrated by the fact that Socialist countries following the Soviet model ordinarily require the defendant, once shown to have caused the injury, to prove that he was *not* negligent. This also used to be the old common law rule for trespass, which made all direct and immediate injury to person or property prima facie actionable unless excused. The rule that in these cases the burden of disproving negligence was on the defendant has survived to this day in Canada, perhaps even in Australia, though no longer in England.[5]

The converse has also found support, viz. to require the defendant, once found negligent, to prove that his negligence did not cause the injury. German law, for example, does so in cases of statutory violation.[6] Common law courts have occasionally applied the same technique to the problem of identifying the culprit from among several negligent candidates.

Our sense of fairness demands that, all other things being equal, a person shall not be held to account merely because it is clear that either he or somebody else was responsible, though the plaintiff cannot say which one. We reject the notion of collective guilt in the civil as much as in the criminal law unless, that is, the equities are shifted. For example, if both defendants had been engaged in a common design against the plaintiff, such as to rob him, each will be liable

[5] *Fowler* v. *Lanning*, [1959] 1 Q.B. 426. The old trespass rule disappeared a century earlier from highway accidents.

[6] This practice, while condemned in *Vyner* v. *Waldenberg Bros.*, [1946] K.B. 50, retains prestigious advocates like Lord Wilberforce in *McGee* v. *N.C.B.*, [1973] 1 W.L.R. 1,6.

as a 'joint tortfeasor' for all the damage regardless of who actually did it. Similarly there is now good authority for saying that, whenever an accident deprives the plaintiff of his ability to prove who of several negligent actors was responsible for his injury, they may be justly required to exculpate themselves or identify the amount of damage for which each is alone responsible. Thus, when two sportsmen out on a hunt simultaneously shot carelessly in the plaintiff's direction, it was held to be up to each to identify, if he could or would, whose shot had struck the plaintiff.[7] Here the chances were 50/50 and contribution between them, presumably in equal shares, would further mitigate the harshness of holding each liable in full. The only alternative would be to deny all redress to a victim of negligence for the sake of two proven wrongdoers either of whom could have hit the plaintiff.

A recent American extension of this principle is more controversial. A young woman, one among four hundred others, contracted a vaginal cancer after puberty supposedly as a result of her mother's use of a drug during pregnancy. The drug, *DES*, was manufactured by over two hundred companies and no records could be discovered to identify from which particular manufactuer the mother's drugs had emanated. The court adopted the novel solution of holding each company liable in an amount proportionate to its market share, on the theory that the amount each would eventually pay would correspond to the probable number of its true victims.[8] This decision will surely prove unacceptable to those who believe that the law of torts should remain true to its traditional mission of individual liability and leave collectivist solutions to legislative schemes of accident compensation.

3. *RES IPSA LOQUITUR*

Proof may be either by direct evidence or by inference from other facts, called circumstantial evidence. Thus if an intending passenger slips on a station platform on a banana

[7] *Cook* v. *Lewis*, [1951] S.C.R. 830 (Sup. Ct. Can.); *Summers* v. *Tice* (Cal. 1948), 5 A.L.R. 2d 91.

[8] *Sindell* v. *Abbott Laboratories* (1980), 26 Cal. 3d 588.

peel, his case against the railway, that it failed to maintain a proper system of inspection, may be established either by proof that the particular skin had been dropped there the night before and no effort made to remove it, or by simply showing that it was dry, gritty, and black—for this would permit the inference, based on experience, that it had been there long enough to be picked up by any reasonably careful employee charged with the task of keeping the platform reasonably safe. True, there are other conceivable explanations of how it might have come to be there without negligence on the part of the railway or its servants; for instance it could have been dropped less than a minute before from a paper bag carried by an alighting passenger. Still the odds are sufficiently in favour of the first hypothesis to permit the conclusion that the railway was at fault. Yet this conclusion though permissible is not peremptory: it is one that *may*, not *must*, be drawn. If the railway does not make a serious attempt to explain it away, either by proof or argument, it runs a substantial risk that the trier of fact will draw that conclusion and therefore decide against it; in other words, the *risk* of non-persuasion has shifted. But it is only a risk, not a certainty, for the trier of fact may remain unpersuaded and conclude that the hypotheses are too evenly balanced to call the shots against the defendant.

This perfectly intelligible and rather mundane insight into rational thought processes, common to lawyer and layman alike, was invested with an esoteric aura destined for misunderstanding and distortion when in its application to certain cases it came to be tagged with a Latin label—*res ipsa loquitur*—from intellectual conceit rather than any more respectable reason. Now, it is true that sometimes a thing will tell its own story, such as (in the seminal case) that a barrel of flour falling out of a warehouse on top of a passer-by in the street is more consistent with negligence on the part of the warehouseman than any other explanation. 'Putting two and two together', the accident implicates the defendant and will entitle the jury to find for the plaintiff, particularly if the defendant has nothing to counter—rebut—the inference that is open against him.

When does an accident bespeak negligence in the defendant? Although the cases present an infinite variety of fact situations and are, in that sense, beyond meaningful classification, they satisfy the following common test: first, the accident must be one which ordinarily does not happen without negligence; and secondly, that negligence must be the defendant's.

The first requirement postulates a basis in experience that more probably than not this accident was due to negligence. This may be satisfied despite the possibility of some other explanation to account for the occurrence, such for example as that an unauthorized person had gained access to the storeroom and rolled the barrel out of the window for sheer mischief. The odds, however, would be against it, and it is not unfair to call on the defendant to substantiate such a suggestion. On the other hand, the mere fact that the accident is rare is not sufficient. To say that a rare accident does not ordinarily happen is a truism, but to say that it ordinarily does not happen *without negligence* requires a broader basis of experience. Usually founded on common knowledge among laymen, it may, according to the better opinion, be supplied also by the common knowledge of experts, as in cases of alleged medical malpractice. Moreover, progress in human experience and knowledge may well have a bearing on the application of the maxim. In the early days of aviation an air crash could not be confidently attributed to negligence either in the aircraft's design or in its maintenance or operation. Conscious ignorance about aerodynamics not only excluded any inference of negligence, but even supported the argument that flying was so hazardous, fraught with risks which not even the highest care could eliminate, that it warranted the imposition of strict liability. Nowadays, however, the position is reversed.

The second requirement is that the accident must implicate the defendant. As we have seen, the plaintiff is ordinarily required to prove not merely that he was the victim of negligence but also whose. Accordingly, if the accident bespeaks negligence, but points no more to one than the other of two possible culprits, the maxim fails, since legitimate inferences cannot be drawn against either. Thus, a broken drainage tube left in a patient's bladder does not implicate the surgeon when post-operative treatment involved its periodical replacement by the staff of an independent hospital. Of course, whenever one person is responsible for the acts of all others, like a hospital for all its staff, all that is required is an inference that some one of them was negligent.

The necessity of linking the accident with the defendant also accounts for the common pronouncement that the defendant must have been in 'exclusive' control of the thing that caused the injury. Now, if he was, this would tend to eliminate alternative causes. But there are many accidents which clearly incriminate a particular person without his having been, literally at any rate, in control of the 'thing' at the time of the mishap. Once, for example, an explosion of a carbonated bottle has been traced to a probable defect in the glass, eliminating the likelihood of damage through handling after it left the bottler's plant, it points sufficiently to the latter to justify an adverse inference against him. All that need be postulated, therefore, is that the apparent cause of the accident is one for which the defendant's negligence would be responsible.

Procedural effect

It was suggested earlier that *res ipsa loquitur* is but an aid in the evaluation of evidence and, as the preceding discussion has borne out, the conditions that bring it into play are compatible, and compatible only, with the premise that sometimes certain facts are rather telling, sufficiently so to permit belief in what they tell (viz. the defendant's responsibility) in the absence of an explanation to the contrary. But there is no *inherent* justification for attaching to it any greater weight, such as that of a presumption which would actually shift the burden of proof and require the defendant to establish on a balance of probabilities that he was *not* negligent, with the result that, if he fails to tilt the scales in his favour, the trier of facts must, not merely may, decide against him. To go that far would be to give more weight to circumstantial than to direct evidence. It is true that, when a thing tells its own story, it may do so in a whisper or it may scream from the roof tops, but this depends on the strength of the inference to be drawn from the particular facts of each case. It will accordingly vary from one to another and is not capable of any generalization.

In England, however, in contrast to most other common law or, for that matter, civil law jurisdictions, the heresy has gained ground of treating the maxim as shifting the burden of proof to the defendant. In part this may have been in psychological reaction to the impressiveness of its Latin brocard, in part to the insidious tendency mentioned earlier of treating as a binding proposition of law what in a given case was only meant to be a particular conclusion of fact. This distortion is seriously abetted by the disappearance of jury trial, for a judge's lengthy disquisition on what prompted him to reach a verdict for the plaintiff may be easily misinterpreted to mean that the facts not only justified, but compelled such a verdict. Jury trial, on the other hand, reduces this risk by focusing more sharply on the procedural consequences of the distinction as it bears on the allocation of functions between judge and jury, and because jury verdicts are laconic and clearly devoid of precedential value.

In practice, of course, all this makes little difference, because the trier of facts, and especially juries, will rarely resolve lingering doubts against the plaintiff, unless the defendant's attempted exculpation was truly impressive. In some cases, indeed, there is little, if anything, that a defendant can do to dispel the case against him, whether it be classified as an inference or presumption. This is true whenever he knows as little as the plaintiff about what went wrong, as in so many cases where a foreign substance entered a product in the manufacturing process (mice in Coca-Cola bottles) or when the defendant was killed in the very same accident. In these cases, then, *res ipsa* comes close to strict liability. And as experience, particularly in America, illustrates, it can also be deliberately exploited for the purpose of promoting transcendent policy objectives, as, for example, to offset the 'conspiracy of silence' among doctors by inducing them to talk on pain of suffering an adverse judgment.[9]

[9] *Ybarra* v. *Spangard* (1944), 25 Cal. 2d 486, 162 A.L.R. 1258 (burden of proof shifted to all members of a surgical team to explain external injury to a patient's shoulder during appendectomy).

VIII

STRICT LIABILITY

1. RATIONALE

MOST, if not all, systems of law, committed though they may be to the general philosophy of fault, are prepared to countenance strict liability in some exceptional situations. What are the factors that exert so strong a pull as to displace occasionally the ordinary axiom that injury neither intended nor negligent does not constitute an actionable wrong?

One explanation, more pertinent to English law than to systems based on a systematic Code, is simply that some instances of strict liability have survived the vagaries of precedent as relics of a past which used to espouse a stricter theory of civil liability. Such perhaps is the rule of cattle trespass, which stems from a time when all trespass, i.e. direct and immediate injury to the person or property of another, involved the actor in presumptive responsibility. Another example is what remains of the erstwhile strict liability for escaping fire. Not too much, however, should be made of pure historicism as a reason for lingering strict liability, because in all too many instances ancient tradition proved no insuperable obstacle to the reform-minded judiciary of the nineteenth century. If, then, a few did survive, it is more probably because some other, modern reason militated in their favour. Thus, whatever solution might have commended itself to a present-day court if the matter were of first impression, the stringent liability for cattle trespass, which allows of no excuse except perhaps act of God or the malicious intervention of a stranger, can be as readily sustained now as at its beginning in the thirteenth century on the ground that it constitutes an excessive hazard to agriculture which is best eliminated by placing the risk even of a non-negligent escape on the cattle owner rather than on his hapless neighbour. Expressed in modern terms, our law insists on fencing-in rather than fencing-out, though the latter has understandably proved more appealing in the preponderatingly open grazing areas in the western parts of the United States.

As the preceding discussion has already implied, the most cogent argument for raising responsibility beyond the conventional standard of mere reasonable care is that the activity or enterprise is fraught with exceptional peril, that the risk is practically uncontrollable in the sense of posing a threat despite all proper care being taken, and that it is therefore not unfair to place the burden of compensation on him who chooses to subordinate the safety of others to his own personal advantage. An ever-growing number of pursuits is inherently so dangerous that even the observance of all safety precautions commensurate with the high risk of the enterprise offers no prospect of adequately controlling their potentiality for mischief. Often enough it would arguably be negligent to embark on them at all, because of the unreasonable hazard they present to others, were it not for the fact that their high social utility or some other balancing factor might be deemed to justify taking such a risk consonant with the conventional formula of negligence—a formula which takes for its model ordinary activities that are safe enough when conducted with all reasonable circumspection, but not exceptional activities fraught with high danger despite all reasonable precautions.

The problem is therefore closely linked with modern technology, with the awesomely enlarged human capacity to release energy. A prosaic illustration would be that of an oil driller who decided to 'blow out' a well and proceeded to do so in accordance with established procedures. These, however, were in no way proof against unknown and harmful substances being belched from the bowels of the earth, including the arsenic that was spewed over neighbouring pastures. Here the operator had resolved the dilemma facing him by subordinating the interests of others to his own. The chance of something deleterious coming up might have been comparatively small though clearly recognized, and the more perplexing because it was irreducible by anything short of not proceeding with the blow-out. Yet the latter was a necessary and accustomed procedure in oil drilling—an industry of paramount economic importance which it would not be justifiable to impede for less than absolutely compelling reasons. To say that the operator's choice was negligent would imply that for him to proceed would be unlawful and could be enjoined by injunction. It is precisely to resolve this dilemma that the law may say to him: 'What you propose to do is not prohibited and we therefore cannot stop you. Yet if you proceed, you must be prepared to foot the bill should anything go wrong, as you hope it will not though well aware that it might.'

This rationale strikes an unfamiliar chord only because of the traditional identification of tort with reprehensible conduct, which is reflected in its very name.[1] For, to repeat, strict liability ensues although neither the activity nor the manner in which it is conducted is wrongful in the ordinary sense. The defendant must pay, not because he should have known better and prevented the accident, but because that was the condition attached to his being permitted to conduct his activity in the way in which it was, in view of its irreducible risks. This result can be defended on grounds of fairness, even economic efficiency.

The case for fairness is that the defendant deliberately chose to put others at exceptional risk in order to promote his own interests. That the risk was irreducible might not have made it negligent but obligated him to meet the cost he foisted on others for his benefit. This is akin to the principle of unjust enrichment, although here the defendant does not have to disgorge the benefit he has gained (as when he has committed a deliberate wrong like selling stolen goods[2]) but need only compensate for the loss he has caused. Another celebrated application is the rule in *Vincent* v. *Lake Erie Transportation Co.*, that a ship's captain who seeks refuge from a storm by tying himself up without the dock owner's consent, must compensate the latter for the damage to the dock. Because the captain acted under necessity, he did no wrong (indeed, the dock owner would himself have incurred liability for resulting injury if he had resisted the exercise of the captain's privilege and pushed him off), but this did not preclude his having to compensate for the damage he caused in order to benefit himself.[3]

[1] Tort, *delit, unerlaubte Handlung.*

[2] The owner may sue the thief either for the value at the time of conversion (tort) or the thief's proceeds (restitutionary action 'for money had and received').

[3] (Minn. 1910) 124 N.W. 221; *Restatement, Torts, Second* § 197, 263;

The economic justification for strict liability is more debatable. On the one hand, it can be argued that if the defendant is acquitted of negligence, it must be because he had employed all cost-justified precautions and the activity was so useful that he was entitled to carry it on despite the unpreventable hazard it posed to the public. Therefore, to impose liability on him would create the wrong incentive, viz. to invest in cost-*un*justified procedures. On the other hand, strict liability does a more complete job than negligence of internalizing the risk to the harmful activity. For one thing, the risk ought to be allocated to the activity rather than to the public because it is non-reciprocal (unlike motor traffic) and the enterpriser is the superior cost-avoider. Strict liability therefore adds an incentive for him to reduce accidents, which spell economic wastage; but if he does not, the cost of accidents should be reflected in the pricing of his products with the hoped-for result that, in a competitive market, the demand for the product would lessen and so would the accident rate.

The latter argument has proved most persuasive as a justification of strict liability for defective products. As we have already seen,[4] this principle has long been accepted in American law and has been recommended in England in train with its likely adoption by the EEC Directive for the whole Community. It will be noted, however, that in this instance[5] strict liability is being extended to an activity or things that cannot pretend to pose exceptional risks. Why then apply it to products but not to services and other harmful conduct which the logic of cost-internalization would also reach? The reasons for singling out products are manifold: the consumer's peculiar vulnerability and dependence on the manufacturer for product safety, his lack of resources in proving fault and sustaining fault litigation, familiarity with strict liability between seller and buyer, the notion that perfection can be expected and achieved in products but not in services and other activities, and finally the 'deep pocket' of

German *BGB* § 904. English courts have hitherto proceeded on the simplistic assumption that if the act is permitted, the actor cannot be liable for compensation.

[4] *Supra* p. 87.

[5] As perhaps in others recommended by the Pearson Commission, like vaccine and aircraft injuries.

manufacturers and their ability to pass on the cost to the consumer, the very person who will ultimately be footing the bill in higher prices.

2. THE PRINCIPLE OF *RYLANDS* v. *FLETCHER*

Strict liability for extraordinarily hazardous activities is peculiarly associated with the famous decision in *Rylands* v. *Fletcher*, in which the House of Lords in 1867, in the hey-day of economic liberalism, drew sustenance from the sparse growth of a few sporadic precedents dealing with cattle trespass, spreading fire, and escape of filth from a privy to launch the generalized principle that anyone 'who for his own purposes brings upon his land anything likely to do mis-chief if it escapes must keep it in at his peril'. This formula-tion soon proved to be too embracing to survive second thought. Indeed, the judicial record is manifest with per-sistent endeavour, if not to stifle, at least to keep under closest trim this odd growth foisted on the common law at a moment of apparent imbalance.

First, it soon became clear that the principle was applic-able only to substances and activities fraught with more than the normal level of common risks. Taken literally of course almost anything is likely to do mischief, *if* it escapes; and indeed not too fine a point has been put on this requirement: the quality may be present either because it is inherent in the matter itself (e.g. because of its volatility as in the case of gas or dynamite) or by reason of its bulk or volume (like water in a large reservoir as distinct from a goldfish bowl).

Secondly, the dangerous object must have been brought upon the land by human effort (though not necessarily the defendant's) rather than originating there 'naturally' like an outcrop of rocks or water collected in a hollow. Far from the latter being the object of strict liability, the common law was not even anxious to insist on a duty of care to keep them in, for fear that this would expose landowners to an inordinate burden of estate management. Only lately has this immunity fallen into disfavour, first in the case of falling trees, even-tually in regard to all conditions of natural origin, even weathering rocks on a promontory.[6] (Understandably it

[6] *Leakey* v. *National Trust*, [1980] Q.B. 485 (C.A.).

continues to enjoy greater vogue in countries, like America, with large areas of uncultivated bush and forest.) Strict liability pertains only to things 'brought upon the land'. It would be wrong, however, to interpret this requirement too literally so as to exclude for example an explosion in an oil well, still less vibrations set up in blasting, for modern uses and techniques often entail increased danger and furnish all the less justification for relaxing the standard of liability.

Thirdly, the most drastic limitation, evolved after protracted experiment, was that the principle of strict liability pertained only to 'abnormal uses'. For some time the disposition prevailed of equating 'abnormal or non-natural' with 'artificial'. This trend rightly evoked the criticism that it discriminated against all efforts to improve the lot of mankind above the most primitive level of agricultural or domestic existence. It drew some semblance of support from the very facts of the parent case itself, where a Lancashire mill-owner employed some independent contractors to construct a water reservoir in connexion with his factory. The job was badly done, connoting negligence on their, but not on his, part, with the result that water seeped into the workings of an adjacent mine. He was held liable for having created the source of danger (not for the negligence of the contractors) despite the obvious utility of the project and what appears to have been a normal adjunct of industrial operations at the time and place. The explanation would appear to be that what tipped the scales was the extraordinary danger inherent in collecting so large a mass of water—a menace to which the court was much alive in memory of recent dam disasters in the same area. The mill-owner, having exposed his neighbours to so great a menace for his own personal advantage, was felt, not unfairly, to deserve the concomitant burden of having to make compensation if anything went wrong.

Progressive experience in applying the distinction has proved that it can be handled with more discrimination. At all events since 1913 the accepted guideline is that, in order to attract strict liability, there 'must be some *special* use bringing with it increased danger to others and . . . not merely the ordinary use of the land or such a use as is proper for the general benefit of the community'.[7] For example,

[7] *Rickards* v. *Lothian*, [1913] A.C. 263, 280 (P.C.).

gas, electricity, or water for domestic purposes is treated as a 'normal user', demanding no more than reasonable care, whereas their storage or supply in bulk by commercial concerns or public utilities is classified as an 'abnormal user', attracting strict liability. The difference in treatment is due in the first instance to the greater magnitude of the risk entailed: both because the larger volume is more difficult to keep under control and because any mishap may assume catastrophic proportions. Somewhat perplexingly, however, liability is by no means restricted to disaster damage on the theory that strict liability should be limited to the exceptional risks that called it into existence. Far from this being the case, all but two or three of the English decisions have been concerned with claims for damage typical of 'normal risk' accidents, such as small fires or minor personal injuries sustained by a single casualty. All the more, then, it suggests as a transcending reason for imposing strict liability on bulk suppliers that, in contrast to domestic consumers, the risk is part and parcel of their business in handling the particular commodity. Here then is once again the golden thread of enterprise liability.

Lastly, the imposition of strict liability on bulk suppliers, often municipalities or other public authorities, underlines the important lesson that neither reasonableness nor social utility furnishes a reason for exemption. True, Justice Blackburn's original formula spoke of 'anyone who for his own purposes . . .', but this has been consistently understood as synonymous with 'conducting his own affairs' rather than 'for private profit as distinct from public service'. And this is as it should be, for there is no justification whatever for subordinating in this manner private rights to public welfare. If the enterprise enures to the public good, then let the public also shoulder the cost, the more because it can thus be spread among its beneficiaries. For the same reason the courts are open to criticism for giving excessive berth to the defence of statutory authority. Many of the undertakings here in question (public utilities, railways, oil refineries) operate under statutory authority. If the damage they cause others is a *necessary* incident of the activity expressly authorized, as when a railway empowered to run steam locomotives causes sparks, a tort immunity for resulting damage may perhaps be legitimately inferred even in the absence of a special compensation clause,[8] although it is a democratic imperative that public authorities expropriating private property for the public good shall pay compensation. The immunity has, however, been extended even to cases of water or gas mains bursting or electricity wires becoming dislodged, which are not necessary corollaries of the authorized enterprise. The Pearson Commission rightly recommended abolition of the defence.[9]

The Pearson Commission in general favoured a more expansive role for strict liability. It envisaged two categories: first, unusually hazardous 'things or operations', like explosives and flammable gas or liquids; and secondly, those which, although normally perfectly safe, are likely to cause serious and extensive casualties, like large public bridges, dams, major stores, and stadiums.[10] The second criterion is novel in principle since it lacks the crucial element of uncontrollability, but may well have influenced in the past the widespread statutory imposition of strict liability on nuclear facilities.[11] Rather than leave such open-ended categories to judicial implementation, the Commission recommended a listing of qualifying 'things or activities' by statutory instruments in order to avoid the uncertainty of judicial legislation.[12]

3. ANIMALS

Strict liability pervades responsibility for damage done by animals.[13] As already mentioned, the ancient rule of cattle trespass furnished one of the inspirations of *Rylands* v. *Fletcher.* It makes the owner of straying livestock liable for damage done to the land or property on it, except premises adjoining the highway whose owner is presumed to have accepted the risks of ordinary traffic, including a bull wandering into the china shop—an idyllic view of English rural towns.[14]

[8] *Allen* v. *Gulf Oil,* [1981] A.C. 1001 (nuisance).

[9] *Report* I para. 1653.

[10] Ibid., paras. 1640–5.

[11] The Nuclear Installations Act 1965 limits the operator's liability to £5 mill.

[12] *Report* I, paras. 1646–51.

[13] In England the law was codified in the Animals Act 1971.

[14] Sect. 4, 5.

Dangerous animals attract *scienter* liability.[15] They are divided into two categories: those belonging to a dangerous species, like lions, bears, and monkeys, which are not commonly domesticated in the British Isles and when fully grown are prone to cause 'severe damage';[16] the others comprise the familiar denizens of the farmyard from bulls to lambs. For mischief perpetrated by the first group the keeper is responsible without any more ado, whilst with respect to the second there must first be proof that he knew or had reason to know of the dangerous propensity of the particular animal. In the first, knowledge of the risk—*scienter*—is conclusively presumed as a matter of law; in the second it must be established as a matter of fact. But in neither case is liability dependent on any particular negligence in the manner of controlling the animal: the mere keeping of it is considered a sufficient threat to the safety of others to warrant a shifting of the legal risk even for non-negligent injuries. There is enough social usefulness in most dangerous animals, whether wild beasts in zoo or circus or ferocious stud bulls on the farm, to preclude them from being outlawed, but the special risk they present entails a corresponding obligation for the keeper to keep them at his peril.

The focus of all three rules is on the characteristics of the animal. In the case of livestock, it is their propensity to roam which both justifies the strict liability and limits it to typical damage, excluding personal injury.[17] Liability for dangerous animals, however, covers 'any damage', not confined to vicious acts. Thus it was sufficient when a frightened circus elephant ran after a barking dog, injuring a midget in an adjoining booth.[18] American courts have taken a more restrictive view, confining liability to typical risks and therefore excusing the circus the sight of whose elephants in a street parade caused a horse to bolt.[19] An animal of harmless species, however, must have been 'vicious, mischievous, or fierce' to the knowledge of its keeper, even if the trait is not contrary to its species, like a bitch with pups given to snapping or a ram to butting. But there is no

[15] Sect. 2.

[16] Sect. 6(2).

[17] The common law apparently included it.

[18] *Behrens* v. *Bertram Mills Circus* [1957] 2 Q.B. 1.

[19] *Scribner* v. *Kelly* (1862), 38 Barb. 14.

liability in the absence of negligence for the playfulness of an unbroken filly or of dogs running across traffic. Dog Acts commonly dispense with proof of *scienter* but differ as to the damage. The English Act confines liability to killing or injuring livestock; American legislation, on the contrary, to biting persons, thereby perhaps revealing a national difference in the scale of values.[20]

Negligence

The victim of an animal, though unable to pursue his claim under one or the other head of strict liability, may always fall back on negligence. That a horse, for example, is not dangerous does not absolve the person in charge from so riding or leading it as not to expose other road users to unreasonable danger. In controlling animals no less than inanimate things he owes a duty of care not to imperil people within the foreseeable range of risk.

In this connection, however, English law long perversely clung to an archaic immunity. Stemming from a time before the English countryside assumed its characteristic hedgerows, it exempted a cattle owner from any duty of care to fence in his livestock or otherwise prevent them from straying on to the highway. Until the advent of fast-moving motor traffic this could perhaps be tolerated as a choice, biased no doubt but still defensible, between the respective burden on farmer and traveller. Nowadays, however, it constitutes an outrageous subsidy shamelessly exacted by the farming lobby at the expense of public safety. Eventually the immunity was abolished in England in 1971,[21] but it has demonstrated continuing tenacity in the Commonwealth, particularly in Australia, despite persistent judicial protests and recommendations by Law Reform bodies.

4. VICARIOUS LIABILITY

The common law holds a 'master' *vicariously* liable for torts committed by his 'servant' in the course of employment. This principle is not confined, as its archaic terminology might suggest, to relations of menial service. Nor is it in any

[20] Cf. *Salmond & Heuston on Torts* (18th ed. 1981) § 121.
[21] Animals Act 1971, s. 8.

way dependent on proof of managerial fault in the selection or supervision of the culpable employee, as under German law. Vicarious liability is a liability without fault on the part of the employer, the employee's fault being simply imputed to him as a matter of law. This way, therefore, an overwhelming proportion of all accident losses is today allocated to an individual without reference to culpability; the more when account is also taken of the concomitant tendency to demand in practice less in the way of proof from an injured plaintiff where it is evident that the bill will be met, not by the vulnerable servant, but out of the deep pocket of his employer. The transcendent justification is frankly functional: to assure recourse against a party much less likely to be judgment-proof than the culpable employee and one moreover who is not only in a comparatively better position to bear the loss, but even able to distribute it by spreading the cost (whether direct or in the form of insurance premiums) among his customers. Social and perhaps even moral justice reinforces this result inasmuch as it tends to exert pressure for adopting more rigorous accident-preventive procedures (including the selection, supervision, and disciplining of personnel) and because, after all, the losses were incurred in pursuit of the employer's interest. Last of all, from the point of view of economically sound cost allocation, injury and damage done by employees 'in the course of employment' is as proper a charge to production expenses as injury sustained by them in accidents 'arising in and out of the course of employment': in short, vicarious liability, like workers' compensation, represents production costs which should be reflected in the price of goods or services charged to the customers of the enterprise.

That the liabilty is 'vicarious' might suggest that the employer substitutes for the employee.[22] Actually, the employee is liable jointly with his employer. In practice, however, judgment is rarely enforced against the employee. Nor would the employer as a rule seek an indemnity from the employee, unless he was guilty of a severe transgression or carried his own liability insurance.[23] The modern trend is

[22] A vicar represents God.

[23] A right of subrogation by the employer's insurer was narrowly upheld in *Lister* v. *Romford Ice Co.*, [1957] A.C. 555.

to limit or abolish such a right of indemnity[24] or to abolish the employee's direct liability as well. Thus in Socialist countries the victim can direct his claim only against the employing enterprise, which in turn may discipline the employee by reducing his pay without imperilling his existence.

The master's vicarious liability is not unlimited, for unlike a husband of old who used to be answerable for all the torts of his wife (perhaps because a woman's work was never done in those days), it does not extend, as just mentioned, beyond torts committed by the servant in the course of his employment. Not that the tort must have actually fallen within the express or implied authority of the servant, nor even that it occurred in doing something that was strictly of any concern to the master, like negligently throwing away a burning match after lighting a cigarette on the job. The notion is wider than that, encompassing (according to the accredited formula) all acts of the servant that can be regarded as wrongful and unauthorized *modes* of performing an authorized task. Not even a prohibition relating merely to manner, time, and place, as distinct from actually delimiting the sphere of employment, will furnish an excuse. This is well illustrated by the case of the bus driver who, in defiance of express instructions, pulled across the road in front of a rival bus, causing it to overturn. His employer was held responsible on the ground that this was merely an unauthorized manner of doing his job, viz. driving a bus.[25] In contrast when a bus *conductor* took it upon himself to turn the bus round for the return trip during a momentary absence of the driver, he was held to have stepped altogether outside the scope of his employment: driving could by no stretch be deemed incidental to his assigned job as conductor.[26]

Even wilful wrongdoing may fall within the range of vicarious liability, though there has been decidedly more hesitation than in cases of negligence. Undoubtedly there is least cavil where the servant's motive was to advance the interests of his employer, like the porter who mistakenly ejected a passenger from a train. But although it is now settled

[24] E.g. in several Australian jurisdictions, and Germany. In England, *Lister* was overcome by a 'gentlemen's agreement' regarding accidents between co-employees.

[25] *Limpus* v. *London Gen. Omnibus Co.* (1862), 1 H & C 526.

[26] *Beard* v. *London Gen. Omnibus Co.*, [1900] 2 Q.B. 530.

that a master may be liable even for his servant's fraud, yet if it was committed solely for the servant's own benefit, it would seem that the master must have at least placed him in a position to appear as his representative in the relevant transaction. Such, for example, was the case where a solicitor's managing clerk misappropriated some mortgage moneys of a client to whom he had misrepresented the nature of the proposed deal. Thus the agency doctrine of 'ostensible authority', rejected as unduly narrow for the stock situation of negligent injury, seems to have retained a hold in marking the outer perimeter of vicarious liability for wilful wrongs of a servant.

Independent contractors

The employer of an independent contractor as distinct from a servant does not ordinarily incur vicarious liability. This is because, as a matter of common understanding and business convenience, the contractor assumes sole responsibility for the accident losses in doing the job, being better able to make provision for absorbing them in the first place, while no doubt eventually debiting the cost to the customer as part of the price of his services. Typically, contractors like plumbers, builders, and taxi-drivers are in a much better position than the householder or casual passenger to guard against the risks of their specialized work and equip themselves to carry appropriate insurance. In short, the risks of accidents are incidental to the contractor's enterprise rather than to the employer's.

This basic principle has, however, gradually become eroded by exceptions. The reason for this is not altogether clear. Since the principal, if held liable, is entitled to an indemnity, his role is in effect only that of a guarantor against the contingency of the contractor's insolvency. Apparently it is thought that, because the job was after all undertaken for the benefit of the principal, he should in such an emergency bail out the contractor and stand the loss however crippling, rather than the hapless victim of the contractor's tort. It has become fashionable to conceal this form of vicarious liability by predicating that in the relevant situations the principal is cast under a so-called 'non-delegable' duty, meaning that he remains responsible for the manner in which the work is carried out. Not its least perplexing feature, however, is the absence of any visible thread linking the various instances in which, in somewhat random fashion, such a special duty has been found.

Most plausible are the conventional instances of strict liability, like those pertaining to ultra-hazardous substances (*Rylands* v. *Fletcher*) and the near-strict duty to maintain premises abutting the highway in sound repair. Analogous also is the responsibility for the use of inherently dangerous implements, like blow-torches, and for work involving a high risk of nuisance. Much more difficult to account for, however, is the inclusion of many other duties, like those incumbent on employers to provide a safe system of work or on occupiers towards contractual entrants (e.g. with respect to the safety of a grandstand in a football stadium)—which have nothing to do with specially risky activities and yet are considered candidates for elevation from the ordinary mundane duty to take reasonable care to the higher duty to guarantee that care is taken.

Somewhat blurred as the distinction in responsibility for servants and independent contractors has thus become, the critical difference still remains that the employer of a contractor is never liable for any mere 'collateral' negligence, like an accident in bringing up machinery to the working site as distinct from operating the machine on the job itself.

Yet another factor whittling away at the old immunity is the reformulation of the test for distinguishing between servants and independent contractors, which over the years has resulted in many a relation being reclassified as one of master and servant and thus subject to the traditional rule of vicarious liability. The hallmark of that relationship has always been the close control exercised by the one over the other, typically—according to the accredited test—not only over *what* the subordinate should do, but also over *how* he is to do it. The growing dissociation between management and technical skills in advancing stages of business and industrial organization demanded some corresponding adjustment of that test. Accordingly it no longer matters whether the employer had the know-how to tell his employee how to do his work; it is sufficient that he had managerial control, that the employee was a cog in the employer's organizational structure. Thus, even highly skilled professionals, like doctors and nurses on a hospital staff, have come to be classified as servants, since they are at least subject to managerial control in such critical matters as working rosters, routines, remuneration, and discipline. An alternative theory for pinning responsibility on hospitals is to postulate that, by offering a complete range of treatment, the institution assumes a personal, non-delegable duty to ensure safe treatment at the hands of such staff as it provides, regardless of their specific status. The same approach has also been applied to schools.[27]

Car owners

The overriding quest for financially responsible defendants accountable to traffic victims has also led to a consistent dilution of the conventional prerequisites of vicarious liability. Since car owners rather than drivers carry insurance, a number of devices has been deployed for saddling them with responsibility for any tortious injury arising out of the use of vehicles registered in their name. Most far-reaching is the statutory imputation of vicarious liability widely adopted in Australia, Canada, and America, whereby all drivers, or at least those who have the owner's permission, are conclusively deemed to be agents acting in the course of the owner's employment. Somewhat the same result is achieved by the equally prevalent technique of requiring liability insurance covering all or all authorized drivers of the car, often as a condition precedent for its annual registration. This in substance is the position in Britain under the statutory scheme of compulsory insurance.[28]

But these statutory reforms are in general applicable only to personal injuries and fatal accidents. In addition the common law has strained to make its own contribution, most important in the residuary cases of property (e.g. collision) damage or where legislation has not otherwise lent a helping hand. In their various forms all work with the pliable clay of 'agency'. They range from the American 'family purpose' doctrine which makes the owner as head of the household answerable for all uses of the car by its members, including

[27] *Commonwealth* v. *Introvigne* (1982), 41 Austr. L.R. 577.

[28] But *Launchbury* v. *Morgans*, [1973] A.C. 127, discouraged further extension as impinging on the legislative function.

the sixteen-year-old taking his girl-friend to the pictures on a Saturday night. Its English counterpart is that, first, any owner actually in the car at the time of the accident incurs responsibility as a corollary of his right to control the manner of its driving, whether the driver be a relative, friend, or prospective purchaser; and secondly, even if the owner be not in the car, the driver is considered his 'agent' so long as he is driving for a purpose not entirely his own, presumably like a housewife doing the family shopping. In addition every driver is initially presumed to be the owner's agent, so that it is for the owner to dispel, rather than for the victim to establish, the existence of 'agency' in its current, embracing sense.

5. MOTOR TRAFFIC

Probably the most eligible candidate today for strict liability or compensation is motor traffic. In retrospect it may well be a source for regret that the courts themselves missed no less than two critical opportunities in the past of subordinating running-down actions to strict liability. The first occurred in the third quarter of the nineteenth century, when they finally yielded to the pervasive challenge of the fault theory and edged out the erstwhile strict liability of trespass from collisions on the highway;[29] the second when they failed to avail themselves of the invitation to treat the new apparition of the motorized 'devil wagon' as an inherently dangerous object that deserved the attribution of strict liability.[30] They thus showed themselves more timorous than the French who first ingeniously converted an unprepossessing Code section, dealing (like *Rylands* v. *Fletcher*) with a duty to keep things under one's control, from negligence to strict liability and by 1927 applied it to motor accidents.[31] In England, any radical reform thereafter required the helping hand of Parliament.

The present system

The sheer size of the road toll pre-eminently calls into question the adequacy of the negligence system as a fair,

[29] *Holmes* v. *Mather* (1875), L.R. 10 Ex. 261 (C.A.).
[30] See *Walton & Co.* v. *Vanguard Motor Bus Co.* (1908), 25 T.L.R. 13.
[31] See e.g. Zweigert & Kötz, *Introduction to Comparative Law* II, 322.

adequate, and efficient method of accident compensation in our highly motorized society. Each year in Great Britain about 7,600 people are killed and 400,000 injured in road accidents, most of them involving a motor vehicle.[32] This amounts to more than 10 per cent of all injuries, about half as many as injuries at work which have now been under a special compensation regime for almost a century. Road injuries, moreover, are more likely to be severe or fatal. The principal source of compensation for the cost of medical care and disability is, of course, the National Health and Social Security systems. The role of tort is therefore only complementary, although not insignificant. It compensates a proportionately high number of claimants estimated at 25 per cent, compared with 10.5 per cent for work injuries and 6.5 per cent over all. Compulsory insurance since 1930 and provision for the victims of uninsured or untraced motorists (Motor Insurance Bureau Agreement) help to achieve this record. But the administrative cost is high, considering that of all tort claims 41 per cent relate to motor vehicle injuries, even if only 1 per cent reach the courts.

The high transaction costs of the tort system, to be explored at greater length in the following chapter, bear particularly heavily on motor accidents, if only because of the high percentage of such claims. In addition, the negligence doctrine itself operates with unusual capriciousness in this context.

Reform models

There are several basic reform models. One division is between those that retain the principle of individual liability and others with a collectivist structure. The first take the form of strict liability backed by compulsory insurance, as in Germany since 1909. This has the disadvantage of retaining the adversary posture between victim and injurer's insurer, but perhaps offers more incentive for penalty rating and thereby improving the client's driving record. At the opposite end of the spectrum are compensation funds centrally administered on the model, or as part, of the Social Security system. This invites the criticism of increasing bureaucracy

[32] The *Pearson Report* I, chap. 18 (1978).

and of weakening incentives to accident reduction. The Pearson Commission, however, favoured this model and recommended the setting up of a fund within the Social Security system which would provide benefits on the same preferential scale as for industrial accidents but separately funded by a levy on petrol.[33]

A third model is that of the no-fault legislation in about half of the United States. It is built on the principle of first-party insurance covering all occupants of the insured car[34] who therefore address claims to their own insurer, not the insurer of some third party as under the tort system. This has several advantages: it ensures a better relation between claimant and insurer, and premiums can be better aligned to benefits.[35]

Any of the above-mentioned models may either become substitutes for, or be complemented by residuary, tort damages for negligence. The choice is more likely to be influenced by politics (assuaging the legal profession) than by principle. Even the Pearson Commission's majority yielded to this pressure; and only a few countries (Québec, Puerto Rico, Israel) have resisted it successfully. Critical for the relative success of a 'mixed scheme' is, of course, the level of no-fault benefits. For the higher they are, the less incentive remains for seeking damages for non-pecuniary injury and other uncompensated loss. Some of the American statutes seek economies by setting 'thresholds' below which tort claims for relatively trivial injuries are abolished.

Benefits under all schemes are limited, either by tariffs (social security), by ceilings or thresholds, by limiting damages to pecuniary losses, or combinations of these. The determining factor is how to husband the resources earmarked for the scheme. Almost invariably the aim is merely to capture the existing sources of paying for traffic accidents but use administrative economies to spread benefits more widely. If the benefits that can be afforded on that basis would not always be acceptable as adequate, retention of a residuary tort remedy becomes inevitable.

[33] *Report* I, chap. 18.

[34] And pedestrians struck by the car. It is therefore just like optional insurance for damage to one's own car, except for being compulsory and covering personal injury.

[35] Low income owners of cheap cars who, under the tort/third party system subsidize the rich, would fare better.

The relative attractions of these models, as between themselves and in comparison with the unreformed fault doctrine, are better judged after reading the following chapter.

Property damage

Unlike most other European countries, Britain does not require compulsory third-party insurance against property damage, although pursuant to an EEC Directive of 1983 will soon have to fall into line. Compensation systems have as a rule confined themselves to personal injuries because this is where the need is greatest, because property is more likely to be already insured by its owners and because the extra premium cost would make the scheme politically less attractive.

A distinction should be made between damage to motor cars and to other property such as structures. Some compensation plans have abolished all tort claims for damaged cars on the ground that such losses should be borne exclusively by their owner. This would eliminate the disproportionately high transaction costs of third-party claims for such relatively small amounts and benefit owners of cheaper cars who would no longer have to help pay for the luxury cars of the wealthy. In England so-called 'knock-for-knock' agreements between different insurance companies already ensure that the first-party insurance of the car owner pays for the damage rather than the third-party insurance of a tortfeasor. If tort claims were formally abolished, first-party insurance could well remain optional.

IX

TORT OR COMPENSATION

COMPENSATION plans are increasingly replacing tort liability as a more attractive device for accident compensation. The modern reform proposals for road accidents discussed in the last chapter are symptomatic of this trend. It all started with Bismarck's first Workmen's Compensation Act in 1883 and has gathered pace with the growing quest for social security in the modern welfare state.

Workers' compensation, whether in its original structure or merged into a comprehensive social security system, provides preferential benefits for job-related injuries. Specialized plans for particular types of accident are proliferating in such areas as road traffic, aircraft crashes, victims of violent crimes, drug and vaccine, even sporting injuries. Recently, the Pearson Commission, not content with proclaiming that social security in Britain had already reduced tort to the role of 'junior partner',[1] recommended adoption of several specialized compensation plans or strict liability, with a view to eventual displacement of all tort damages.[2] This ultimate objective of comprehensive and exclusive no-fault accident compensation has already been blossoming in New Zealand since 1974 and by a hair's breadth came close to realization in Australia in 1975. In the meantime, the law of torts is being manipulated, especially in the United States, by compensation-minded judges and juries, sometimes looking more like handmaidens of collectivism than the traditional guardians of liberty. The death of tort?[3]

What, then, are the comparative attractions and shortcomings of the principal competitors: tort, special compensation programmes, or comprehensive social insurance?

Scholarly views on accident compensation policy inevitably

[1] *Royal Commission on Civil Liability and Compensation for Personal Injury* I para. 1732 (1978).

[2] Strict liability for defective products, vaccine injuries, expanded loss of 'exceptional risks', rail transport; compensation for road accidents.

[3] With apology to Grant Gilmore's *The Death of Contract* (1974).

reflect social perceptions and values of their time. The most important objectives advocated have been (1) deterring socially undesirable conduct, (2) allocating resources efficiently by holding to a minimum the waste to society from accidents, (3) compensating deserving victims and widely distributing losses to minimize individual catastrophe, (4) minimizing transaction costs, and (5) fairly distributing the cost of compensation.

While all these objectives may seem desirable, there is no agreed calculus for balancing them; nor is it simply a matter of ascertaining which of the competing systems would attain the greatest number of these goals. Some goals may seem far more important than others; for example, compensating the injured may or may not strike different policy-makers as worth sacrificing deterrence, let alone increasing costs.

1. PUNISHMENT AND DETERRENCE

Emphasis on punishment rests primarily on a moral basis, while emphasis on deterrence looks more to efficiency. The first seeks to inflict pain in retribution for the wrong done to the victim; and since it is the victim, not the state, that calls for the punishment in torts cases, punishment and vengeance are closely related. In contrast, deterrence principally aims at the reduction of accidents by imposing a toll on unsafe conduct. Since unreasonable injury to person or property causes a reduction in society's wealth, any deterrent therefore serves the aim of economic efficiency.

Although the twin purposes of punishment and deterrence have furnished the classical rationale of tort liability, their credibility has increasingly declined under the changing conditions of modern society. This, of course, is a criticism not of these objectives themselves but rather of the common law's failure to attain them. Perhaps the principal cause is that the admonitory effect of an adverse judgment is today largely diffused by liability insurance which protects the injurer from having to pay the accident cost and instead distributes it among a large pool of premium payers and thereby 'socializes' the loss. In many countries the victim no longer even in form addresses his claim to the injurer but proceeds directly against the latter's insurance carrier, thereby even eliminating the symbolic tokens of individual blame.[4]

Other realities of tort litigation may undermine the vengeance objective. Thus, although the victim's psychic satisfaction in making his adversary 'pay' is claimed by some legal psychologists as a significant rationale of tort liability,[5] the delays and aggravations of tort law in action probably impose psychological hardship and anxiety on victims that more than make up for what little satisfaction some victims receive.

None the less, some admonitory effect of a tort award is still retained. Insurance premiums are commonly adjusted in the light of the insured's accident record, and fear of substantial rises and possibly even policy cancellation may have some effect on individual conduct. The broad American consensus in favour of basing premiums for both liability and workers' compensation insurance on the insured's past accident record rests largely on this belief. Other countries, including Great Britain, however, are sceptical about the effectiveness and worthwhileness of such finesse;[6] or, like Australian politicians, prefer flat rates for third-party motor insurance, for the sake of their imagined popular appeal.

The admonitory effect of liability probably varies with different classes of potential defendants. Some are peculiarly sensitive to the stigma of an adverse judgment wholly apart from any financial detriment. The most obvious example is the medical profession whose members dread the notoriety of being sued, even more than being held liable, for its adverse reflection on their professional competence or integrity. More immediate and quicker response to an adverse judgment is also likely to be forthcoming when the censure falls on managerial failings in industry or business rather than on random human frailties like inattentiveness in factory or on the road. By the same token, large, stable, and well managed enterprises are far more likely to recognize and act on the potential rise in insurance premiums they face than are small firms fighting for economic survival.

[4] The *action directe*, pioneered by French Courts (1926), has since been emulated in many countries, less often in common law jurisdictions with jury trial.

[5] E.g. Ehrenzweig, 'A Psychoanalysis of Negligence', 47 *Nw.U.L.Rev.* 855 (1953).

[6] See, e.g. Atiyah, 'Accident Prevention and Variable Premium Rates for Work-Connected Accidents', 4 *Indust. L.J.* 1, 89 (1975).

Tort law may also play a key role in stimulating the market to work. Tort litigation in the United States has repeatedly served as 'Ombudsman',[7] giving publicity to dangerous products (Pinto, tampons, etc.), often with far more devastating financial consequences to the producer in terms of lost future sales than in damages awarded to the injured.

Still, one must be sceptical about the effectiveness of tort law in promoting accident prevention as compared with other legal or social mechanisms. The three most important of these are government regulation, criminal sanctions, and ordinary economic pressures.

Regulations can play an educative role in prescribing clear procedures designed to avoid accidents. Negligence law, by contrast, condemns people after it is too late. Also, while regulatory standards are established by experts, tort law leaves to inexpert juries or judges the bewildering task of resolving disputes between partisan expert witnesses. While tort law has come to take advantage of statutory standards by sometimes (though quite erratically) treating their violation as fault without more (*per se*), it is unwilling to treat compliance with prescribed standards as conclusively exonerating. Thus even licensing of products after a rigorous official testing procedure, as in the case of drugs, is not accepted as necessarily acquitting the manufacturer. An important advantage of the criminal sanction is its concern with punishing the offender for engaging in prohibited conduct; it will fall on the culprit regardless of whether he happened to victimize anyone. By contrast misconduct, however reprehensible, remains outside the reach of civil process so long as it does not injure anybody. That is why motorists today fear criminal penalties more than civil sanctions.

Even if there were no public controls and no tort law, potential injurers would face other substantial pressures favouring safety. Adverse publicity has repeatedly proved itself a potent sanction against defective products or accident-prone activities. Recall of motor cars by the American regulatory agency is one example. Drivers' concern for their own safety surely counts for more than the fear of having to pay damages. Potent deterrents for management against

[7] See Linden, 'Tort Law as Ombudsman', 51 *Can. B. Rev.* 155 (1973).

work accidents are interruption of work schedules, demoralization of employees, and, of course, sanctions under industrial safety legislation.

In any event, the tort system's residual effects in deterrence and punishment, such as they are, can also be enlisted by no-fault compensation.[8] While social security and general welfare systems have a tradition of flat-rate premium rates, accident compensation plans such as workers' compensation and road accident schemes do—and, in the opinion of many observers, should—employ differential rates as reward or rebuke of individual accident records.[9] Grave misconduct can also be sanctioned by means of withholding benefits, imposing fines, or indemnification as in the case of drunk drivers under some road accident compensation plans.

2. EFFICIENT LOSS ALLOCATION

Advocates of individual responsibility received a timely boost of morale from the current fad of lawyer-economists. One theory, already noted,[10] applauds the negligence principle as an ideal standard for promoting the most efficient allocation of resources because its economic calculus encourages, but encourages only, cost-justified precautions. In other words, the actor is penalized only for under-investment in accident prevention.

There are several basic problems with this thesis. Its model is the calculating 'economic man' with full information on the balance of costs. This character will rarely be found in the 'real world'. But let us concede that at least in the case of continuing industrial processes, such as the mass production of cars, experience may permit reasonably reliable forecasts of the cost of accident-preventive measures as well as the *rate* of future accidents. But how do we measure the *cost* of such accidents? Surely, it is a bizarre

[8] See Craig, 'Deterrence and Accident Compensation', 17 *U.W. Ont. L. Rev.* 111 (1978).

[9] In New Zealand industry differentials have been employed from the outset and computerization will now permit experiments with individual bonuses. However, the Road Accident Scheme levies a flat rate on motor vehicle owners. Professor A. R. Prest strongly advocated differential rates for work injuries in his Minority Statement in the *Pearson Report*, paras. 940–8.

[10] *Supra* p. 29. Its principal exponent is Richard Posner. See his *Economic Analysis of Law* (2nd ed. 1977) ch. 6.

distortion of the common law to postulate that the calculus of negligence calls for striking a purely economic balance between benefits and losses, the losses being assessed solely in cold-blooded terms of the damages that would be awarded to the victim or his survivors. While it is true that risks are sometimes worth taking and therefore considered reasonable either because the benefits from taking the risks or the cost of avoiding them are wholly disproportionate, the judgment is social, not economic.

Admittedly the production manager of an assembly line will likely be guided by an *economic* judgment of the cost-justified level of quality control, obedient to Coase's famous theorem that (in a perfect market) the most efficient (wealth-maximizing) use will prevail regardless of the initial assignment of legal rights.[11] But would not a fair-minded observer be tempted to conclude that if our manager chose to run the risk of accidents because it is the cheaper alternative, he should at least pay for such accidents as occur rather than escape altogether because the risk was cost-justified and therefore not negligent. If the latter hypothesis were right, it would add another plausible argument for imposing *strict liability* for defective products and thus making the producer compensate the casualties of industrial efficiency!

A different economic argument is Calabresi's theory of 'general deterrence'.[12] Under no illusions about tort liability's potential for 'specific' deterrence, he argues from the postulate of Pigou's welfare economics[13] that all costs ought to be debited to the activity that causes them so that they are reflected in the price of the resulting product or activity. The cost of accidents, in short, is properly an item of the overhead costs of a particular enterprise. In this way activities with higher accident rates will have lesser attraction in the market place and will thus be carried on to a lesser, more socially desirable extent. By contrast, it is claimed that if activities do not bear their accident costs, they are in effect subsidized and will thus be overproduced. This creates both an inefficient allocation of resources and excessive accidents

[11] Coase, 'The Problem of Social Cost', 3 *J. Law & Econ.* 1 (1960).

[12] See Calabresi, 'Some Thoughts About Risk Distribution and the Law of Torts', 70 *Yale L.J.* 499 (1961); *The Cost of Accidents* (1970).

[13] Pigou, *Economics of Welfare* (4th ed. 1932).

to boot. Thus, the market mechanism can be enlisted in pursuit of 'general deterrence' of accidents.

Although it has become fashionable to argue that tort law should serve to internalize costs, there are many problems also with this line of analysis. First, *negligence* law does not in fact attempt to assign all accident costs to activities that cause them. Rather, it purports to assign only the cost of accidents that reasonably should have been avoided. To some, like Calabresi, this is an indictment of negligence and an argument for strict liability. To others it reveals a fundamental ambiguity about the internalization argument. What is the cost of what? Facile assumptions abound. For example, work injuries are by general consensus regarded as part of the cost of industrial operations: 'the product should bear the blood of the worker'.[14] But on closer examination, the problem can become very thorny indeed. Is an accident caused by failure of an industrial tool to be internalized by the maker or by the user of the tool? Is a plane crash caused by a defective altimeter a risk attributable to manufacturing altimeters or aeroplanes or to flying of, or in, aeroplanes? While it has even been argued that no *economic* choice is possible between attributing a car-pedestrian accident to either driving or walking, Calabresi resolves the impasse by selecting the motorist as the 'best cost avoider', having the better information and means to reduce such accidents—both questionable assumptions.

Moreover, in the real world it is frequently impossible to internalize accident costs to the specific offending product or activity. For example, not only would a drug that eventually reveals itself as dangerous in all likelihood be totally withdrawn from the market, but the cost of compensation will in any event probably be spread among all or most other products of the particular manufacturer, with the result that the consumers of safe drugs will in effect be bearing the accident cost of the dangerous drug. This would raise the cost of all drugs and—following Calabresi's thesis—to that extent deter their use: a result that might have an adverse effect on public health.

The most problematical feature of these economic theories is of course their assumption of the rationality of human

[14] A dictum attributed to Lloyd George.

behaviour. But experience does not suggest that market control, any more than monitoring cost efficiency, is likely to make a substantial contribution to accident prevention.

How do compensation systems measure up to Calabresi's prescription? The more you fine-tune internalization or risk-avoidance, the more you get away from the principle of insurance, i.e. risk spreading. Strict liability and *special* compensation plans, for example for road traffic victims, function alike in focusing on one specific target, arguably so as to internalize and place the cost on the best cost-avoider, for example motorists. By contrast, *comprehensive* accident compensation, precisely for the sake of wide loss-distribution, sacrifices the opportunity for such channelling in so far as funding is undifferentiated, as when premiums are levied on all tax-payers. Even road traffic compensation plans would 'externalize' the cost of accidents due to equipment failures by placing the cost on motorists rather than on manufacturers or repairers. It is however possible to reduce such externalities even within the framework of a general compensation scheme by distributing the cost on a more differentiated basis. In New Zealand, for example, the road traffic scheme is financed separately from the general accident fund, and even a road traffic scheme could place separate levies on car *manufacturers*, were it not for the fact that the cost would ultimately also be passed through to motorists.

3. COMPENSATING DESERVING VICTIMS

Many years ago a distinguished British scholar concluded that the only defensible *Aim of the Law of Torts* was compensation.[15] Yet the law signally fails to achieve that purpose. For, the most controversial aspect of the negligence system is that it discriminates between different accident victims not according to *their* deserts but according to the culpability of the defendant: a claimant's success is dependent on his ability to pin responsibility for his injury on an identifiable agent whose fault he can prove. Put differently, negligence deems as deserving only those who can trace their harm to someone's wrongdoing. To critics, this causes

[15] Glanville Williams, 'The Aims of the Law of Tort', 4 *Cur. Leg. Prob.* 137 (1951).

unfairly unequal treatment in several ways: between victims of the same kind of injury, one of whom can but another cannot point to a responsible cause, for example one who breaks his leg in a car accident and another who slips in the bath-tub;[16] between one who does and one who does not succeed in proving fault in a defendant—a distinction exacerbated by the vagaries of jury trial long after the accident in question and the fine line that often divides minimally acceptable and culpable conduct; between those with especially effective lawyers and those without and between those who are personally attractive victims and those who are not—both of which are thought by critics to influence juries unduly. Not least of all is the fortuitous exclusion of victims unable to collect from responsible defendants who turn out to be judgment proof, i.e. lacking liability insurance or other financial resources to pay.

By contrast, compensation plans avoid most, if not all, the preceding inequities by focusing not on the injurer's misconduct but on the victim's injury. Compensating the injured by 'spreading the loss broadly' instead of crushing the random victim has wide appeal to modern man: as a mark of compassion and social solidarity, arguably even for aiding rehabilitation and thus reducing the cost of accidents. The only constraint is society's willingness and ability to bear the cost. This constraint is reflected in a number of ways.

In the first place, benefits are usually less generous than the 'pot of gold' promised by torts. Mostly, they are limited to out of pocket loss, i.e. medical expenses and loss of earnings, the latter sometimes with low ceilings. Non-pecuniary losses are usually excluded in order to spread benefits over a much wider class of beneficiaries and in order to save the high administration cost of evaluating such losses. However, some schemes, especially those replacing rather than complementing tort liability, give hostage to our cultural legacy of non-pecuniary tort damages, such as the Schedule lump-sum awards for loss of faculty under workers' compensation (now replaced in England by disablement benefits) and somewhat similar awards under the New Zealand comprehensive accident compensation scheme. Besides, compensation

[16] Hence widely known as the 'bathtub argument'. Home accidents account for about 50 per cent of all injuries.

systems often set ceilings on their total liability corresponding to the maximum available insurance cover or other limits on funding. For example, the liability of nuclear facilities under British law is limited to £5 million (under the U.S. law to $560 million), that of the German drug compensation scheme to about £60 million (DM 200 million). It thus serves to protect not only victims but also would-be defendants from financial catastrophe. The technological advances of our time have armed individuals with a capacity to cause almost unimaginable losses which, under the individualistic principles of tort damage assessment, can entail the ruin of whole industries, as illustrated by recent spectacular bankruptcies of asbestos producers in the United States.

The second constraint affects coverage. The broadest schemes would provide compensation for income loss entirely regardless of cause, including illness and even unemployment. But pessimism about the political prospects of such ambitious plans has caused most reformers to narrow their focus. A first line of retreat is to limit compensation to the disabled, perhaps including even congenital defects and illness, as contemplated in the two-stage Woodhouse proposal for Australia. More practical, however, is to retreat another step and cover only *accidents* on the model of tort liability, as in New Zealand since 1974, implementing the celebrated *Woodhouse Report* (1968). Least ambitious but politically best negotiable are compensation plans limited to particular kinds of accident, like workers' compensation, compensation for victims of crime, and so forth. Depending on the breadth of their coverage, accident compensation funds raise two main problems.

The first is the administrative burden of determining boundary issues. For example, has someone who bicycles into a parked motor car suffered an injury that was 'caused by or arose out of the use of a motor vehicle'? Or, more familiarly, has a worker who suffers a heart attack incurred 'personal injury from accident arising in and out of the course of employment'?

This administrative burden is overshadowed by a more insidious philosophical problem. What are the credentials for preferential treatment of these beneficiaries compared with others who fall outside the coverage of the plan? In the case of ethical drugs, why do some plans, in order of increasing breadth, cover only research volunteers, others vaccine victims, and yet others victims of drugs in general? Why not extend compensation to all dangerous products, not limited only to drugs? One way out of this dilemma is to argue that the proposed change is a politically ripe part of an evolving pattern that over the long haul is headed towards consistency. In short, when public and official attention is focused on a specific class of injuries, the opportunity should be grasped for reform, even if it is only part of the package eventually desired. This seems to have been the lodestar of the Pearson Commission. On the other hand, there are those who strenuously criticize special plans, not only for the horizontal inequity they entail, but for diverting efforts from enacting a system of comprehensive social insurance.

4. MINIMIZING TRANSACTION COSTS

The most formidable criticism against the tort system is its inordinate expense. The Pearson Commission estimated that in England it cost 85p to deliver £1.00 in net benefits to the victim.[17] By comparison, the administrative costs of the New Zealand compensation scheme lie under 10 per cent. The resulting savings account far more than somewhat lower benefits for the ability to provide compensation for *all* accident victims for the same price.

The high transaction costs of the tort system are inherent in the system itself. Primary is the adversary relationship between claimant and the compensation source. Liability to compensate is dependent on issues of causation and fault, which require investigation and are frequently contested. The assessment of damages, tailored to each case, invites additional controversy. In sum, the system is geared to individualized processing and does not favour economies of scale. Moreover, these costs are incurred in the processing of all claims, not only those that are eventually successful.

[17] *Report* I para. 261. Otherwise expressed, operating costs amounted to 45 per cent of the premium.

5. FAIRLY DISTRIBUTING COSTS

Fair allocation of the cost of accidents (the 'justice factor') is at the core of the fault theory of torts. Damages are awarded not on the basis of the plaintiff's merits but the defendant's demerits; the rationale being that only fault justifies imposing the loss on a defendant. Opposition to no-fault is based principally on two grounds. First, such liability is considered unfairly onerous; second, it tends to discourage enterprise. These suppositions have become largely falsified by the advent of liability insurance and the ability of most typical tort defendants to pass on the loss to their customers in the form of higher prices. Thus the beneficiaries of the dangerous activity will eventually be footing the bill. In some situations, it will be the class of potential victims, like consumers of defective products, airline passengers, and so forth. This may explain the greater appeal of strict liability or no-fault compensation in the latter instances, since they operate in effect as a form of compulsory self-insurance.

In summary, the actual operation of the tort system nowadays rarely fits the classical model of individual loss bearing but rather results in collectivization of losses much as under compensation plans. This effect largely undermines the argument that it is unfair to allocate costs to the non-negligent.

Conclusion

As mentioned at the outset, there is no objective calculus for deciding which of the three basic methods of dealing with the accident problem—tort, special or comprehensive compensation—best meets the several goals we have considered. For debatable is both the degree to which each method meets these goals as well as the relative order of priority among them. Moreover, even a principled choice along these lines must confront political realities, like power relations at the legislative level and the resistance of vested interests, not least that of the legal profession.

X

NUISANCE

NUISANCE is a field of tort liability rather than any particular type of tortious conduct. Its unifying element is the type of harm, not (like negligence) the type of conduct causing it. Its purpose is to secure an individual's claim to enjoy the amenities of his land unimpaired by noxious odours, noise, and other annoyances, whether of tiles dropping from a neighbouring roof, roots encroaching from an elm tree, or pollutants emitted from industrial smoke stacks—anything short of a direct physical intrusion or ouster which falls to the province of trespass.

Nuisance, like trespass, long antedated the rise of the modern tort of negligence. Both these older branches of law define property rights and especially relations between neighbours. In most legal systems which are organized systematically in a Civil Code, these matters are part of property law rather than torts. But the focus on remedies rather than rights, which set its mark so characteristically on the English common law from the beginning, pushed nuisance into the remedial corner of torts.

Protected interests

Many property rights—rights with respect to land or chattels—are absolute in the sense that, except in so far as abridged by legislation in the public interest for example for the purpose of zoning, they may be asserted without making any allowance for the competing interests of others. Thus a landholder may intercept underground water percolating in undefined channels (as distinct from river water) without regard for the wish of his neighbour down the hill to get a share of it for his own well. More important, the law of trespass offers categorical protection against intrusion by physical entry unqualified by any consideration for the reasonableness of the defendant's conduct: no countervailing interest on his part being heeded save such narrowly limited pleas as imminent necessity to save himself or his property from destruction. In contrast many other rights relating to the enjoyment of property are qualified in that the law will not protect them except against *unreasonable* infringements. Such rights in other words must be balanced against those of others and may require subordination at least partial or temporary to competing interests of neighbours. That is the realm of the law of nuisance.

One can no more claim an absolute right to noiselessness than a right to absolute noiselessness. In an industrial area a home-owner cannot presume to bring all industry to a halt for the sake of enjoying a tranquil mid-morning nap in his back garden. Only when the noise level exceeds the limits of tolerance, having regard to ordinarily prevailing standards in this or similar localities and to the use of available devices to mitigate its effect, has he good ground to complain. Thus the controlling standard for protection is unreasonable interference. It is the law of 'give and take', an application of the Golden Rule 'do not do unto others as thou wouldst not have done unto you'. I must tolerate occasional smoke from my neighbour's incinerator, as the price for obtaining the same indulgence from him. Nor can I protest against his using household electrical equipment because it interferes once in a while with my television reception, since it would be unfair to require him to subordinate his own legitimate activities, otherwise not injurious to anybody, to my own extra-sensitive uses.

It can make all the difference, therefore, whether a given interference is classified as trespass or nuisance. The test is supposedly whether the interference is physical or not. But is 'physical' to be defined by the scientist or the untutored layman? By modern insights or old shibboleths? The problem is illustrated by two cases. In one,[1] an open-air cinema sought an injunction against a neighbouring night race track for casting floodlights on its screens. The interference was classified as not 'physical' and therefore subject to the defence that the plaintiff's use was abnormally sensitive; yet to the physicist light is a physical force just like others that are tangible. In another case,[2] pollution was held to be

[1] *Amphitheatres* v. *Portland Meadows* (Ore. 1948), 198 P. 2d 847, 5 A.L.R. 2d 690.
[2] *Martin* v. *Reynolds Metals Co.* (Ore. 1959), 342 P. 2d 790.

a physical interference ('breaking and entering') because minute particles, not visible to the naked eye, were identified as having fallen on the plaintiff's crop and poisoned his cattle with the result that the farmer could avail himself of the longer period of limitation for trespass. Because 'balancing' was considered the clue to the first case, the harm was classified as nuisance; because the plaintiff in the second case deserved to recover on either theory, the court gave him the benefit of the doubt on the procedural point. But if that decision were generalized, it could carry environmental protection to extravagent lengths by depriving industrial users of the nuisance defence that the interference did not exceed the limits of reasonable tolerance in its location.

The other side of the coin is that because the protection afforded against nuisance is qualified, it becomes possible to redress a landowner's grievances and thereby recognize 'rights' which, standing alone, are still outside the pale of legal protection as being altogether too refined and precious.

Thus in this instance smell and noise may well be actionable, although neither would qualify as 'personal injury' in a negligence action, unless so severe as to cause cancer or a broken ear-drum. Privacy interests receive protection in complaints such as that a neighbouring residence is being used as a house of ill fame or that a lady is being persistently pestered by solicitations over the telephone. Nervous shock owing to fear of low-flying aeroplanes or bullets fired through the air supported recovery for 'parasitic damages' long before redress came to be allowed for this form of injury independently of occupation rights. Nor does it matter that only recreational amenities are at stake, as in the case of domestic television reception, since this has long become prominent among the 'ordinary uses of property' for residential purposes. Most often of course economic values are primarily involved, as when unnecessarily noisy building operations drive away the patrons of a hotel next door, when the advent of a factory or smallpox hospital in a predominantly residential neighbourhood threatens to impair property values, or when a building falls into such disrepair as to become a safety menace. Not that claims to all conceivable amenities by property owners are thus supported: to mention but one example, no right is recognized to an unimpeded view or prospect.

Reasonable user

The touchstone of the law of nuisance for balancing competing claims to land use was eventually found in the concept of 'reasonable use'. This was the uneasy compromise reached in the latter part of the nineteenth century in the conflict between residential claims and industrial development. A number of factors, none necessarily alone decisive, call for consideration.

Foremost is the gravity of the harm involved: there is little if any margin in the case of actual physical injury or even damage to property, but it increases proportionately as the annoyance or inconvenience recedes into the finer and more subtle reaches of sensitivity. Some dicta go so far as to say that 'sensible material damage' precludes all balancing and can never be justified by competing values, especially location. Such a categorical distinction however raises difficulties: for one thing, 'material damage' may be as difficult to define as 'physical intrusion', besides suggesting an affinity with trespass; for another, it seems to assume, erroneously, that physical discomfort cannot have serious effect on property values.

The gravity of the injury may also be affected by its length: an occasional or merely temporary interference such as that caused by repair work or building construction, may have to be tolerated when a similar, but incessant or permanent, operation would be condemned as excessive. As already mentioned, the standard of comfort and convenience is largely influenced by the character of the locality: 'what would be a nuisance in Belgrave Square would not necessarily be so in Bermondsey'. This zoning function worked fairly efficiently in keeping noxious trades out of residential areas. But the locality standard was also invoked to furnish an excuse for the industrial polluter during the rapid industrial expansion of the nineteenth century. The staggering rate of respiratory diseases among the working population nearby, we now know, contradicted both the contemporary denial that these were 'physical' injuries caused by the poisonous smoke and the claim that it was in any event a not unreasonable degree of 'discomfort' for an industrial neighbourhood.[3] Thus a double standard arose, the more exacting protection traditionally afforded in rural and better-class residential districts and the forgiving attitude towards industrial pollution. The plight of the industrial population was further aggravated by the reluctance to issue injunctions against factories and the disinclination to prosecute public nuisances.

Next in importance in its bearing on reasonable user is the purpose behind the objectionable activity or enterprise. The higher its position on the scale of social values, the greater its claim to forbearance by others. If all practicable means of reducing its injurious effect have been employed, its great utility may present a hard choice between closing it down altogether or bearing with it despite the inconvenience or other detriment it inflicts on a small minority. Quarries or mines cannot be moved, railways must be accessible to their customers, and even airports cannot be placed too far from centres of population. One solution is to solicit the legislature's aid in authorizing the undertaking, which has the effect of impliedly relieving it from liability for any harm it necessarily entails, like the stench of oil refineries[4] or the noise of aircraft near airports. Special compensation Acts or even constitutional provisions like the Fifth Amendment of the U.S. Constitution may mitigate the sacrifice this exacts by requiring compensation to be paid for this form of expropriation. And this is as it should be (but unhappily is not always so), because there is no reason whatever why any single one or more members of the community should have to shoulder the cost of something calculated to be of great benefit to the majority. To the contrary, the expected community benefit makes it all the more desirable that the cost be passed on to a large section of the public, spread either by means of rates and taxes or by inclusion in the price charged to the consumer public.

Looked at in this light, then, the fact that an enterprise poses as the champion of public interest, far from being

[3] See Brenner, 'Nuisance Law and the Industrial Revolution', 3 *J. Leg. Stud.* 403 (1974); McLaren, 'Nuisance Law and the Industrial Revolution', 3 *Oxf. J. Leg. Stud.* 155 (1983).

[4] See *Allen* v. *Gulf Oil*, [1981] A.C. 1001.

a good reason for, is actually a better reason against, acquitting it from liability for the nuisance to which it subjects a minority. Where the annoyance or detriment is less grievous, however, it is proper to demand some allowance on account of its utility and social acceptance, like church bells ringing at reasonable hours on Sunday, milk deliveries at night, and so forth. By the same token an anti-social purpose must be given weight in the opposite scale: the firing of explosives, acceptable perhaps at a public celebration, becomes intolerable when done for the sole purpose of spiting a neighbour.

Strict liability?

Although the standards of reasonableness, and indeed of neighbourliness, on which Lord Atkin drew so heavily for inspiration in formulating his embracing notion of negligence, are at the core of nuisance, the two are only distant cousins. 'Unreasonable user' in nuisance calls for a balance being struck between competing uses of land; 'unreasonable risk' in negligence depends on an appraisal of how likely the danger is to materialize. The one has to do with calculated injury, the other only with contingent injury. Responsibility for the first is by no means necessarily discharged by taking all reasonable precautions, responsibility for the second almost always is.

Does this mean that liability for nuisance is strict—that, if the damage or *nocumentum* (nuisance) can be stigmatized as an unreasonable interference with a plaintiff's rights, it matters naught whether or not the defendant was in any sense remiss in not taking proper safeguards? To be sure, when the conditions of actionable nuisance took shape long before tortious negligence was even emergent, there was little disposition for such refinements. But eventually nuisance turned out to be no more proof against the pervasive fault philosophy than was the kindred remedy of trespass. In the first place, as we have just seen, the issue of 'unreasonable user' draws sustenance from much the same taproot as negligence. Secondly, modern law has progressively insisted that there be no liability without knowledge or means of knowledge that a nuisance was occurring.[5] This adjustment came about first in cases where the source of the nuisance

[5] *Sedleigh-Denfield* v. *O'Callaghan*, [1940] A.C. 880.

was due to a predecessor, a treapasser, or an act of nature, like a tree set afire by lightning. In cases such as these where the defendant is charged not with having actively set up a nuisance but merely with responsibility for maintaining his land nuisance-free, his duty as occupier to abate dangerous conditions whatever their origin was already sufficiently onerous when limited to situations where he had reason to be aware of the need. No more could fairly be asked from him—indeed, as already noted,[6] until quite recently he was flatly excused from doing anything at all to rectify conditions of natural origin, like weathering rocks or seeding weeds.

The position is less clear where the nuisance was actually created by the defendant himself or by someone for whom he is responsible like his servants or agents. In most nuisance cases the remedy asked for is an injunction to prevent *future* interference, which should obviously issue without reference to whether the defendant had been aware in the *past* that a nuisance was emanating from his land. The issue under consideration therefore cannot be tested except in relation to claims for damages that occurred prior to the time when he acquired or should have acquired knowledge. Such cases are rare, but what little authority there is seems to negate liability. In absolving the defendant in a leading case the court expatiated on the 'very serious' burden that would be involved if an occupier had 'at his peril to insure that nothing *done* or omitted by him shall injure something buried beneath it', like a pipe laid along an underground easement, of which he did not know or could not reasonably be expected to know.[7] It is now also settled that liability for nuisance does not extend beyond foreseeable consequences so as to harmonize it with alternative claims for negligence.[8] Finally, this conclusion alone is compatible with the principle of *Rylands* v. *Fletcher*, which limits strict liability to the escape of such dangerous things alone as were brought upon the land and employed for an 'abnormal use'. To attach strict liability to any other type of nuisance would be to inject an indefensible element of incongruity into a body of doctrine

[6] *Supra* p. 157.

[7] *Ilford U.D.C.* v. *Beal*, [1925] 1 K.B. 671, 674. Strikingly enough, it was in just such a case that it was held (in *N.C.B.* v. *Evans*, [1951] 2 K.B. 861) that there was also no liability for *trespass* (to goods) in the absence of negligence.

[8] *The Wagon Mound (No. 2)*, [1967] 1 A.C. 617 (P.C.).

that has long been painfully striving towards a semblance of cohesion.

The only modern if controversial support for a stricter liability concerns nuisances due to non-repair of artificial structures or fixtures, for which an occupier may apparently be held responsible whether or not he knew or ought to have known of the danger, unless it be that the condition was created by a trespasser or a secret and unobservable operation of nature, such as a subsidence under the foundation of the premises. This of course relates to conditions menacing personal safety, like tiles or guttering falling from adjacent buildings, where the need for the law's pressure to adopt accident-preventive measures is greatest.

Public nuisance

The type of nuisance so far discussed is commonly called 'private' in contrast to 'public' nuisance. Whereas the law of private nuisance protects landholders against interference with the beneficial use and enjoyment of their land,[9] the law of public nuisance is concerned with interference with public rights, especially those of free and safe passage along the public highways and waterways. But it encompasses also all manner of other petty crimes, like houses of ill repute, street queues, lotteries, and so on. Redress for public nuisance is primarily by abatement or indictment at the instance of governmental authority. Yet as early as the fifteenth century private citizens were permitted to sue if they suffered 'special' or 'particular' damage, different from that of 'everyman'.

What qualifies as 'special' damage defies preciser definition. It clearly includes all personal injury and property damage, for example, such as might be caused by an obstruction of the highway or masonry falling on passers-by in the street. In this way, some traffic accidents have become actionable as nuisances, for example collision with an unlighted truck parked in the road, although it is now settled that the plaintiff must prove negligence just as if he had sued for negligence. Mere inconvenience and delay, on the other hand, would not ordinarily support a private claim. Thus while water pollution would not cause 'special damage' to a recreational

[9] Only occupiers can sue, which according to the English view, excludes even their families.

angler, it well might to commercial fishermen. This distinction effectively denies resort to public nuisance as a weapon for private enforcement of environmental protection.[10] American law, which is in general more sympathetic to private initiative in law enforcement, has tended to be more helpful by increasingly expanding 'standing to sue' for abatement (as distinct from damages) and by permitting class actions to provide a financial incentive for costs.

Remedies

The remedies available for nuisance are damages and injunction. Common law damages can be awarded only for past losses, without prejudice to later claims for additional loss. Equity, on the other hand, was empowered by statute[11] to award damages in lieu of injunction, which would be assessed once and for all, for the past as well as the future. Because this would be tantamount to allowing the defendant to buy out the plaintiff and thus compulsorily acquire an easement to commit a nuisance, courts are understandably reluctant to grant this remedy against an unwilling plaintiff. It would in effect confer on the defendant a power of compulsory acquisition which is, by statute or constitution, confined to public authorities acting for the public benefit.

On the other hand, should a court not be influenced by the *public* interest, where appropriate, in denying an injunction and confining the plaintiff to damages? In particular, is it permissible to heed pleas of economic efficiency that, to shut down a cement works or power station for the benefit of an odd private residence in the country would make no sense because the value of the offending enterprise, including employment opportunities, far outweigh the plaintiff's private stake? English courts, unlike some American ones, purport to exclude such considerations and treat the contest as purely inter-personal. In reality, the issue is less stark than it appears.[12] For if the court grants an injunction, it remits the parties to private bargaining,

[10] But private individuals may make complaints of statutory nuisance under the Public Health Act 1936, s. 99.

[11] Chancery Amendment Act, known as Lord Cairns Act, 1858.

[12] See Calabresi & Malamed, 'Property Rules, Liability Rules and Inalienability', 85 *Harv. L. Rev.* 1089 (1972); Ogus & Richardson, 'Economics and Environment', 1977 *Camb. L.J.* 284.

whereas if it grants damages the price is set by the court. The latter method would be preferable in some situations where the transaction costs of private bargaining are high, for example where it is difficult to strike a bargain with numerous parties, especially 'hold-outs'; otherwise, however, the most efficient allocation of economic resources would probably be achieved by private bargaining stimulated by an initial injunction. An injunction would also vindicate non-financial environmental interests which tend to be inadequately compensated in damage awards.

Conclusion

The preceding account has revealed the severe limitations on the effectiveness of nuisance in promoting environmental objectives. These limitations range from substantive rules, like the ambivalence of the standard of 'unreasonable interference', to the procedural restrictions on private initiative especially in regard to public nuisance. Most limiting of all is that its zoning effect is prescribed by the fortuity of litigation between single individuals, in which the larger issue of public welfare rarely gains recognition. The law of nuisance is therefore no substitute for zoning and environmental protection agencies and can aspire at best to only a subsidiary role in these endeavours.

XI

PROTECTION OF HONOUR AND REPUTATION

1. TRESPASS, FALSE IMPRISONMENT, AND MALICIOUS PROSECUTION

UNDERSTANDABLY the law's primary concern is with protecting individuals' interests of substance by assuring recovery for personal injury and property damage. But man does not live on bread alone. Increasing sophistication has, with the advance of civilization, fostered demands for extending legal protection to non-material interests of personality like self-respect, reputation, and privacy. In actual fact the common law's entry into this field (like the Roman law's) occurred remarkably early, not so much because it felt any singular tenderness for such claims, as that they happened to become identified with the early law's unremitting concern for public order. Thus it came to pass that, among its earliest remedies, it afforded redress against mere offensive contact, actual or just apprehended: it was not necessary for battery, assault, or false imprisonment that there be any bodily injury (external trauma). Anxious to reduce the temptation for duels, for men taking the law into their own hands, royal justice offered damages, even punitive damages, for the insult, embarrassment, or distress caused by the defendant's outrage. Many centuries later it added to the stock of this armoury an action against outrageous conduct other than by threatening physical movement (to which trespass remained tied), such as practical jokes or threats conveyed by word of mouth calculated to cause serious nervous shock or other physical injury.[1] Noticeably a common bond of these various trespass wrongs and their kin is that the culprit either intended or 'as good as intended' to inflict the mental distress or other disagreeable sensation which constitutes the wrong.

Closely related to false imprisonment, both in regard to the defendant's conduct and the plaintiff's injury, is the tort

[1] *Wilkinson* v. *Downton*, [1897] 2 Q.B. 57.

of malicious prosecution. Both involve the exertion of constraint, typically by means of legal authority, upon an individual who, in consequence, suffers humiliation, partly for its own sake, and partly because of fear for his reputation among his fellows. The difference between them lies only in this that false imprisonment, a trespass, requires that the defendant must have either laid hands on the plaintiff himself or have used somebody else to do it for him, like *ordering* a policeman to make an arrest; whereas in malicious prosecution the exercise of an independent judgment by the police or a judge is interposed between the defendant's initiative and the eventual prosecution of the plaintiff. Since the law strongly favours the co-operation of private citizens in law enforcement, even now that the police have assumed the major role, it naturally views with jealousy the deterrent effect upon this, if suspects once cleared could readily recover damages from those who set the law in motion. While it has a lesser stake in encouraging private arrests (and consequently imposes on the citizen in general the risk that someone has actually committed the crime),[2] it reveals its sympathy for the private prosecutor or denouncer by imposing the severest handicap on his victim striving for revenge. Thus a plaintiff, in order to succeed in the first tort, need only show that his imprisonment was false, i.e. unlawful, but for the tort of malicious prosecution he must overcome the twin almost insurmountable hurdles of proving that the defendant's prosecution of him, besides terminating in his favour, was undertaken without reasonable and probable cause as well as 'maliciously', i.e. for a purpose other than to vindicate the ends of justice. The difference between them, despite the identity of interests involved on the plaintiff's side, is due entirely to the disparate weight of the countervailing interest represented by the defendant.

2. DEFAMATION

English law has traditionally evinced a solicitous regard for safeguarding reputation against defamation. The threat to

[2] In other words, 'reasonable and probable cause' provides a defence only for arresting the wrong person, not for making an arrest when, in fact, no crime had been committed at all. By contrast police officers are given the benefit of a reasonable mistake on both counts.

public safety and the established order, it is true, was never far from the forefront of this concern. Thus it was that, almost on the heels of the first printing press, the ominous Star Chamber was set on the task of countering the menace of seditious libels, primarily by meting out repulsive punishment, but also by an occasional award of damages to an aggrieved individual. From this practice sprang the generalized jurisdiction of the common law courts, after the fall of the accursed strong-arm of Tudor government, to provide civil redress against libel, complementary to the criminal law against, in the main, its blasphemous and seditious varieties. It is a unique feature of English law that the criminal side of defamation has in the course of time become practically obsolete, while civil claims, as ever, occupy a prominent place on the legal stage; in contrast to many other legal systems, which offer the petty criminal courts as the principal or sole arena for assuaging outraged reputation.

The interest protected by the law of defamation is the loss of esteem among one's fellows. It is essential that the offensive allegation be 'published', i.e. conveyed to someone other than the plaintiff, though it need be to no more than a single individual. Merely hurling a defamatory charge at the plaintiff within no one else's earshot is not sufficient, because redress is not afforded for outraged pride or *self*-respect as such. The interest that is protected is accordingly relational —not self-esteem, but the esteem in which one is held by others. Such may be at stake whether the attack strikes at the plaintiff's private reputation (e.g. that he persistently beats his wife) or his reputation in business or profession (e.g. that he is tardy in paying his debts). Though the law has been alert to the special menace of defamation causing economic loss, it has not closed its door to claims founded only on ridicule or loss of reputation in a purely private respect.

To be defamatory the imputation must be calculated to make people think the less of the claimant. Usually this will consist in attributing to him some dishonourable conduct; but so embracing is the law's protection that it includes also imputing to him some condition over which he has no control, so long as it is apt to expose him to ridicule or contempt, like accusing him of being a bastard. Even insinuating of a lady that she has been raped is enough, because, taking people as they are with their frail standards of propriety and compassion, the sympathy that is her due may not suppress altogether feelings of embarrassment, even a shrinking from her society.[3] The relevant reference is evidently to attitudes prevalent among ordinary folk in the community, neither ideal on the one hand nor yet anti-social on the other.

The last-mentioned qualification is designed to exclude such complaints as that by a professional gangster that he has been falsely accused of refusing an order to rub out a rival mobster or of turning stool-pigeon. The reason for this is not that the law will discountenance minority views, since it is clearly as defamatory to accuse the member of a small religious sect like a Jehovah's Witness of so eclectic a sin as accepting a blood transfusion as it would be to denounce someone for beating his mother. Indeed, as the above-mentioned instance illustrates, it does not even seem to matter that the impugned conduct is regarded by the overwhelming bulk of the community as not only perfectly proper but actually desirable. What makes the case of the Jehovah's Witness so different from that of the criminal is the fact that the value system accepted by the former, unlike that of the latter, is not regarded as positively anti-social. In any event the law should not be too censorious and take the view, as courts have done on occasion,[4] that it is incompatible with their duty of upholding the criminal law to recognize as defamatory any imputation, however damaging, that a person has turned informant to the police. There is a wide range of criminality; and at any rate with regard to offences which involve no moral turpitude and are widely condoned like gambling on club premises, it would be shutting one's eyes to reality without any corresponding social benefit whatever to withhold the protection of the law of libel from someone *falsely* accused of having informed the police.

Finally it should be noted that not every falsehood concerning a person is defamatory. If it does not reflect on his reputation, as where it is said of someone that he has

[3] *Yousoupoff* v. *M.G.M.* (1934), 50 T.L.R. 581 (C.A.).
[4] *Byrne* v. *Deane*, [1937] 1 K.B. 818 (C.A.).

closed down his business, he may well suffer loss of custom but must content himself with the more limited redress, if any, offered for the tort of injurious falsehood, or trade libel as it is sometimes called, which, unlike defamation, requires proof that it was uttered with malice and knowledge of its falsity.[5]

Slander

Endemic to the law of defamation is the problem of being swamped with trivial complaints, petty squabbles that do not deserve to mortgage the limited resources of the legal system, especially courts of superior jurisdiction. The common law's response to this quandary was to draw the distinction between libel and slander. Libel, comprising the more serious forms of defamation, is actionable without proof of 'special' damage, i.e. for injury to reputation without necessarily any additional material damage, like loss of job or business. Slander, on the other hand, is deemed sufficiently inconsequential or trivial in its likely prejudice to reputation to require some further token in order to qualify for legal redress, viz. actual economic loss. To this a few exceptions are allowed when slander is actionable *per se*: imputations of crime, loathsome disease, unchastity (of women), and words calculated to disparage a person in his office, profession, or business—all, on their face, highly prejudicial to reputation.

What is odd about this distinction is not the consequences attached to it, but the criterion by which it is drawn. For it is the medium of publication that is controlling. Libel consists in defamation conveyed by writing to the eye, slander by the spoken word to the ear. The one is of permanent form, associated historically with the Star Chamber's concern over the printing press, the other is supposedly evanescent and derives from an earlier piracy of jurisdiction from the ecclesiastical tribunals which once held cognizance of 'slander' because of its spiritual implications. Like most distinctions, this is of course also capable of occasional capriciousness, but on the whole serves its purpose pretty well. In Britain and Australia defamation by radio and television has by statute been equated with libel, because of their large area of dissemination and impact on the public's

[5] *Infra* p. 226.

credulity. In contrast, the formidable broadcasting lobby in the United States has promoted a trend in the opposite direction, resulting in an unfair discrimination against the press, which remains subject to the more stringent law of libel.

Some American jurisdictions also require proof of special damage for all *libel* that is not defamatory on its face (*per se*), in effect treating it like slander. Many an allegation looks innocent enough until proof of some extrinsic fact discloses the sinister slant it harbours for those 'in the know'. It is the age-old function of the 'innuendo' to specify in the pleadings a defamatory significance which the words would not carry in the absence of such extraneous background information. To say, for example, that X is about to get married or that he is a coloured man carries no defamatory connotation whatever unless it be the case that he is already married or happens to be white. Yet the only requirement English law has insisted on is that anyone suing for an imputation not defamatory on its face like those just mentioned, must give suitable notice in his pleading (the innuendo) of the special meaning he is taking exception to and be prepared to supply particulars, on request, of the facts on which he plans to rely to substantiate his charge. Some American courts, however, have gone further by not only insisting on this safeguard against unfair surprise, but also by treating such libels as mere bagatelles unless supported, like slander, by proof of pecuniary loss. Thus, not content with treating some slander like libel (designated as slander *per se*), these jurisdictions also treat some libel (designated as libel *per quod*) like slander. In both instances the affix '*per se*' means that they are actionable without special damage, but in the case of slander it all depends on the content of the allegation, whereas in the case of libel what matters is whether it is defamatory on its face (*per se*). Even if one were right in surmising that this refinement had its origin in a basic confusion as to the meaning of the Latin expression, its widespread acceptance undoubtedly reflects the strong appeal it has for excusing innocent publishers.

Innocent defamation

Liability for defamation is strict. Statute apart, it is not necessary to prove that the defendant either intended to defame or could have avoided it by exercising reasonable care. How and why this came about is not altogether clear, especially considering that the old-style pleading never failed to assert that the offensive words had been 'uttered with malice'. It is linked to a mistaken focus on publication, not its contents. Thus while publication must be either intentional or negligent,[6] its author takes the risk that it is defamatory. He is not liable for an accidental publication, but is liable for an accidental defamation.

Many decisions testify to the hazards of this rule. What looks perfectly innocent on its face, and therefore does not prompt caution, may turn out, as we have already seen, to be defamatory in the light of some undisclosed background, as when a notice mistakenly announced that Mrs. X had given birth to twins, but unbeknownst she had only been married for four weeks. Or in another celebrated case, where a journalist had maligned a fictitious person whom he named 'Artemus Jones' and a real person by that peculiar name complained that people who knew him thought he had been meant.[7]

To mitigate this burden English legislation since 1952 permits retraction and apology as a suitable means of redressing innocent defamation[8]—an acceptable compromise which neither deprives the victim of an opportunity to vindicate his reputation nor bears harshly on defendants without moral blame. Another ameliorative measure of longer standing is to permit newspapers to publish an apology for any libel printed without actual malice or gross negligence; and thereby to reduce their liability to 'special damage' only, as is commonly the case in America, or at least as under the prevailing British legislation to avoid litigation expenses by the subtle device

[6] For example, he would not be liable if a defamatory letter properly addressed to the *plaintiff* himself fell into the wrong hands. (Remember that publication must be to a third person!)

[7] *Hulton & Co.* v. *Jones*, [1910] A.C. 20.

[8] The Defamation Act 1952, s. 4. defines 'innocent publication' as one where 'the publisher did not intend to publish [the obnoxious statement] of and concerning [the plaintiff] and did not know of the circumstances by virtue of which they might be understood to refer to him; or [where] [the statement] was not defamatory on the face of it, and the publisher did not know of circumstances by virtue of which they might be understood to be defamatory of the plaintiff; and in either case the publisher exercised all reasonable care in relation to the publication'.

of depriving a plaintiff of his costs if he proceeds to sue and is awarded less than the sum paid into court by the defendant.[9]

The U.S. Supreme Court has gone further and, in its prolonged efforts to bring the law of defamation into conformity with the constitutional guarantee of free speech, now insists on fault as a prerequisite for all actionable defamation, of private individuals no less than public figures.[10]

Truth

Whether truth should be an unqualified defence to defamation presents a more complex issue than one might have thought at first. Quite obviously truth is least calculated to mitigate the sting of the offence to the person attacked, yet society may feel too far committed to the value of accurate information, let alone be willing to afford a monetary award to a complainant for loss of a reputation which he did not deserve. The criminal law, understandably looking to the adverse effect of libel on public order, did not admit truth as a defence at all, though for more than a century now this is qualified if the publication was for the public benefit.[11]

The civil law on the other hand took precisely the opposite tack. But while in principle refusing to redress truthful defamation, in practice the dice are heavily loaded against the traducer by casting on him the burden of establishing its truth. This allocation of proof constitutes a shrewd compromise, because only too obviously there is a world of difference between knowing a thing to be true and being able to prove it to the satisfaction of a jury. It is therefore bound to have a decidedly chilling effect on speech, particularly on investigative reporting by the media.

Is there any value in publicity of shameful episodes, however true, if they are devoid of legitimate public interest? English law continues to deny a specific remedy for invasions of privacy that consist in giving publicity to private facts, such as dredging up long-forgotten events in a person's past to satisfy a prurient public. Some Australian statutes

[9] Lord Campbell's Act 1843, s. 2.
[10] *Gertz* v. *Welsh* (1974), 418 U.S. 323.
[11] Lord Campbell's Act 1843.

long ago took up an originally English idea[12] of denying the defence of truth in civil as well as in criminal proceedings if the publication was not for the public benefit. Initially intended to aid the integration of convicts into society, it has been deliberately retained to combat gratuitous invasions of privacy.[13]

Absolute privilege

In certain situations the importance attached to free speech demands some subordination of the individual's claim to vindicate his reputation even against false defamatory attacks. In order to justify such an exceptional departure from the normal pattern of legal adjustment, the public interest must be seriously engaged to exact so drastic a sacrifice. Sometimes it is so overwhelming as not to brook any qualification whatever: these are the occasions of absolute privilege. Being so drastic in effect, they are both rare and jealously harnessed. More often the privilege is conditional on being exercised for its proper purpose and is accordingly forfeited by abuse. These are the occasions of qualified privilege, and because of their built-in safeguard they are more readily tolerated.

Absolute privilege is accorded to protect communications necessary for the efficient functioning of government: for speeches in Parliament, for anything said in the course of or preparatory to proceedings in a court of justice (whether by judge, counsel, or witness), and for communications between high officers of State, like inter-departmental memoranda between ministers. The reason for conferring an unqualified privilege in these cases is not because of any tenderness for unmitigated liars in high places, but because the protected individuals should not be deterred from speaking freely by fear of harassment in having to justify themselves and repel a charge of malice before a jury. Likewise it is no coincidence that these situations offer varying safeguards against abuse: witnesses in legal proceedings are under the control of judges, intra-mural government communications enjoy but a limited circulation, and irresponsible demagoguery by legislators can be pilloried not least by soliciting the help of members of the other party.

[12] A recommendation not adopted in Lord Campbell's Act of 1843 for civil actions.

[13] This provision has become a stumbling block in impending uniform legislation.

Qualified privilege

No simple formula embraces the various occasions of qualified privilege, except in the most general terms whenever prevailing social needs justify people communicating with each other in good faith relative to certain matters without fear of having to back up the truth of everything they say in a court of law. Sometimes this is found because the defendant is under an obligation, at least social if not legal, to convey the relevant information to someone with a correlative interest or duty to receive it. One example is a father talking to his daughter concerning her would-be fiancé; but apparently not a stranger, not even a family friend, making disclosures to a wife about her husband's alleged double life. While it is a strong point that the information was solicited, as in the familiar instance of an employer giving a reference concerning a former servant, it is by no means necessary. In other cases the source of privilege lies in the common interest shared by the communicants, as when partners or shareholders exchange information concerning their firm.

But although the public interest is obviously the ultimate credential of all privilege, it cannot be invoked directly by the public media, still less by anyone else, concerning matters of general interest or concern. In this respect, English law has struck a noticeably different balance from American law between private reputation and the public's 'right to know'. Straddling the defences of qualified privilege and fair comment, the difference is reflected on two major questions: first, does privilege cover false and defamatory allegations of fact as well as defamatory expressions of opinion?; and secondly, does it protect all expressions of opinion or only honest or reasonable ones? English law has taken a narrower view of both questions in the interest of limiting the sacrifice of individual reputation.

In the first place, English law does not recognize as such a qualified privilege for false allegations of fact in the public media, no matter how great the public interest in the revelations. At first blush it may perhaps seem peculiar that qualified privilege should be readily accorded to unfounded charges addressed to a prospective employer against an applicant for private employment, but be denied to someone who in good faith informs the public of charges against an election candidate who is in effect an applicant for service with them. This paradox finds at least a partial explanation in the fact that the former is concerned only with private communications to one, perhaps two, individuals, whereas the principal reason for denying a blanket privilege based on public interest is precisely that the radius of dissemination is too large when weighed against the vast potentiality for ruining reputation. This has been so keenly felt in England that even the limited privilege recognized at common law for communications concerning a candidate addressed to electors alone, as in leaflets or handbills distributed locally, was eventually abrogated by statute.[14] In origin the paramount reason for so circumscribing the scope of the critic was the tenderness evinced by Victorian judges for the sensitiveness of gentlemen, who, they feared, might otherwise be deterred from entering the public arena; indeed so ardent was their sympathy that attacks on a person's morals were and still are categorically beyond the pale even of fair comment. Evidently this attitude has had an appeal lasting into our own day of more prosaic politics and politicians.

The public interest in the dissemination of news concerning public affairs is accommodated only by the qualified privilege for fair and accurate reports in newspapers and elsewhere of a large number of specified matters. At the head of it stand reports of parliamentary and judicial proceedings; and, apace with burgeoning faith in an educated electorate, legislation has progressively added many others, from reports of decisions of professional associations to public meetings and inquiries. Contemporary English legislation has engrafted the refinement that reports of the last group, unlike those of the first, lose their privilege if the defendant neglects to publish a correction upon request.[15]

By contrast, American law is much more solicitous of the public's 'right to know'. Taking at once a more robust view of the fibre of politicians, and dedicated to the peerless importance of public debate as a check on despotism and corruption, criticism of public officials and public figures

[14] Defamation Act 1952, s. 10.

[15] See Defamation Act 1952, Schedule, Parts I and II.

has been elevated to a constitutionally protected right which is lost only on proof of clear and convincing evidence by the plaintiff that the defendant knew his allegation to be false or was recklessly indifferent to the truth.[16] Not surprisingly, American investigative reporting, which earned much credit in the Watergate affair, thrives under these permissive auspices.

The second major difference relates to the scope of the defence accorded to expressions of opinion and comment. American law has adopted the categorical view that 'under the First Amendment [freedom of speech] there is no such thing as a false idea. However pernicious an opinion may seem, we depend for its correction not on the conscience of judges and juries but on the competition of other ideas.'[17] This absolute privilege is justified by several arguments, the principal one being that so long as the statement is one of opinion on known facts a sceptical public can judge for itself what credence it deserves. This is reinforced by the premise that only falsehoods can constitute actionable defamation and that opinions and ideas cannot, of course, be proved to be either true or false.

By contrast, English law has qualified its defence of 'fair comment' in two particulars. First, the comment must be based on true facts.[18] Hence truth is material not only to justify such allegations of fact as are defamatory (that being the function of the distinct defence of *justification*) but also as the first step in establishing that the comment itself is fair.

Secondly, not all comment but only fair comment merits protection. Yet despite the quite misleading name of the defence, 'fair' his criticism need never be, provided only that it is honest. He may freely dip his pen in gall, indulge his own idiosyncratic prejudices, neither mealy-mouthed nor fearful of being judged by what is reasonable and prudent. For the day of the critic would be over once juries were free to substitute their own judgment for his and thereby repress his imagination to the level of their own conformist mediocrity. Belief in the golden mean is far from incompatible

[16] *New York Times* v. *Sullivan* (1964), 376 U.S. 254.

[17] *Gertz* v. *Welsh* (1974), 418 U.S. 323, 339.

[18] But since 1952 (Defemation Act, s. 5) it is no longer necessary that the facts stated as the basis of the comment are correct in every detail, so long as they are substantially true and thus support the comment as fair.

with furnishing a platform for radical views, for what is unpopular today may become the accepted creed of tomorrow, and we must ever insist on keeping open the arteries for change. Thus the range of tolerance is not what a reasonable but what an honest critic, however obstinate, prejudiced, and exaggerated, would have expressed.

But like qualified privilege, fair comment is forfeited if the *purpose* of the communication was improper; if, under the cloak of criticism, the defendant sought to promote an ulterior motive, such as gaining some financial advantage or silencing opposition to a controversial venture, or if he did not honestly hold the opinion he professed. This is commonly expressed by saying that malice defeats the defence.

That an improper motive should defeat a comment that is objectively fair has not passed without serious criticism. It seems to be based on a confusion between qualified privilege and the distinct defence of fair comment and exposes the critic to scrutiny not only for what he said but also for why he said it. In the process the public's interest in scrutiny of public affairs receives short shrift.

Remedies

An individual anxious to vindicate his reputation against a recalcitrant traducer has no alternative to seeking the publicity attendant on a successful verdict in an action for defamation. Most men of honour would be satisfied with thus clearing their name, rather than insist upon additional damages for heart-balm. Accordingly they may well be content with an injunction—a remedy, however, that once more raises the troublesome spectre of infringing free speech. In America 'prior restraint' is proscribed altogether as a form of judicial advance censorship, incompatible with the constitutional guarantees alike of jury trial and free speech; but while these scruples are not shared in England in anything like so categorical a manner, the relief is given only reluctantly when a jury would clearly condemn the publication as defamatory and no defences like privilege or justification (truth) are raised.

The ordinary remedy therefore consists in damages. These range widely, from 'contemptuous' awards of one penny in token that the plaintiff's reputation if infringed at all was really worthless, to substantial awards of many thousands of pounds, rather out of proportion when compared with the strict and censorious attitude prevailing with regard to personal injury awards. In this context, however, juries have traditionally been given a free rein.

The plaintiff is entitled to damages both for economic injury, like loss of job or customers, as well as for injury to reputation. The former he must prove, the latter is presumed. Since the prospect of heavy damages has a specially chilling effect on freedom of the press, the U.S. Supreme Court has limited awards, as a constitutional requirement, to actual damages, including loss of reputation, which must now be proven.[19] In England, exemplary damages were abolished by judicial fiat in 1964 except for the rare case where the defendant specifically sought to make a profit by defaming the plaintiff.[20] Commonwealth courts have refused to follow this lead in the belief that the remedy was necessary to discourage malicious defamation. In any event, 'aggravated damages', which in practice are often difficult to distinguish, are still permissible: although damages may no longer be awarded solely to punish the defendant, the plaintiff is entitled to compensation for injury aggravated by the manner in which, and the motives with which, the defamation was made or persisted with. In sum, while defamation is an injury to reputation, i.e. the esteem in which the plaintiff is held by others, yet its effect on his own sense of self-respect and honour can thus be vindicated.

The preoccupation of our law of defamation with damages has been a crippling experience, starting with the ill-fated distinction between libel and slander. The remedy is not only singularly inept for dealing with, it actually exacerbates the tension between protection of reputation and freedom of expression, both highly treasured values in a civilized and democratic community. Tradition has it that the amount awarded should reflect the worth of the plaintiff's reputation. Adequate vindication can therefore be achieved only at a high price from those on whom we depend for information. Moreover, where freedom of expression is particularly urgent, the law has no alternative to depriving a plaintiff of all means

[19] *Gertz* v. *Welsh* (1974), 418 U.S. 323.
[20] See *Cassell* v. *Broome*, [1972] A.C. 1027.

for vindication by recognizing absolute or qualified privileges.

Alternatives to damages do exist. Voluntary retraction and apology may reduce damages and, in the case of certain reports, may condition qualified privilege.[21] But there is no machinery for compelling retraction and contrition. Nor is there a right of reply, as in many countries, for anyone wishing to vindicate himself in his own words.

3. PRIVACY

Outrage and distress are often caused by wanton invasions of a person's privacy. The call on the law's protection against such practices has become the more urgent as the trying conditions of modern urban life make some sheltered retreat from the scarring impact of communal existence a virtual necessity for maintaining one's emotional balance, rather than an idle luxury for the pampered or an indulgence for the anti-social recluse. This greater need of the individual is unhappily matched by an increasing lack of scruple on the part of professional snoopers, whether in the avowed service of public security (crime detection or spy-catching) or as agents of the mass media catering for the voracious appetite of the prurient public. Fantastic electronic devices, moreover, like ultra-sensitive microphones, have made it possible to pursue many of these activities without infringing the narrow limits set by the law of trespass, which once provided substantial protection against the familiar forms of intrusion.

What has been the law's response to this menace? In a famous article published in 1890 by Warren and Brandeis, the latter eventually to become the celebrated Justice of the U.S. Supreme Court, the authors concluded that the existing stock in the doctrinal armoury of the common law, if yet sporadic and perhaps unorganized, justified a broader generalization towards protecting the interest of privacy. Probably no article has ever had a more profound impact on the future direction of the law, for the clarion call was heeded almost instantly, and progressively over the years American courts have bent to the task of putting flesh on the skeleton of this new tort.

[21] *Supra* p. 204.

The British reaction has been less sanguine, and to this day the courts have displayed no more initiative in responding to the challenge than merely to sustain those interstitial shoots which Warren and Brandeis had encouraged to break through the crust of judicial inertia. This negative attitude has its source as much in timidity to balance the demands of privacy with the public interest in the free flow of information as in the prevailing view that it would trespass on the legislative function for courts these days to recognize a 'new' cause of action. Inevitably this counsel of despair condemns us to the status quo because the media lobby, as experience has shown, vehemently opposes legislative reform with the main argument that judges should not be entrusted with the sensitive task of striking that balance in individual cases. The success of American courts is not accorded much relevance.

Intrusion

Privacy is really a compendious name for several quite distinct interests liable to be impaired by different kinds of invasions, linked, however, by the common bond that they interfere with a person's wish to be let alone. Perhaps its most typical version consists in intrusion on the plaintiff's desire for seclusion or solitude. In some measure this is now vindicated by resort to the conventional theory of trespass, which affords protection against all forms of entry upon private territory without the occupier's permission or legal authority. Recovery against an intentional trespasser is not contingent on proof of actual damage to the 'close', and affront to the plaintiff's dignity and sensibilities may be fully compensated, even now that punitive damages are no longer permitted.

Trespass does not however cover all objectionable intrusions into the sphere of privacy. In contrast to American law, it would not be tortious for a landlord to secrete a bugging device in the bedroom of an incoming tenant, to engage in unauthorized telephone tapping or in excessive public surveillance.

One of the most bitterly resented but persistent outrages is the publication of intimate photographs surreptitiously obtained by crashing a private party or breaking into a home. Indeed, it was just such an occurrence at his daughter's wedding that aroused Warren's anger to write his seminal article. Trespass would have provided a remedy against the intrusion but not for the unwanted publicity of the offending photographs. The latter would have constituted a different invasion of privacy—public disclosure of private facts—which can be committed without obtaining possession of those facts by illegitimate means.

Some intrusions not involving actual entry may be actionable as nuisance, such as constant watching and besetting a house or persistent telephone calls during day and night soliciting a lady's favours. But against many annoying practices on neighbouring property there is no remedy, because they do not, in contemplation of law, constitute an unlawful infringement of any right. Examples are the obstruction of a view, perhaps enjoyed over many years, which will not even by prescription (twenty years' open user) ripen into an easement, as a right to light ('ancient lights') or air used to before 1959. In this connection mention is often made of a well-known decision by the High Court of Australia[22] denying an injunction to restrain the broadcasting of races from a high structure on neighbouring land overlooking the plaintiff's race course. The dictum that our law did not recognize 'a general right of privacy' betrays a faulty analysis of the situation. For the nub of the complaint was not an offence to the plaintiff's sensibilities but an appropriation of an economic asset; an exploitation not of his personality but of his business values. The former alone falls to the province of the law of privacy, the latter to legal protection against unfair competition. The decision is therefore a perhaps regrettable pointer to the inadequacy also of the English law of injurious trade practices, but should not cast its benighted shadow on privacy.

Appropriation

A similar distinction should be observed in connection with misappropriation of a person's name or likeness. In one form this constitutes invasion of another prominent type of privacy interest, viz. the commercialization of the plaintiff's identity, causing him anguish and distress because he wished to keep it 'private' instead of having it exposed to publicity.

[22] *Victoria Park Racing Co.* v. *Taylor* (1937), 58 C.L.R. 479.

One of the cornerstones for Warren and Brandeis's generalization was a mid-nineteenth-century decision, enjoining on Prince Albert's behalf the unauthorized reproduction of some sketches made by him and his queen of their children. Quite obviously, though the ostensible basis for issuing the injunction was the protection of a property interest, viz. the common law copyright or right of first publication, the Prince's real concern was to be saved the embarrassment of publicity—an interest in privacy—rather than to protect the commercial value that might have been his from exploiting it. This non-economic interest on the part of an author—commonly identified abroad as a *droit moral*—may since 1911 be vindicated as a statutory copyright, sanctioned with punitive damages in suitable cases, such as that of the photographer of a wedding group who improperly sold a negative some years later to the press, which included the bridegroom's father-in-law who had recently been murdered, and the publication of which was therefore calculated to cause deep distress to the surviving family.

Sometimes the law of defamation will support redress, if need be by stretching a little the rather pliable notion of what is defamatory. An amateur golfer, for example, portrayed without his consent in an advertisement for chocolate, was awarded substantial damages for the implication that he prostituted his amateur status.[23] Similarly a nurse whose picture was enlisted (by mistake) for advertising a whisky was once granted redress by the U.S. Supreme Court on the coventional basis of libel rather than for invasion of privacy *eo nomine.*[24]

Quite a different evaluation is prompted by cases where the gist of complaint is that the misappropriation of his name or likeness has violated the plaintiff's right to exploit it himself for material gain. Far from being a wallflower, soliticious of maintaining his anonymity, this plaintiff—professional sportsman, entertainer, or other popular idol—merely wishes to secure for himself the fruits of commercial sponsorship rather than have a stranger divert it to his own profit. This is an invasion, not of any right of privacy, but a right of publicity; what is jeopardized is not an interest of

[23] *Tolley* v. *Fry*, [1931] A.C. 333.
[24] *Peck* v. *Tribune Co.* (1909), 214 U.S. 185.

personality but of the pocket-book. Redress for this grievance must appropriately be sought by appealing once more to the law of unfair competition. It is a version of the tort of passing-off, which, in its simplest form, consists in palming off one's own goods as those of the plaintiff and thus misappropriating his goodwill for one's own gain and his detriment. It has been easy to extend this remedy to false attributions of sponsorship, for while it may not lose the plaintiff a sale in the conventional sense (since he is not in competition with the defendant), yet his goodwill has been jeopardized, possibly diluted, and almost certainly its economic value diverted.

Publicity of private affairs

The most notable gap in legal protection under the present law, but also one posing the greatest difficulty of adjustment with the competing interest in free dissemination of information, concerns disclosure of the private affairs of a person usually through the mass media. To the extent that the facts disclosed are false the law of defamation usually furnishes an adequate remedy; but, as already intimated in discussing the defence of justification, English law does not afford any curb, as Australian law does,[25] against publicity of true facts, however distressing, even when such publicity serves no sound public purpose. The problem is well illustrated by a celebrated Californian case.[26] The plaintiff had once been a prostitute who gained considerable notoriety as the accused in a murder trial. But after her acquittal she had given up her life of shame, got married, and assumed a place in respectable society. This curtain of anonymity was rent asunder some seven years later by a motion picture called 'The Red Kimono' which rehashed the old story, cleaving to the truth even to the point of identifying her real maiden name. In what has become a landmark decision, this was held to be an actionable invasion of her right of privacy.

Its most interesting aspect is that it subordinated in her favour the competing interest in giving publicity to public facts. Hers had not been a 'private life', especially in relation to those incidents portrayed in the motion picture, nor was this a wanton disclosure of the private life of a 'public

[25] *Supra* p. 201. [26] *Melvin* v. *Reid* (1931), 297 Pac. 91.

figure': the story was one of public record and in a sense notorious. The critical factor of course overshadowing all this was the public interest in promoting her rehabilitation which was callously jeopardized by the defendants' taking not the slightest trouble to use pseudonyms and otherwise mitigating its impact, for the purpose not of conveying to the public newsworthy information but idle entertainment.

The line in such cases may not always be easy to draw, but it really makes no greater demand on the craft of judges than those which confronted their predecessors in working out the nice balances in the law of defamation. A remarkably workmanlike formula for striking the right balance was proposed in Lord Mancroft's Bill in 1961, which would have conferred a cause of action on a person against anyone 'who without his consent publishes [in newspaper or by broadcast] any words relating to his personal affairs or conduct if such publication is calculated to cause him distress or embarrassment'. Apart from admitting the defence that the publication was not intended to refer to the plaintiff or that the occasion was privileged under the law of defamation, it was also to be a defence that at the time of publication the plaintiff was the subject of reasonable public interest either by reason of some contemporary event directly involving him personally (and it was reasonably necessary to disclose his identity) or by reason of some office or position or conduct of his, and the matter published relating thereto was the subject of reasonable public interest or fair comment thereon.[27]

In the absence of such enabling legislation the protection now afforded is at best interstitial. A *tabula in naufragio* is the equitable jurisdiction to enjoin breaches of trust and confidence. Conventionally enlisted in support of proprietary rights such as an employer's whose trade secrets or lists of customers are being pirated by former employees, it also holds a modest potential as a weapon to combat humiliating and offensive disclosures of private information. Its most ambitious and notorious application by far, from this point of view, was the injunction granted to the Duchess of Argyll against the Duke for betraying

[27] See also the recommendation of the Australian Law Reform Commission, *Unfair Publication*, Part III (1979).

confidential information imparted to him by her concerning their private life.[28] If the court was prepared to protect non-proprietary confidences in token merely of contractual relations, as it has on occasion in the past, surely it was warranted in doing so all the more in support of the marriage relation, which has the strongest claim of all in terms of social policy for respect of the mutual trust in which the secrets of private life are exchanged between spouses. If the immorality of the Duchess had undermined the confidences of the future, it had not betrayed the confidences of the past and did not therefore license the Duke to publish unchecked the most intimate confidences of earlier and happier days.

[28] *Argyll* v. *Argyll*, [1967] Ch. 302.

XII

ECONOMIC TORTS

IN quest for an ever more inclusive formula for tort liability the boldest generalization has been to postulate that at least all *intentional* injury should be actionable in the absence of some specific lawful justification.[1] Modest as this may be by the standards of some legal systems accustomed to broad Code formulations, it has yet proved too ambitious for the common law which has, as we have repeatedly seen illustrated, no penchant for abstractions. The most that might conceivably pass the sceptical test of authority is that all intentional *physical* injury is prima facie wrongful.[2] For, transcending all the ancient distinctions between direct and indirect injury, between the writs of trespass and case, modern law is understandably so clearly biased against intended physical harm that it is prepared to brand it as anti-social, criminal as well as tortious, unless the defendant can enlist one of the accredited excuses, like self-defence, lawful arrest, or necessity.

This generalization, however, can hardly be extended to embrace also all intended economic or pecuniary loss. The reason is plain. A great deal of human activity, especially economic activity, involves conflict with opposing interests of others. The very notion of competition, foundation stone of our capitalist system, countenances if not actively encourages friction in which one enterpriser advances himself at the cost of another for the assumed good of society generally. The inefficient, the weaker, are thus eliminated from the economic process. Obviously rules of law which would flatly condemn conduct calculated to cause economic disadvantage or ruin to a competitor would be so flagrantly at odds with the basic tenets of the political economy as to be altogether *hors de concours*. Not even the concession that only prima facie liability was contemplated, susceptible

[1] Pollock, *Law of Torts* (15th ed. 1951), 17–18.

[2] *Wilkinson* v. *Downton*, [1897] 2 Q.B. 57; *supra* p. 49.

to justification, was apt to make such a proposition more acceptable, because it would still approach the question with a misleading bias, and in any event tend to fudge the really critical issue of what would qualify as lawful justification. At best the formula would be acceptable only at the cost of being either question-begging or circuitous.[3]

In this connection one must also obviously eschew the trap of being carried away by the emotive wash of the evil connotation usually associated with the idea of intended injury. Of course, in contrast to negligent or other accidental harm, the actor must have desired the consequence in question, at least in the sense of being aware that it was substantially certain to happen or being consciously indifferent to whether it would happen or not (a state of mind often designated as 'recklessness'). This has nothing to do with motive or the purpose prompting the actor's desire to accomplish a particular aim. Someone firing a gun at an assailant is not doing so any the less intentionally because he is acting in self-defence. Accordingly in many a competitive situation a person may be 'intending' pecuniary detriment to an adversary, although behaving perfectly in accordance with the canons of accepted conduct. This means not only that intention to inflict economic injury is far from sufficient as a general proposition to warrant liability, but also that purpose or motive assumes a singularly critical role in this context.

The important case of *Abbott* v. *Sullivan*[4] serves as a good illustration of both points. A cornporter had been removed from the register of the Cornporters' Committee in disciplinary proceedings, which in doing so acted beyond its powers. Having thereby lost his livelihood, the aggrieved plaintiff sought damages from two committee members, but failed. In the absence of his establishing a claim against them for the conventional torts of defamation, conspiracy, or procuring wrongful dismissal, the court declined to recognize any residuary right to recover damages for intentionally depriving him—even pursuant to *ultra vires* proceedings—of his 'right to work', at all events in the absence of malice.

This decision is illuminating in the present context for two

[3] But cf. the 'prima facie tort' doctrine, which has some vogue in the U.S.A., for the infliction of intentional harm without excuse or justification by an act that would otherwise be lawful.

[4] [1952] 1 K.B. 189 (C.A.).

reasons: First, it furnishes a poignant illustration in a particularly 'hard' case of an express refusal to accept any general postulate that it was an actionable tort in the absence of justification—and here there was plainly none—intentionally to pursue a course of action calculated to inflict pecuniary injury on another person. Secondly, the court considered it wise as a matter of policy not to venture beyond existing precedents and recognize any such new claim to damages in the circumstances. It is one thing for the judiciary to intercede, as they have readily done, in protecting a man's livelihood or right to work against abuse of powers or mistaken interpretation of their rules by 'domestic' tribunals when this can be accomplished by merely setting aside an unlawful decision or ordering reinstatement of the aggrieved individual.[5] But it is quite another to award him damages, for harsh as may be his plight it could only have been done at the cost of defendants who, as likely as not, were merely acting under some innocent mistake concerning the ambit of their powers and in the absence of malice were not otherwise at fault at all. True, they would surely have been reimbursed out of the coffers of their organization, and the cost thus spread among all members, but this is a viewpoint which does not readily occur to most English judges, more accustomed to the focus of an individualistic (rather than collectivist) morality and reluctant to look beyond the most immediate parties and the effect on them of a particular decision.

Malice

If intended injury is not a talisman to recovery, would malice make the difference? Generally in the law of torts malice is used compendiously to embrace not only what Justice Cardozo once felicitously called 'disinterested malevolence'[6] but any improper purpose, like launching a prosecution against somebody in order, not to vindicate justice, but to exert pressure on him in relation to a collateral matter (e.g. to induce him to marry his daughter or cease business competition).[7] Let us, however, in the present context be

[5] E.g. *Lee* v. *The Showman's Guild of Great Britain*, [1952] 2 Q.B. 329. See Lord Lloyd, 'The Right to Work', 10 *Cur. Leg. Prob.* 36 (1956).
[6] *Nann* v. *Raimist* (1931), 255 N.Y. 307, 319.
[7] As in the tort of malicious prosecution, discussed *supra* p. 195.

content with a narrower meaning of malice as a desire to inflict damage for its own sake. Would that be a sufficient ground for liability?

Judicial pronouncements have not been altogether wanting in support of the proposition that malice can make no difference, because 'if it was a lawful act, however ill the motive might be [the defendant] had a right to do it'.[8] But this, like so many of Lord Halsbury's observations, was as dogmatic as it was shallow. For the conditional 'if' injects an assumption that cannot be made unless one has already answered the very matter at issue. It is a linguistic or rhetorical trick of stating nothing more than a bald conclusion under the deceptive pretence of furnishing a reason. Besides, it flies in the face of the accumulated experience of the common law which, in a number of instances, makes malice the linch-pin of liability. Such, as we have already seen, are malicious prosecution, injurious falsehood, and qualified privilege in defamation.

The heresy draws some strength, however, from the celebrated decision in *(Mayor of) Bradford* v. *Pickles*[9] where the defendant, for no better reason than alleged 'spite', intercepted water percolating in undefined channels in the bowels of his land and thereby deprived the City of Bradford, owners of the upper as well as lower adjacent land, of this water which they desired for the purpose of a conservation scheme. Despite some incautiously wide speculations concerning the effect of malice, of which the preceding dictum is the most notorious and unguarded, the decision denying all relief to the plaintiff simply meant that a landowner's right to such water is absolute and not in any way conditioned by reasonable use or any similar requirement of social utility. Thus, as subsequent decisions have placed beyond doubt, it did not purport to eliminate the relevance of malice from liability for nuisance generally, for most 'natural' rights incident to occupation, like making noise, smoke, etc., are qualified by reasonable user and thus very much dependent on the purpose of the activity causing the inconvenience.[10] Besides, the facile assumption commonly made that Pickles was guilty of spite deserving censure must be modified in the light of the fact that actually he was only

[8] *(Mayor of) Bradford* v. *Pickles*, [1895] A.C. 587, 594.
[9] Ibid. [10] *Supra* p. 189.

holding out for a higher price for his land which the City wished to acquire. In a sense, therefore, he had a purpose, selfish as it might be, not wholly incompatible with the mores of our culture; at all events not anti-social like a desire to inflict injury from sheer caprice or mischief-making.

In another landmark case, *Allen* v. *Flood,*[11] their Lordships only a few years later applied the same philosophy to an inter-union dispute. A union of ironworkers objected to the plaintiffs' employment, as woodworkers, on a ship because they had previously done iron work on another ship without belonging to the union. The defendant, a union delegate, informed the employer that unless he discharged the plaintiffs, the ironworkers would be called out on strike. The plaintiffs were accordingly discharged at the end of the day. But notwithstanding a finding by the jury that the defendants had acted maliciously, it was held that they had committed no tort in the absence of employing unlawful means to effect their purpose.

Unlawful means

'Intent to injure' and 'malice' having been found wanting, the quest for a plausible generalization has shifted with renewed urgency to the doctrine of unlawful means.

Although an early, but obscure, decision had it that 'he that hinders another in his trade or livelihood is liable to an action for so hindering him',[12] this proposition was firmly disavowed in the later nineteenth century by judges who, in the majority, had lost their stomach for intervening in industrial relations any more than in the market. Indeed, as we have just seen, even malice was not considered sufficient. Moreover, the statutory immunities for trade unions and for most forms of industrial action 'in contemplation or furtherance of a trade dispute' not only reinforced the prevailing judicial caution but gave little scope for deploying tort remedies.[13] The right to strike thus seemed secure.

[11] [1898] A.C. 1.

[12] *Keeble* v. *Hickeringill* (1707), 11 East 574n.

[13] Commencing with the Trade Disputes Act 1906, now the Trade Union and Labour Relations Acts 1974 and 1976, s. 13. Trade unions have a general privilege, their officials only the below-mentioned limited privileges. Criminal penalties were removed as early as 1875.

However, the last twenty-five years have witnessed a noticeable change in increased judicial intervention, accompanied by some reduction in the statutory immunities. Not surprisingly, the trade union movement has bitterly resented this development as inspired by judges who never became reconciled with *Allen* v. *Flood.*

The catalyst was a decision in 1964, *Rookes* v. *Barnard,*[14] in which the House of Lords extracted from earlier, opaque judgments a tort of intimidation, consisting in threats of unlawful action for the purpose of causing economic injury to another. In the instant case, the defendant coerced an employer to dismiss the plaintiff under threat of calling out his men in violation of an anti-strike clause. This was held to constitute 'unlawful means', actionable at the suit of the dismissed employee. The outer reaches of this decision still await authoritative definition.

Most important perhaps is its potential for a wider generalization. If threatening to do an unlawful act is actionable, all the more should be the doing of it. If this logic is accepted, the tort of intimidation can be seen as an illustration of a more general tort of unlawful interference with economic interests. What is more, the well-established specific economic torts of 'procuring breach of contract' and 'conspiracy', to be noted presently, can be recognized also as illustrations of the wider principle of tort liability for intentionally causing economic loss by unlawful means.

Tempting as such a rationalization might be to an orderly mind, it would have to await clarification in several respects. At the outset, what is included among 'unlawful means'? Drastic enough as was the inclusion of a mere breach of contract, would every act one is not free to do qualify? This could undermine the established axiom that statutory violation does not confer a private cause of action unless the statute's specific purpose was to prevent the harm that occurred.[15] Caution is also suggested by the important recent decision in *Lonrho* v. *Shell Oil Co.*[16] where the owners of a pipeline failed in their claim for the loss they allegedly suffered from prolongation of the Rhodesian crisis due to

[14] [1964] A.C. 1129. The decision itself was reversed by statute in 1965.
[15] *Supra* p. 98.
[16] [1982] A.C. 173.

the defendants' violation of the oil embargo. This decision teaches that breach of a statute does not constitute 'unlawful action' for present purposes so as to confer a cause of action on claimants whom the statute was not intended to benefit. Besides, consequential loss like the plaintiffs' would not qualify as 'intended injury' even if the defendant had known that it was substantially certain to occur. In the present context, it must have been the purpose of the defendant's action to inflict the harm in question.

Whatever the ultimate fate of the greater generalization, the remaining specific economic torts display a cleaner profile.

Interference with contract

The tort of intentional interference with the performance of a contract by unlawful means developed out of feudal conditions which, viewing employment relations in terms of status rather than contract, gave a master a right to sue a stranger for persuading his servant to leave his employment prematurely, much as he would have had an action for trespass for forcibly abducting him. This link with menial service was not discarded until the great case of *Lumley* v. *Gye*[17] in the middle of the nineteenth century, when it was successfully invoked by an operatic impresario against a competitor who had induced the famous star, Miss Johanna Wagner, to break her contract and sing for him instead. Soon after, the remedy was generalized to protect all manner of contractual relations, ranging from employment to resale covenants, typical during the motor-car shortage in the immediate post-war period, and exclusive franchise agreements between an oil company and service stations.

In its simplest form, the tort consists in 'procuring breach of contract' by persuading one of the parties to commit some act inconsistent with his obligations. The aggrieved party is of course free to pursue his remedy against the latter for breach of contract, but may also, or alternatively, seek redress against the interloper in tort. Moreover, in line with the trend to generalize the principle of 'unlawful interference', it is now well recognized as also actionable to employ other unlawful means, like maiming or abducting one party in

[17] (1853), 2 El. & Bl. 216.

order to prevent him from performing his contractual obligations with the plaintiff. One familiar version is the so-called 'secondary action (or boycott)' when, in order to strike at B, the defendant instigates A's employees to strike (in breach of their employment) so as to prevent A from fulfilling his contract obligation to B—as occurred in the leading modern case when union officials placed an embargo on the supply of newsprint to a printer by ordering their members, lorry drivers in the employ of his paper supplier, to refuse loads destined for him.[18] Such secondary boycott is now specifically declared unlawful.[19]

Although malice is no longer required, intent to strike at the plaintiff remains essential for the good reason that otherwise freedom of manœuvre would be unduly curtailed. Almost every strike aimed at one business entity is known almost certainly to prejudice its performance of contract commitments to others, and it would be an undue deterrent to 'direct industrial action' (at least by contemporary standards) to expose the striker to liability to such others—unless, indeed, the strike was specifically aimed at them rather than the first, as in the case of a secondary rather than primary boycott. Still less is anyone guilty of mere negligence liable for any loss resulting therefrom in increasing the cost of his performing a contract or in depriving him of the benefit of an expected contract performance by someone else. Thus, when a ship negligently sank a barge that was being towed to port, the tugmaster failed to recover from the culprit his lost remuneration.

But even if malice is no longer a necessary element, a socially approved purpose may furnish justification. Thus, a father may counsel his daughter in good faith to break her engagement, and even an artists' protection society was once excused for persuading a theatre to cancel the engagement with the manager of a troupe who paid his chorus girls so low a wage as virtually to drive them to prostitution.[20] The action has all but disappeared from the field of industrial relations as the result of the specific statutory immunity for, *inter alia*, any act 'in contemplation and furtherance of a trade

[18] *Thomson* v. *Deakin*, [1952] Ch. 646 (C.A.).
[19] Employment Act 1980.
[20] *Brimelow* v. *Casson*, [1924] 1 Ch. 302.

dispute' which would have been actionable on the ground (only) that it induced some other person to break a contract of employment.[21]

Conspiracy

Most notorious of all the economic torts, though now but an empty shell, is that of conspiracy. It consists of two branches. The first is the classical specimen, derived from the criminal law, of a combination by two or more persons to injure the plaintiff by use of *unlawful* means. The taint may derive from anywhere along the broad spectrum of illegality, including the commission of a crime, tort, or breach of contract. Thus redress becomes available not only to the immediate victim of violence, but also to any person who was intended to suffer pecuniary or other loss in consequence, like an employer whose loyal servants are beaten up by strikers. Since the recent expansion of the tort of intimidation just noticed, this aspect of the conspiracy doctrine has lost much of its earlier importance inasmuch as this type of conduct would now seem to be actionable even if committed by a single individual alone.

In its second aspect, a combination to injure may become tortious, however lawful the means employed, if its purpose is considered 'unjustifiable'. This changes the focus from means to ends, and offers an opportunity for active judicial intervention in setting the boundaries of tolerance to which men (at all events when acting in concert) must confine their selfish pursuits. The weapon thus fashioned was indeed for a time wielded, with civil as well as criminal sanctions, to promote the economic interests of the dominant entrepreneur class against the aspirations of the emerging labour movement. But well before the turn of the twentieth century this bald partisanship came to falter and was eventually replaced by the current doctrine of judicial neutrality.[22]

Today, as a general rule, the pursuit of economic self-interest is recognized as providing its own justification for any combination aimed at subjugating an adversary or

[21] Now the Trade Union and Labour Relations Act 1974, s. 13.

[22] Reinforced since 1906 by statutory immunity for acts 'in contemplation and furtherance of a trade dispute'. Now Trade Union and Labour Relations Act 1974, s. 13(4).

competitor. This is as true when unions strike an employer for better conditions as when business rivals are bent on internecine competition amongst themselves. It applies to jurisdictional disputes between unions as much as to unions seeking to maintain a closed shop against non-union interlopers. Freedom to trade, to sell one's goods or labour, has been anointed as a justifiable end, even if this freedom is to be exploited for the purpose of preventing others from enjoying it themselves.

The permissiveness of the modern law, which has virtually eliminated the tort of conspiracy from the effective legal armoury in the field of industrial and business relations—in large measure precisely as a mark of the scepticism, even revulsion, over the partisan policy of activism in the past—was finally clinched in the great *Harris Tweed* case in 1942.[23] The famous cloth was, and still is, traditionally produced by mills on the Island of Lewis, spinning yarn woven manually by crofters on the island. This alignment was threatened by the more economic use of imported yarn from the mainland by certain modern mills. In order to ward off this threat to the livelihood of the crofters' home industry, the Transport and General Workers Union (which counted among its members both spinners in the mills using hand-woven yarn as well as dockers in the island port) struck a bargain with the old-style producers to destroy their competitors in return for a 'closed shop'. Accordingly, a total embargo was imposed on the importation of yarn from the mainland, which brought the plaintiff's production to a halt. The courts, however, refused to intercede on his behalf, judging the union officials as within their rights to act in concert, no less among themselves as in conjunction with the old-style mills, in advancing their own objective—the closed shop—by making an arrangement which committed them to injure the plaintiff with whom they actually had no quarrel at all.

Modern case law furnishes few, if any, examples of combinations which failed this forgiving test of 'furthering legitimate trade or business interests'. Among those that have been mooted as candidates for exclusion are agreements inspired by hostility to the religion, race, or colour of the plaintiff, or those stemming from pure motives of

[23] *Crofter Hand Woven Harris Tweed Co.* v. *Veitch*, [1942] A.C. 435.

vengeance, wantonness, or spite, unmitigated by any socially acceptable purpose. On only one reported occasion was a union committee condemned—for persecuting a member solely from a desire to punish him for his public opposition to them personally. In sum, the sting has all but been drawn from a tort remedy that was once counted among the most effective instruments of judicial intervention with the free interplay of economic forces in the market-place.

Industrial relations

The proceeding torts—injury by unlawful means, interference with contract, conspiracy—have a special relevance to industrial relations. Indeed, most of the modern decisions which have clarified and developed these doctrines where concerned with the right to strike, first with 'primary', later with 'secondary' strikes as industrial strategy changed. The first period ended with the taming of the torts of procuring breach of contract and conspiracy by statutory privileges for such actions in 'contemplation and furtherance of a trade dispute'.[24] After a longish period of acquiescence, the courts from the mid-fifties onwards increasingly intervened particularly against secondary industrial action (i.e. directed against suppliers and customers of the target), a process which added 'indirect' interference with contract rights and the development of the torts of intimidation and injury by unlawful means. Repeatedly Parliament, at the behest of the unions, attempted to neutralize these judicial advances by creating new immunities, only to be foiled at the next confrontation.[25] The judicial distaste of secondary boycotts has at last been reinforced also by statutory prohibition.[26]

But neither side of industry has cause for satisfaction, if only because of the endemic uncertainties of the law and the practical difficulty of planning industrial strategy in conformity with it. Another drawback is that the focus of the law has been primarily on 'unlawful action' instead of on 'justifiable ends', no doubt in quest for 'neutral principles'.

[24] Trade Disputes Act 1906.

[25] Acts of 1965, 1971, 1974, 1976. Currently, the Trade Union and Labour Relations Act 1974 as amended.

[26] Employment Act 1980.

Would it not have been preferable to define a 'right to strike'?

In most other common-law countries, unlike Britain, the tort remedies are rarely deployed in the industrial arena. In the United States, for example, they are pre-empted by the federal Labor Relations Act; in Australia by the system of compulsory arbitration and a general reluctance by both sides of industry to appeal to the ordinary courts of law.

TABLE OF CASES

INDEX